But ONE Race

But ONE Race

The Life of Robert Purvis

Margaret Hope Bacon

STATE UNIVERSITY OF NEW YORK PRESS

Published by
State University of New York Press, Albany

Printed in the United States of America

For information, contact State University of New York Press, Albany, NY
www.sunypress.edu

Production by Judith Block
Marketing by Susan M. Petrie

Library of Congress Cataloging-in-Publication Data

Bacon, Margaret Hope.
    But one race : the life of Robert Purvis / Margaret Hope Bacon.
        p. cm.
    Includes bibliographical references and index.
      978-0-7914-7007-7 (hardcover : alk. paper)
      978-0-7914-7008-4 (pbk : alk. paper)
    1. Purvis, Robert, 1810–1898.   2. African American abolitionists—Biography.
3. Abolitionists—United States—Biography.   4. African American civil rights
workers—Biography.   5. African Americans—Pennsylvania—Philadelphia—Biography.
6. Philadelphia (Pa.)—Biography.   7. Antislavery movements—Pennsylvania—
Philadelphia—History—19th century.   8. Philadelphia (Pa.)—Race relations—History—
19th century.   I. Title.

E449.P983B33 2007
973.7'114092—dc22
[B]

2006012419

10 9 8 7 6 5 4 3 2 1

In grateful appreciation for the help and support of my husband

S. Allen Bacon

Contents

Acknowledgments

The origins of this book date back to 1997 when I published an article on Robert Purvis in the *Pennsylvania Magazine of History and Biography*, entitled "The Double Curse of Sex and Race: Robert Purvis and Human Rights." I found the research for this essay difficult because of the absence of family correspondence, on which I had relied in all my previous biographies. Intriguing as I discovered Purvis to be, I could not believe it would be possible to write a full-length biography under the circumstances.

At this point, I met Dr. Julie Winch, author of the prizewinning *A Gentleman of Color: The Life of James Forten*. Julie Winch was still at work on James Forten; she collected a considerable amount of material on Robert Purvis. This she generously shared with me, encouraging me to undertake further study of Purvis. To read my footnotes is to discover how deeply indebted I am to her continuing generosity in sharing data. In addition, she read drafts of my manuscript and made many corrections. Julie Winch also introduced me to Reginald Pitts, a professional genealogical researcher, specializing in black families. He was an important helpmate. The footnotes at the end of the text make clear how much he has helped.

I must also acknowledge continuing help from John Purvis of Scotland, who has collected information on the worldwide Purvis family and shared all his work on the Robert Purvis branch.

Another source of unfailing help throughout this long project has been Beatrice Walton, librarian of the Byberry Friends Meeting, who has supplied much material on Byberry Hall, Byberry School, and the community of Byberry, where Robert Purvis spent many years. Dr. Joseph Borome, who has written a number scholarly articles on Robert Purvis, was encouraging and helpful.

I would especially like to thank the Friends Historical Library, the Historical Society of Pennsylvania, Dr. Theo Fair, president of the Pennsylvania Abolition Society, and James Livingston, for their permission to use materials found in their collections throughout this book.

Much of the work on this book I conducted at the Friends Historical Library, Swarthmore College. I am indebted to the former curator, Mary Ellen Chijioke, as well as the present curator, Christopher Densmore, and archivists Susanna K. Morikawa and Patricia C. O'Donnell. Patricia also helped with developing the genealogical chart. The Swarthmore College Library's Department of Interlibrary Loan was helpful in obtaining many books and tapes for me.

Phillip Lapsansky, Charlene Peacock, and Linda August of the Library Company of Philadelphia; Rachel Onfu, and Linda Stanley of the Manuscript Division of the Historical Society of Pennsylvania; John Pollack of the Rare Books Collection, University of Pennsylvania; and Emma Lapsansky-Werner, Curator of Special Collections at Haverford College, were helpful in the project. At Special Collections in addition I would like to thank Ann W. Upton, Joelle Bertolet, and Diana Franzusoff Petersen. I must also thank Dr. Roger Lane of Haverford who generously lent me the microfilm tapes of William Dorsey's scrapbooks of Philadelphia.

This book would have been impossible to write without the generous support of the staff of various research libraries, who made photocopies of letters pertaining to Robert Purvis and granted me permission to quote from them. These include: Marianne Cawley of the South Carolina Room, Charleston County Public Library; the staff of the South Carolina State Department of History and Archives, and of the South Carolinian Library in Columbia, South Carolina; the Sophia Smith Collection, Smith College; the Anti-Slavery Papers, Boston Public Library; Sydney Gay Collection, Columbia University Library; Wendell Phillips Papers, Harvard University Library; Moorland-Springarn Research Center, Howard University; George Arents Research Library, Syracuse University; the Jones Library, Amherst, MA; the Library of Congress; Historical Society of Pennsylvania, Rare Books, University of Pennsylvania; and the American Antiquarian Society.

Dr. Ira Brown supplied a great deal of material from his own researches on Pennsylvania black history; Dr. Marie Agnew-Marcelli gave me invaluable assistance in tracing Ann Hathaway Purvis; Jean Yellin Fagan helped me understand the connection between Robert Purvis and Harriet Jacobs; Mary Sewell-Smith of St. Thomas Episcopal Church aided me in searching church records; Helen Ganay Toppins helped me with research in New York City; Marcus Huey, and Barbara Graf aided with pictures of artifacts passed down in the Purvis family; and Bill Pepper assisted me in scanning pictures. Teresa Engeman proofread the manuscript. Judith Block handled the production at SUNY Press.

Beverly Palmer of Pomona College encouraged me, and I am as always indebted to my husband, S. Allen Bacon, for his patience and his belief in me.

Ancestral Chart
of the Purvis Family

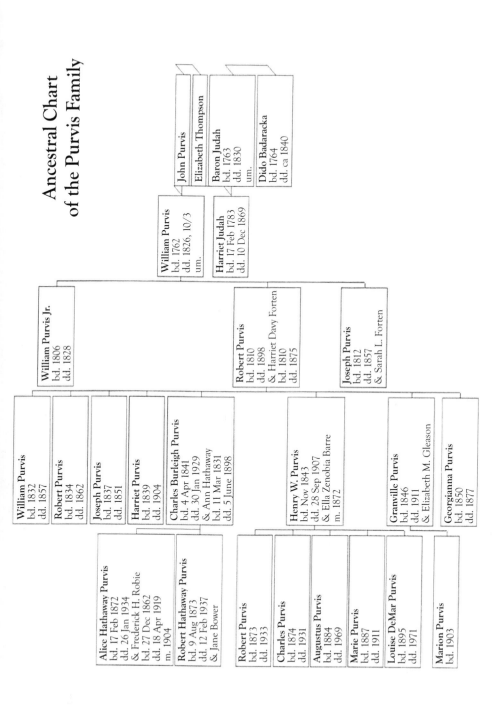

John Purvis

Elizabeth Thompson

Baron Judah
bd. 1763
dd. 1830
um.

Dido Badaracka
bd. 1764
dd. ca 1840

William Purvis
bd. 1762
dd. 1826, 10/3
um.

Harriet Judah
bd. 17 Feb 1783
dd. 10 Dec 1869

William Purvis Jr.
bd. 1806
dd. 1828

Robert Purvis
bd. 1810
dd. 1898
& Harriet Davy Forten
bd. 1810
dd. 1875

Joseph Purvis
bd. 1812
dd. 1857
& Sarah L. Forten

William Purvis
bd. 1832
dd. 1857

Robert Purvis
bd. 1834
dd. 1862

Joseph Purvis
bd. 1837
dd. 1851

Harriet Purvis
bd. 1839
dd. 1904

Charles Burleigh Purvis
bd. 4 Apr 1841
dd. 30 Jan 1929
& Ann Hathaway
bd. 11 Mar 1831
dd. 5 June 1898

Henry W. Purvis
bd. Nov 1843
dd. 28 Sep 1907
& Ella Zenobia Barre
m. 1872

Granville Purvis
bd. 1846
dd. 1911
& Elizabeth M. Gleason

Georgianna Purvis
bd. 1850
dd. 1877

Alice Hathaway Purvis
bd. 17 Feb 1872
dd. 26 Jan 1934
& Frederick H. Robie
bd. 27 Dec 1862
dd. 18 Apr 1919
m. 1904

Robert Hathaway Purvis
bd. 9 Aug 1873
dd. 12 Feb 1937
& Jane Bower

Robert Purvis
bd. 1873
dd. 1933

Charles Purvis
bd. 1874
dd. 1931

Augustus Purvis
bd. 1884
dd. 1969

Marie Purvis
bd. 1887
dd. 1911

Louise DeMar Purvis
bd. 1895
dd. 1971

Marion Purvis
bd. 1903

Introduction

$\mathcal{T}$hroughout the nineteenth century the struggle to end slavery, to assist escaping slaves to make their way to safety, and to achieve full rights for black citizens, was conducted by a number of free blacks in the Northern states, in concert with white liberals. Not until Benjamin Quarles published his pioneer study, *Black Abolitionists*, in 1969 was attention shifted from the white abolitionists, especially those clustered around William Lloyd Garrison, to their black colleagues. While the general public has been aware of the contributions of such stars as Frederick Douglass, Harriet Tubman, Sojourner Truth, and William Still, the outstanding work of many heroic black men and women has remained largely veiled.

Robert Purvis, the subject of this study, has been one of these unsung heroes. A wealthy, light-skinned, and very handsome businessman, he was part of Philadelphia's black upper class of which Julie Winch has written so helpfully in *Philadelphia's Black Elite*.[1] In his day, he was best known not only for his stirring oratory on behalf of the rights of black people to full and equal citizenship, but also his continuing rage that such rights were denied. Short-tempered with the enemies of his race, he was a mild and loving husband, father, and friend.

He was also recognized in his day as the pioneer of the underground railroad. At the time of his death *The New York Times* said he was "known to the present and past generations alike for his great work in behalf of the emancipation of slaves"; the paper called him the "President of the Underground Railroad." "Throughout the long period of peril, his house was a well-known station where his horses and carriages and his personal attendance were ever at the service of the travelers upon that road."[2]

Purvis was the principal organizer in 1837 of the Vigilant Committee, which engineered the escape routes through Pennsylvania for slaves heading for Canada—one of the first two such organized underground railroads. There is evidence that more slaves were forwarded under his aegis than during the period following the passage of the Fugitive Slave Law in 1850. One slave he helped escape was Harriet Jacobs, who later wrote *Incidents in the Life of a Slave Girl.*[3]

Unlike some of his colleagues, Purvis understood that all human rights are interlinked. He worked for justice for Native Americans, supported Home Rule for Ireland (despite Irish opposition to black rights in Pennsylvania), and was a strong advocate of women's rights. When the American Anti-Slavery Society split into two groups in 1840 over the question of seating a woman, Abby Kelley, on a committee, Purvis voted for Abby, and when the American Equal Rights Association also split into two groups in 1869 over the Fifteenth Amendment, Purvis was alone among black men in taking the feminist position of Susan B. Anthony, Elizabeth Cady Stanton, and others, declaring that "he would rather that his son never be enfranchised, unless his daughter could be also, that, as she bore the double curse of sex and color, on every principle of justice she should first be protected."[4]

Writing about men such as Purvis in *The Souls of Black Folk*, W. E. B. Du Bois said:

> The free Negroes of the North . . . began to change the basis of their demands; they recognized the slavery of slaves, but insisted that they themselves were freemen, and sought assimilation and amalgamation with the nation on the same terms of other men. Thus, Forten and Purvis in Philadelphia, Shadd of Wilmington, and Du Bois of New Haven, Barbadoes of Boston, and others, strove singly and together as men, they said, not as slaves, as "people of color," not as "Negroes." The trend of the times, however, refused them recognition save in individual and exceptional cases, considered them as one with all the despised blacks, and they soon found themselves striving to keep even the rights they formerly had of voting and working and moving as free men. Schemes of migration and colonization arose among them; but these they refused to entertain, and they eventually turned to the Abolition movement as a final refuge.[5]

Despite Du Bois's statement, many of these free black abolitionists were from time to time attracted to the idea of migration, especially when they began to despair of making any significant changes in their rights as citizens. Abraham Shadd moved his family to Ontario, Canada in 1852, and made it his home for the rest of his life, while his daughter, Mary Ann Shadd Cary, became a black journalist who urged free blacks to consider migrating to Canada. Henry Highland Garnet, black minister and journalist, came to support migration and helped to found the African Civilization Society in 1859. He himself spent four years in Jamaica, and in 1881 became U.S. Ambassador to Liberia. Alexander Crummell, a black minister, moved to Liberia in 1853. While he attempted to gain a medical education, Martin Delaney, sometimes called the "father of black nationalism," assisted Frederick Douglass in editing the *North Star*. Frustrated in this, he moved his family to Ontario, and in 1859 led a party to explore the Niger Valley in West Africa, where he hoped to found a settlement; ultimately, however, he returned to the United States. Edward Blyden, a native of St. Thomas, refused admission to Rutgers Theological Seminary in 1850, migrated to Liberia in 1851, where he taught in the Liberian College and held various government posts.[6]

Even the strongest foes of colonization sometimes considered migration. Frederick Douglass, who consistently rejected the concept, once thought of moving to Haiti; he became ambassador to Haiti after the Civil War. And Robert Purvis himself, whose fame was based on his implacable belief that he had every right to be an American citizen and enjoy the privileges thereof, briefly entertained the idea of migrating to England after the Dred Scott decision.[7]

The debate within the black community over emigration was compounded by the organization in 1817 of the American Colonization Society. All white originally, this group believed that black Americans had a responsibility to bring Christianity and civilization to native Africans by emigrating to Liberia. They were able to attract the interest of many influential men in and around government, and had substantial support in the Deep South, where many slaveholders believed that the existence of free blacks in the North helped to persuade their slaves to escape. Conservative Northerners supported the colonization movement also, believing that blacks could never be assimilated into American society without producing the dreaded "amalgamation" or intermarriage of the races. As the Industrial Revolution began to increase the need for laborers in northern industry, prejudice against blacks deepened, especially among new white immigrants, who feared competition for their jobs. In this increasingly hostile climate, blacks saw their rights actually curtailed, as in Pennsylvania, which voted down its black suffrage in 1838.[8]

Distrusting the American Colonization Society from its beginning, many blacks perceived it as a trick to lure free blacks into leaving the Northern states, and thus lessening the opposition to slavery. Fear of this effort began with working-class blacks, and was quickly taken up by the elite.

Among opponents of colonization, none was more fiery or more persuasive than Robert Purvis, who followed his father-in-law, James Forten, in taking leadership in the opposition movement. He based his arguments against slavery and for rights for blacks on human rights, and refused to be called an African-American. "There is not a single African in the United States," he told a Philadelphia audience in 1886. "We are to the manner born; we are native Americans."[9]

The question of separatism versus integration came up in other aspects of the struggle of black Americans against slavery and for equal rights. Should blacks work with white allies, or should they develop their own reform movements? As a very young man, Purvis followed the lead of black activist William Whipper in arguing that they should make common cause with white allies in such organizations as the American Moral Reform Society, and should not belong to societies developed wholly on a "complexional" basis. He remained devoted, however, to William Lloyd Garrison and the American Anti-Slavery Society, of which he became vice president, and he frequently bankrolled Garrison's *Liberator* and other enterprises. He quarreled with Frederick Douglass, when the latter broke with Garrison following the founding of Douglass's newspaper, *The North Star*. The two remained estranged until they were both old men, working in Washington.[10]

A man of fiery temperament, he also broke with Garrison when the latter believed that the Civil War had solved the problems of slavery and discrimination, and there was no longer any reason to keep the American Anti-Slavery Society functioning. Purvis sided with Wendell Phillips, who believed the organization should continue its efforts until the black man had the vote. Only in his old age did he reconcile with Garrison.[11]

Always hopeful that white society would see the error of its ways in denying the blacks equal rights, Purvis was thrown into despair when the state of Pennsylvania withdrew black suffrage in 1838, when the Fugitive Slave Law was passed in 1850, and when the Dred Scott decision came down in 1857. Yet he knew epiphanies: when the Emancipation Proclamation was made in January, 1863, and when the ratification of the Fifteenth Amendment restored the black vote in 1870.[12]

In Purvis, in short, we see the struggle of the double consciousness, as a black man and as an American, of which Du Bois wrote, played out in a lifetime of struggle for dignity and recognition of his personhood, and that of other men and women of color.

At the time of Purvis's death, the Afro American League of Philadelphia published a selection of Purvis's speeches and letters, revealing the pride the black community took in the oratorical and epistolary skills of this well-known and well-beloved spokesman. In this, the first biography of Purvis, I have included significant quotations from his speeches, hoping that his golden-tongued oratory will contribute to bringing his memory and his message alive for another generation, while introducing a passionate and important advocate for equality for all to the general public.[13]

CHAPTER 1

❧

Of Southern Birth

ℛobert Purvis, destined to become a major figure in the abolition of slavery, was born in Charleston, South Carolina—a state second only to Virginia in its slave population—on August 4, 1810. The Neck, an unincorporated section of Charleston, north of what was known as Boundary Street, was then a place of lawlessness; it was home to many free blacks, and the black mistresses of white slave owners. William Purvis, a white cotton merchant and his mixed-race wife, Harriet Judah, lived here on Elizabeth Street from time to time. The couple had three children; Robert was the second.[1]

Among the devastating effects of chattel slavery was its destruction not only of family ties, but also of a family's past. Instead of the family Bibles, the gravestones, the family letters and journals, and other memorabilia with which many American families trace their ancestry, the descendants of slaves were left with legends, some of them colorful, most of them difficult, if not impossible, to trace.

Such was the case with Harriet Judah, Purvis's mother. When he was eighty years old, and had become famous, Robert Purvis told reporters that Harriet was the daughter of a slave, Dido Badaracka, "a full-blooded Moor." Purvis described her as a woman of "magnificent features and great beauty. She had crisp hair and a stately manner." By Moor, Purvis apparently meant what was known as a Blackamoor. Dido was not an Arab; she was dark-skinned and had tightly curled, "crisp" hair, which Harriet inherited. Many years later, when a critic falsely accused Robert Purvis of trying to pass for white, she described Harriet as a "tight headed negro lady and a dear good woman."[2]

According to the legend which Robert Purvis repeated several times, Dido Badaraka was born in Morocco. At the age of twelve, she was captured by a slave trader, along with an Arab girl. Both girls had been lured to go a mile or two out of the city where they lived to see a deer that had been caught. They were seized, bound, placed on the backs of camels, and carried to a slave market on the coast. Here they were loaded onto a slave ship and transported to Charleston, South Carolina in 1766. At the slave market, the Arab girl was freed. (In order to keep peace with the Barbary pirates, in none of the British colonies were Arabs or Moors enslaved.[3]) However, Dido was sold to a white woman, a Miss Harriet Deas, who educated her, treated her as a companion, and left instructions that Dido was to be freed and given an annuity of $60 when Miss Deas died, which she did nine years later.[4]

Subsequent biographers have accepted this story, but it has proved impossible to verify. The date of 1766 appears to be wrong, for Dido had a child, Mary, Harriet's half sister, in 1804, when she would have been fifty years of age. It seems far more likely that the date of Dido's capture was 1776. Among slaves whose sales were recorded in Charleston between 1773 and 1810 there were twelve Didos, but none owned by a person named Deas. A search of manumission records reveals only that a Mrs. Elizabeth Deas left a will asking her descendants to free "old Dido" in 1802. Even if Dido Badaraka had been born in 1754, rather than 1764 as we now think, she would scarcely be described as "old Dido" at the age of forty-eight.[5]

When Dido was still a young woman, Purvis said, she had attracted the attention of Baron Judah, a member of a prominent Jewish family. There was such a person living in Charleston at the time, who may have been Purvis's grandfather. Baron or Baruch or Barry Judah (1763–1830) was the third of ten children of Hillel Judah, a German Jew, and his wife Abigail Seixas Judah, a Sephardic Jew, originally from Spain or Portugal. This family moved to Charleston sometime between 1766 and 1783, becoming part of a tiny Jewish community, numbering 188 according to the U.S. Bureau of the Census of 1790. Recently scholars have estimated that the numbers might be higher, possibly as many as 225.[6]

Jews began arriving in Charleston as early as 1695, although their numbers remained small until 1750. The first Jewish settlers in Charleston, as well as elsewhere in South Carolina and Georgia, were mainly Sephardic from Spain or Portugal. Many were merchants, and brought some wealth into the communities in which they settled. Although they experienced some discrimination, anti-Semitism was considerably less virulent than in the European nations they had left. They were accepted as citizens, and could vote, but not hold office. A number participated in the Revolutionary War as American patriots, several were captured, and at least one died.[7]

The Jews who settled in Charleston and elsewhere in the Deep South found the Southern way of life agreeable. They readily adapted to the institution of slavery. By 1790 at least 83 percent of Jewish households in Charleston owned slaves. They liked the leisurely way of life which slavery provided, and the mild climate. They participated in the cultural life of the city, though they did not mingle socially, that is, with a few exceptions. Several southern Jews spoke of the South as "this happy land," or "this promised land."[8]

At the time that the Judah family arrived in Charleston, the largest Jewish population, comprising 242 Jews, primarily Sephardic, lived in New York City. The second largest population chose Charleston as their home. The two groups were interrelated and kept in close touch. A friend of the Judah family, visiting Charleston from New York, writing to his sister in 1783, described Baron Judah, who would have been about twenty, as "A fine manly young fellow." It must have been about this time that Baron became involved with Dido. Purvis stated that they were married in a Methodist church, but this would have been unlikely. Many white men had black mistresses, but interracial marriage was extremely rare and frowned upon. The Judahs were a prominent and proud Jewish family and owned slaves at the time. It is probable that Dido was either a slave in this family, or an indentured servant. Whatever their relationship, Baron and Dido had two children, Harriet and a son who was possibly named Daniel. Harriet, born in 1785, became Robert Purvis's mother. A third child of Harriet's, Mary, had a different father.[9]

The relationship between Baron and Dido ended in 1790, when Baron moved with the rest of his family to Savannah, Georgia, and then on to Richmond, Virginia in 1791. In Richmond, Baron Judah became a prominent merchant and citizen, a devoted husband and father of at least four children. According to 1820 records, he kept one slave, Mary. He may have owned others but such records were destroyed in the Richmond fire during the Civil War.[10]

More information is available on Baron's younger brother, Isaac, who upon his death in 1827, gave conditional freedom to two of his slaves, Betsy and Maria; he provided for two "free mulatto boys and brothers whom I brought up, and in consequence of their attention and fidelity and my natural regard for them" (probably a euphemism for the fact that he was their father). He left each boy a building lot in Richmond and $500. These boys took the name of Judah, became barbers, and moved to Philadelphia where one of them, Phillip Judah, became active in the colored convention movement of the 1830s, a movement in which Robert Purvis, possibly Phillip's first cousin once removed, became a leader.[11]

If he shared the sentiments of his brother Phillip Judah, and if he were Dido's lover, Baron Judah might have freed Dido and her children upon leaving Charleston. On the other hand, when Harriet and her sons sued for a debt owed William Purvis' estate, they lost the suit because the South Carolina courts considered all four to be slaves. At the time of her death, one Philadelphia newspaper said that Harriet had been William Purvis's slave, but when she foiled an attempt on his life he freed her and married her. Another newspaper stated that she had been born a slave, but had been freed at age nineteen. According to the Pennsylvania Abolition Society's census of 1856, she was living on South Seventh Street with a niece. One of the two was described as born into slavery, another as having been born free in a slave state. The weight of all this evidence seems to suggest that Dido was never freed, and Harriet was born into slavery. It may be that William never legally freed her, since the laws for manumission were becoming increasingly rigorous. It was impossible, for instance, after 1810 to free a slave unless one could demonstrate his/her ability to be self-supporting. This eliminated the possibility of freeing one's children.[12]

Unlike Harriet, William Purvis's pedigree is well-established. He was one of seven brothers born to John and Elizabeth Thompson Purvis, who lived in Ross, Northumberland, England. After John's early death, his widow moved to Dunfermline, Fife, in Scotland, where their sons were educated. The family's patrimony had been reduced by an outbreak of sheep rot, and all but the oldest brother moved to the American colonies to seek their fortunes. John, Alexander, and Robert established themselves in South Carolina as cotton brokers. William and his brother Burridge joined them in 1780. The pioneer Purvis brothers did not take the newly arrived ones into partnership, and William and Burridge went into business for themselves in Columbia, South Carolina. In 1806, they formed a business called William Purvis & Company with a partner, Ainsley Hall, also originally from Scotland. Under this arrangement, Hall managed the business affairs in Columbia, William handled shipping and brokerage from Charleston, and Burridge represented the business in Europe.[13]

Having made his fortune, Alexander Purvis returned to Scotland in 1809, where he eventually purchased an estate and married. He revisited

South Carolina only once, in 1828. John Purvis eventually retired to Pitts-field, Massachusetts, where he died in 1811. Burridge married a Charles-tonian, Polly Brown, in 1798, and had a number of children.[14]

To represent the business he had formed with Burridge, William Purvis established his principal residence in Charleston; by 1799, he had become a naturalized citizen. Sometime around 1805, he met and fell in love with Harriet Judah, and moved to Charleston Neck to be near her, possibly to live with her. The couple had three sons: William, born in 1806, Robert in 1810, and Joseph in 1812.[15]

In 1810 there were 1,472 free blacks living in Charleston, the major-ity of them of mixed race. There were also 11,671 slaves and 11,568 whites, making the majority persons of color.[16] Some of the slaves lived inde-pendently, either as mistresses of white slave owners (such liaisons were more open and accepted in Charleston than in other parts of the south[17]), or as craftpersons allowed to hire out their own time on condition of pay-ing their masters a share of their earnings. Formal manumission de-manded a complicated legal procedure, and was regarded as unnecessary in these cases. The free blacks formed an elite in the black population. Many were of mixed race, and looked down on their dark-skinned neigh-bors. White slave owners supported the free blacks, seeing them as a buffer between themselves and the slave population. Some of the free blacks owned properties and as many as one-third bought, sold, and owned slaves, whom they hired out to bring in additional income. John Judah, who may have been Harriet's nephew, was the slave of Francis M. Weston. John was trained as a butcher and allowed to live in Charleston as a free man, and to own slaves, although retained the legal status of a slave.[18]

Although Robert Purvis probably never knew this, his mother, Har-riet Judah, was a slaveholder. In February and March 1812, when Robert was a baby, she sold a black girl named Betty, aged ten, and bought an African girl named Bella and a black girl named Jenny. Though some free blacks bought relatives as slaves in order to save them from white owners, this was not the case with these two girls. It is possible that she dealt in slaves as a way of helping her lover William Purvis.[19]

Robert Purvis always asserted that his father despised slavery and re-fused to hold slaves. South Carolina records, however, show that William did, in fact, possess slaves at various times in his life. In 1809, William and Burridge bought out their older brothers and acquired their business with headquarters in Charleston, Columbia, and Sumter. This purchase brought William and Burridge into possession of land, mules, and slaves. In 1819,

William purchased a family of slaves from a South Carolinian slaveholder.[20] It may be that Robert never knew of these transactions. It may also be that William acquired slaves reluctantly and divested himself of them quickly.

Instead of keeping slaves, according to Robert's version, William Purvis hired gangs from a local slave owner to transport cotton from Columbia to Charleston on board two vessels he owned, the *Ant* and the *Bee*. Once, Robert claimed, when his father was overseeing the loading of a barge, the elder Purvis removed his watch and placed it on a bale of cotton. A slave, seeing his opportunity, seized it. When young Robert asked his father if he had protested this loss to the slave owner, William Purvis said "no." He did not want to expose the slave to a whipping. This act of kindness made a lifelong impression on the young boy. William Purvis also sought to educate his sons against slavery, giving them such antislavery books to read as Thomas Day's *The History of Sanford and Merton* and Jesse Torrey's *Portraiture of Slavery*.[21]

Other than these memories of his father, Robert Purvis did not speak or write about his childhood in Charleston. With two brothers to play with, and the sights and sounds of the city to explore, it must have been an exciting time for a small boy. Near their house on Elizabeth Street was the Cooper River with its shipping docks and warehouses; the boys swam, however, in the brackish water. If one ventured farther from home, there was downtown Charleston, between Meeting and King Street. Shops and churches crowded the area. Still farther south were the homes of the gentry, which were turned sideways to the street for privacy; their flowering gardens behind wrought iron gates. Farther still was the Battery, as it came to be called, surrounded by a beach of oyster shells.[22]

In the summer, the rich plantation owners from the interior came up to Charleston to escape the fevers of the lowlands. There was also a time in February, known as Race Week, when the South Carolinian aristocracy flocked to the city. At these times, Charleston below Broad Street was abustle with carriages, for the wealthy families paid calls upon one another, or attended social events. Black slaves, dressed in livery, attended the carriages, and black house servants answered the front door. Behind each house were the quarters for the house slaves the families brought with them.[23]

John Facheraud Grimké, a lawyer and judge, was one of those wealthy plantation owners; he owned the Grimké estate in Beaufort, South Carolina, where they grew Sea Island cotton. John Grimké, his wife Mary and their many children in the summer made their home in Charleston in the fashionable Battery district. Did Sarah or Angelina

Grimké, as fashionable young ladies, see the light-skinned Robert Purvis as a little boy, and wonder about him? Later they were to become colleagues in the antislavery struggle.[24]

Near the Cooper River waterfront, just a few blocks above Broad on Chalmers Street, stood the Slave Market, a warehouse where slaves, freshly brought from Africa, or bred on the plantations, were sold singly or in groups from an auction block. Stripped and sometimes greased to make their bodies shine, the individual men and women were humiliated before the unsympathetic white buyers. It was a fearful and dangerous place for children of color to go, because the possibility of being seized and sold into slavery was always present. If Robert and his brothers did venture this far, they must have shuddered at the scene, for they remembered how their own beloved grandmother had once stood upon that very block.

Wandering around downtown Charleston, Robert would have seen the beautiful St. Michael's Episcopal Church established in 1752 on Meeting Street. Still on Meeting Street, he would have passed the First Scotch Presbyterian Church. It cannot be verified but perhaps his father was a parishioner. Off Meeting Street on Hazell Street was the Jewish Synagogue, built in 1790 by the congregation to which his grandfather may have belonged. And he would also have passed the red brick Quaker meetinghouse on King Street between Queen and Broad. This meeting, strong at the time Governor John Archdale was a member, was in decline; most Quakers had left South Carolina to get away from slavery. Later in his life, Robert would find himself closely connected to the Quakers, although he never became a member.[25]

Where the Purvis boys were schooled during their years in Charleston remains an open question. It seems likely that William Purvis might have arranged to have his boys privately tutored. To educate a slave was against a South Carolina law, enacted after the Stono slave insurrection of 1739. What schools were available to free blacks were organized by the free black community. In 1803, well-to-do free blacks formed the Minor's Moralist Society "to educate orphan or indigent colored children, and also provide for their necessary wants." Daniel Alexander Payne, a prominent black churchman, later a colleague of Robert Purvis, was educated for two years by this group. In 1807, a school for free children of color was established by the Brown Fellowship Society.[26]

This society, founded in 1790 by fifty "bona fida free brown men of good character," was an outgrowth of the social stratification of Charleston's black community. This elite group, which excluded full-fledged blacks, not only built a social hall for lectures and other meetings but they also provided burials for their members. Though many of these "brown men" belonged to St. Phillip's Episcopal Church, they were excluded from burial in its burial ground.[27]

Darker-skinned blacks joined the predominately black Methodist church. In 1815, when white members reasserted their control of church affairs, black leaders sought affiliation with the the newly founded African Methodist Episcopal Church of the North, and built their own church. Slave owners feared the AME as a potential source of insurrection. In 1822, following the discovery of the Vessey conspiracy, whites dismantled this new edifice, taking it down in pieces, board by board.[28]

Like slaves everywhere, many of the Charleston slaves dreamed of freedom, and some were prepared to fight for it. Denmark Vesey (1767–1822) was sold as a boy to a Bermuda slave captain named Joseph Vesey, who took Denmark on many voyages and brought him to Charleston in 1783 to settle down. Denmark was a skilled carpenter, and was able to buy his freedom by 1800. He learned to read and began to absorb smuggled antislavery literature. Slowly, the idea of a slave revolt took hold of his imagination. One by one he brought freed slaves like himself into a network of intrigue, planning such a revolt. Although the resulting uprising did not take place until 1822, the spirit of revolt was in the Charleston air in the years directly after the War of 1812. Like all slave revolts, this one was soon put down and the participants severely punished.[29]

We do not know if Harriet Judah or William Purvis knew Denmark Vesey, although it seems likely, nor even how they and their sons reacted when news of the uprising reached them in Philadelphia in 1822, but Robert Purvis was to defend slave revolts resulting from the system of tyranny, oppression and slavery itself. Writing of another uprising, that of Nat Turner in Southampton, Virginia, he said:

> We are sorry to hear of such scenes as that of the Southampton Tragedy; it proceeded from a natural cause; oppression, tyranny, and slavery always give birth to such events, and we can only say to Virginia, and the other slaveholding states, that so long as they continue to raise up Gabriels and Nats,[30] just so long may they expect to see those scenes acted over and over again. So long as slaveholders and their apologists continue to apply the same remedy to abstract and foreign causes, so long the real cause will sleep in safety.[31]

The fortunes of the William Purvis family were tied up with cotton. The War of 1812 between Great Britain and the United States was hard on merchants, such as William Purvis and his brother Burridge. However, at war's end, they recovered quickly. In 1814, they purchased, in the fork of the Black River and Broad Back Run, an additional 532 acres north of Mayesville, South Carolina, presumably to grow cotton. They prospered in this enterprise and in 1816 formed a new business with a man called Henry Bryce. Burridge was to represent the new company in Europe, and returned to Scotland to buy an estate, Glassmont, in Kinghorn, Fife, for his wife and family. He came back to South Carolina briefly to settle his affairs, and, on the return trip to Scotland in 1816, died at sea.[32]

The death of his brother, combined with his growing uneasiness about dealing in slaves, plus the growing harshness of the slave owners, caused William Purvis to decide to leave also and move to England or Scotland, where he felt his three sons could be properly educated. In 1817, he sold his business. In 1819, he took his little family to Philadelphia, intending it to be a temporary stop while he settled his complicated financial affairs. He planned to buy a home for them in Scotland or northern England.

CHAPTER 2

The City of Brotherly Love

$\mathcal{P}$hiladelphia, the city to which William Purvis moved his family in 1819, was a rapidly growing metropolis with a large free black population. From 1810 to 1820, the population of Philadelphia grew from ninety-two thousand to one hundred thirteen thousand while the black community increased from nine thousand five hundred to twelve thousand, or a little less than 10 percent. This made it one of the largest concentrations of black inhabitants in the United States.[1]

Some of the Philadelphia blacks were the children of former slaves. The Commonwealth of Pennsylvania passed a gradual emancipation act in 1780, under which former slave children were to be freed at age twenty-eight. Some were immigrants from the Caribbean, some were free blacks from the Deep South, hoping to find wider opportunities; and some fled the repression that followed the slave revolts. A few were runaway slaves seeking asylum in a city known—rightly or wrongly—for its tolerance.[2]

While the majority of the black residents of Philadelphia were laborers and servants, there was a large black elite, made up of the families of tradesmen, caterers, barbers, and ministers. James Forten, owner of a sail loft, was a man of considerable property. Joseph Cassey, a hairdresser from the Caribbean, was so prosperous that he lent money to his customers, and eventually he was able to retire a wealthy man. Robert Douglass, also a barber, originally from St. Kitts in the Carribean, married Grace Bustill, a hatmaker, and maintained a large home on Arch Street. Jacob C. White prospered as a barber, owned a store, and later established an African-American cemetery. A number of black men served as restaurant owners and caterers, among them Thomas Dorsey and Robert Bogle.[3]

Interested in self improvement, members of the black elite organized literary societies and libraries. By 1836, black men met to discuss literary and social issues at the African Literary Society, the Reading Room Society, the Young Men's Literary Association, the Demosthenian Institute and the Philadelphia Library Company of Colored Persons; black women met in the Female Literary Association, the Female Minervian Association and the Edgeworth Literary Association.[4]

The center of social and cultural life of the black elite was, however, the black churches, with which Philadelphia was rich. St. Thomas African Episcopal Church was founded in 1793 by Absalom Jones, and the Bethel African Methodist Episcopal Church was established in 1794, by Richard Allen. The First African Presbyterian Church opened in 1811. The ministers of these and other churches were members of the black upper class.

Both Absalom Jones and Richard Allen had belonged to the first benevolent society for blacks, the Free African Society, which was founded in 1787. A number of black attenders of Quaker meetings were members of this group, including the black baker, Cyrus Bustill; the organization was conducted somewhat in the manner of a Quaker business meeting, beginning with a period of silence. According to its charter, the role of treasurer was always to be filled by a member of the Society of Friends , and the group met monthly in the Friends Free African School, which was founded by Quaker schoolteacher Anthony Benezet in 1770, a school which both Jones and Allen had attended. The Society concerned itself with the needs of widows and orphans and other poor blacks; it continued in operation until 1799.[5]

Other such benevolent societies followed. St. Thomas's church launched the African Friendly Society in 1795, and the Female Benevolent Society of St. Thomas in 1796. Other black churches followed suit, with both male and female benevolent societies. Some of the trades organizations also organized such societies. In 1809, the black ministers and other prominent blacks came together to organize the Society for Suppressing Vice and Immorality, with Richard Allen as its principal spokesperson.[6]

These benevolent efforts of black clergymen and others had the support of the Pennsylvania Abolition Society. This organization had been founded mainly by Quakers in 1775 to "Provide Relief for Negroes Unlawfully Held in Bondage"; it expanded in 1787 to include non-Friends such as Benjamin Franklin, who became its president. Its full title became The Pennsylvania Society for Promoting the Abolition of Slavery; the Relief of Negroes Unlawfully Held in Bondage, and For Improving the Condition of the African Race. Its Committee for Improving the Condition of Free Blacks concerned itself with promoting industry and morals in the black community; its Board of Education attempted to provide schools for blacks, including Clarkson School, which opened in 1813 on a lot on Cherry Street between Sixth and Seventh Streets. The Abolition Society was the principal white organization to support antislavery until the emergence in 1833 of William Garrison's American Anti-Slavery Society. It did not, however, admit a black member until 1842, when it admitted the light-skinned and wealthy Robert Purvis. The Society lobbied for the abolition of slavery, and the end of the slave trade, kept track of manumissions, called national conferences of abolition societies, and corresponded with abolitionists abroad. Through its Acting Committee, it defended escaping slaves from pursuit by their masters, and free blacks who were seized by unscrupulous slave catchers and threatened with deportation to the South. Richard Allen himself was once seized by such a speculator, who claimed Allen as a runaway slave. Isaac Hopper, a member of the Acting Committee and a Quaker, was consulted. Allen was freed, and a successful civil suit commenced against the slave catcher.[7]

Hopper was a tailor, not a lawyer, but he had familiarized himself with the law. He often worked in conjunction with Thomas Harrison, a craftsman, who was also a lay member of the Pennsylvania Abolition Society. Thomas Shipley, a lawyer and president of the Pennsylvania Abolition Society in 1836, often used his legal skills to defend the rights of free blacks and escaping slaves. Through these activities, the ties between the black community and white abolitionists, many of them Quaker, were forged.[8]

Schooling was important to the black elite. Some had attended the Free African School founded in 1770 by Anthony Benezet, a philanthropic Quaker with an interest in black education. Benezet had begun tutoring black children in his home in 1750, and was impressed with their ability to learn. The school was begun on Willings Alley and moved to Raspberry Street in 1795, where it remained for many years. In the early years there was a rapid turnover of head teachers. In 1782, although old and sick, Benezet was forced to take over the school himself, conducting it in his home.[9] Several individual Quakers opened short-lived schools for blacks, among these Arthur Donaldson, who taught Sarah Mapps Douglass. Prominent blacks themselves also opened private schools, such as the one developed by James Forten and Grace Bustill Douglass in 1819.[10]

In his memoir in Robert Smedley's book on the underground railroad, Robert Purvis stated that when his father arrived in Philadelphia in 1819, "finding there no schools of a higher grade for 'colored children,' he established a school on Spruce Street, near Eighth Street, and paid the teacher's salary for a year." It may be that Purvis did not know of the Forten-Douglass school. At any rate, the Spruce Street school must have lasted a very short time. In January 1820, both William and Robert Purvis were enrolled in the Clarkson School, run by the Pennsylvania Abolition Society, and their brother Joseph followed a year later.[11]

When they were not learning their lessons in the Clarkson school, the Purvis brothers were free to roam the streets of downtown Philadelphia. There was much to see along Market Street, where farmers brought their produce to the city market, or "shambles," for sale to city dwellers. On street corners, the criers advertised their wares, such as "Pepper pot, smoking hot, come and get your pepper pot!" and oyster men pushed their carts and boasted of the freshness of the oysters. Down along the Delaware River, great ships from many ports rode at anchor, and great warehouses stored their cargoes; over at the Schuylkill River barges heavy with iron and coal and all manner of country produce unloaded cargo at the docks. Both rivers were frozen solid in the winter, and they were often dotted with ice skaters dressed in colorful outfits.[12]

The neat gridiron of red brick dwellings which housed Philadelphia's white population now stretched almost to Center Square, where pumps installed by Benjamin Latrobe in 1799 still functioned to bring water to the city. Independence Hall was no longer the seat of the federal government but housed the state legislature. On Walnut Street, actors and actresses from abroad performed in the beautiful Walnut Street Theater. There were occasional balloon ascensions from Center Square.[13]

But for the majority of black Americans, the city presented a different face. They were crowded into narrow alleys and courtyards in Moyamensing, Southwark, and Cedar Wards, with poor sanitation and water supplies, often lacking any heat in the winter. Jobs were sometimes scarce, as more and more white artisans from Europe arrived to take the better positions. Health care was hard to come by. Though the elite blacks lived comfortably, they could not fail to see their less fortunate brothers and sisters, who worshiped with them in the black churches, and sometimes lived in the alleys behind their homes. How much the young Robert Purvis was affected by their plight is hard to gauge, but it fueled his lifelong struggle for equality for his poorer brothers and sisters.[14]

Meanwhile, as a teenager, Robert was becoming acquainted with his counterparts in the black elite who were to play a role in his later life. James Forten and his wife Charlotte had nine children. Eight survived including: Margaretta, Harriet Davy, James Jr., Robert Bridges, Sarah Louisa, Mary Isabella, Thomas, and William Deas. The first four were age mates of the

Purvis boys. They met at St. Thomas Church, which Harriet Judah attended, and at the Clarkson School. Two of the children of Joseph and Amy Williams Cassey, Alfred and Peter Cassey, were also contemporaries.[15]

Another family whom the Purvis boys came to know was that of Robert and Grace Douglass. Their six children: Elizabeth, Sarah, Robert, James, Charles, and William were of the same generation. Grace Douglass, the mother, had been brought up as a Quaker by her father, Cyrus Bustill. Along with her children, she attended Quaker meetings regularly, though she was never invited to join. Robert Douglass, however, was an elder of the First African Presbyterian Church.[16]

William Purvis had rented a house for Harriet and her sons on Paper Alley, and here they lived until 1824 when they moved to 126 S. Tenth Street. William himself was often away from his family, settling his affairs in South Carolina. In 1823, he paid the heirs of his brother Burridge Purvis $62,000 and assumed his debts, thus coming into possession of all of the lands, stores, animals, boats, and "negroes" owned by his brother. What he did about the slaves is not recorded.[17] Burridge's heirs were slow to turn over his assets, and instead borrowed money from William.

The following year, William Purvis sailed to Britain; he planned to move his family there. He may have intended to buy a country home in Northern England or Scotland for his family, as his brothers had done for theirs. On the way he stopped in New York City to take care of a number of business matters, including making his will. He was sixty-seven; he realized that unless he made some arrangements, his common-law wife and illegitimate sons would not be cared for. Under this will, Purvis left the bulk of his estate to his "beloved friend" Harriet Judah, and their three sons. Harriet was to received $10,000; the three boys would share an estate valued at $250,000, made up mainly of stocks and promissory notes, including those of the heirs of Burridge Purvis.[18]

Two years later, while staying with his Philadelphia family, William Purvis contracted typhus and died on October 3, 1826, at the age of sixty-nine. He was buried the next day after a funeral service at the Second Presbyterian Church. His death was mentioned in *Poulson's Daily Advertiser* of October 4, *The Charleston City Gazette*, and *The Columbia Telescope* of October 17, 1826. The latter recorded "Died in Philadelphia on the 3rd inst. Mr. William Purvis, for many years a respectable inhabitant of our town in the 64th (sic!) year of his age." There was no mention of his living in Charleston Neck, and certainly not of his mixed- race family.[19]

William Purvis's will was probated on October 18, 1826, and Harriet learned of its generous terms. Though she was doubtless relieved to be so well taken care of, and to know that the futures of her sons were assured, still, for her and for the boys, the death of their father was a bitter blow. Twenty-year-old William was already showing signs of the dreaded disease, tuberculosis. Robert, sixteen, and Joseph, fourteen, were too young to lose their father. Robert in particular had loved and respected his father, and referred to his influence all his life.[20]

In settling William Purvis's estate, the lawyers discovered that he was still owed one thousand pounds sterling by John Purvis, the son of Burridge. They arranged for Henry Grimké of South Carolina, the brother of Sarah and Angelina Grimké, to sue John in the courts for the return of this money. This law suit was not settled until 1834, when it was ruled that the sum could not be collected, for John was a pauper.[21]

Harriet was determined to carry out William's wish that his sons be educated as gentlemen. William Jr. was too ill to go away to school, but shortly after her lover's death, she sent Robert off to Amherst, Massachusetts in style. According to Robert Purvis's eighty-year-old recollections, he rode his own horse to Massachusetts. It may be that William Purvis had chosen Amherst for the education of his sons because an older brother, John, had lived in nearby Pittsfield. Perhaps he also believed that Robert would be admitted to a New England school because of the lightness of his skin. It has often been said that Robert Purvis attended Amherst College. However, the college has no record of this, nor of the several classmates Purvis mentions. Instead it is likely that he attended Amherst Academy, which was closely affiliated with the college in the early days. Records are missing for his dates, but show that his younger brother, Joseph, attended the Academy from 1828–1830.[22]

At Amherst Academy, Alphonso Taft (1810–1891), who became the United States Attorney General under President Ulysses S. Grant, and Samuel Colt (1814–1862), later the inventor of the Colt revolver, were Robert's classmates. Colt evidently loved gunpowder from an early age. At the end of their first year at Amherst, he persuaded Purvis to help him celebrate July 4 by "borrowing" a cannon from nearby South Hadley and firing it from College Hill just before dawn. When the startled professors began creeping up the hill to investigate, Colt showed Purvis how to fire a second charge. For this escapade Colt was expelled, and Purvis decided it would be wise to withdraw. He took his horse and finished his education in Pittsfield, Massachusetts, likely at the recently opened Berkshire Gymnasium. Here he may have acquired the cultured writing and speaking style which characterized his public expressions and private correspondence for the rest of his life.[23]

During the years of his schooling, Robert returned from Amherst Academy and from Berkshire Gymnasium to see his mother and his ailing brother, William. Despite the hopes of his mother and brothers, William did not recover from the tuberculosis that had been plaguing him. On April 5, 1828 he died, and was buried at St. Thomas Episcopal Church. *Poulson's Daily Advertiser* carried the news of his death on April 7, along with an invitation for friends and acquaintances to attend his funeral, which was to be conducted from his late residence, "in Fourth Street, the 2nd door below Queen Street." A paragraph, probably written at Harriet's urging, spoke of his virtues:[24]

> The deceased was a young man of the most amiable disposition, sound understanding, and excellent principles. His correct deportment won the esteem of all whom he became acquainted with in life; and the qualities of his heart were such as to ensure the lasting regard of his intimate associates.[25]

When William's will was probated, it was discovered that he had left his generous share of his father's estate to his mother in trust to his brothers This money was eventually used to purchase a house at 270 North Seventh Street. Here Harriet lived until her death in 1869.[26]

It has proved hard to trace the movements of Harriet Judah between 1826, when William Purvis died, and 1832, when she acquired the house on Seventh Street. Some time in the period between 1826 and 1828, she met and married a black clergyman. The Reverend William Miller, a minister of the African Methodist Episcopal Zion Church, was from New York, but was frequently in Philadelphia, preaching at the First Wesleyan African Church (Big Wesley) on Lombard Street, and meeting with black civic leaders, with whom he was later associated in the Negro Convention Movement. Harriet must have met him on one of these occasions.[27]

Born as a free black in Queen's County, Maryland in 1775, Miller moved to New York City and became a skillful cabinetmaker. His real interest, however was in religion. It was at his house on Mulberry Street that the African Methodist Episcopal Zion Church was born. He ran a school for black Americans in his home, and helped to found the New York African Bible Society in 1817. He left the Zion connection temporarily in 1814 to found the Asbury Church, but soon returned to AMEZ. In 1819, he was sent to Big Wesley in Philadelphia to confirm its connection with Zion. By 1835 he was living in Philadelphia and frequently preaching at Big Wesley, though he evidently maintained a residence in New York City, for he was listed there in the Census of 1840. He became a bishop in Zion in 1840.[28]

Miller was interested in the abolition of slavery, and in reform movements within the black community. He attended the 1831 Annual Convention of Free People of Color in Philadelphia, and his church, Asbury, was the site of the fourth annual meeting in 1834. Nevertheless, Robert Purvis never mentioned him in his correspondence. One can only conjecture that he may have resented this replacement of his beloved father. It also appears likely that his mother, Harriet, was frequently in New York City with Miller, until the latter moved to Philadelphia sometime prior to 1835.[29]

In 1833, Harriet Judah Miller and William Miller, together with Robert and Joseph Purvis of Philadelphia, sued the heirs of Burridge Purvis, John and another Robert Purvis, for some property in Columbia, South Carolina still owing William Purvis's estate; they again employed Henry and Thomas Grimké of Charleston as their lawyers. They lost the suit, however, since Harriet and her two sons were still considered slaves under South Carolina law.[30]

A young man now, Robert Purvis was considered both well-educated and a gentleman. According to contemporary accounts and the pictures which have come down to us, he was extremely handsome. At the time of his death at age eighty-eight, several papers commented on his continuing good looks. He was six feet tall and graceful, with an erect carriage, dark wavy hair and sideburns, dark eyes, fine brows, high cheek bones, a well-formed mouth and chin, and very light skin. He was a fine horseman and traveled extensively, usually by horseback, or horse and carriage, and sometimes stayed in fashionable places where he was often mistaken for white. Told that he was black, reporters guessed that he had one-eighth, one-sixteenth, or one-thirty-second amount of African blood. Yet he was never tempted to "pass" as white (except once, to play a trick on a slaveowner); his identification with his grandmother's race was perhaps the strongest element in his sense of self.[31]

By 1828, Robert Purvis was living in the city of Philadelphia, and rented his own pew in St. Thomas Episcopal Church.[32] Sometime during this year, he heard an electrifying speech by Benjamin Lundy, a Quaker abolitionist. Lundy was a journalist who had been born in New Jersey but moved to Mt. Pleasant, Ohio where he founded an antislavery society, the Union Humane Society. In 1821, Lundy began to publish an antislavery newspaper, *The Genius of Universal Emancipation*, which he moved first to Greenville, Tennessee and then in 1824 to Baltimore, Maryland.[33]

In *The Genius*, Lundy published many of the antislavery authors of the day, including Elizabeth Heyrick, a British abolitionist whose pamphlet, "Immediate, Not Gradual Abolition," was aimed at Great Britain's policies. The slogan became a rallying cry for American antislavery advocates. Lundy also published the poetry and essays of Elizabeth Chandler, an abolitionist from Philadelphia, who became the editor of the "Ladies Repository" of the newspaper.[34]

Lundy was fervently committed to immediate emancipation of slavery. As a subtitle to his masthead he adopted the slogan, "Let justice be done though the heavens should fall." But he also thought in common with many abolitionists of his day; he believed racial prejudice would make it impossible for former slaves to live in peace and prosperity in the United States. He therefore was at first cheered when Robert Finley, a young man from Basking Ridge, New Jersey organized the American Colonization Society in 1816. The purpose of this group was to send American blacks to Africa, ostensibly to bring civilization, Christianity, and new resources for trade to the native peoples. Many founding members of the American Colonization Society believed that freedom should be given to slaves on condition that they "return" to Africa to take part in the development of that continent. At first some abolitionists supported the movement, believing it might solve the problem of slavery, but they soon became suspicious, discovering that the organization put more emphasis on ridding the country of blacks than on freeing slaves. In his pamphlet, *Thoughts on the Colonization of Free Blacks,* Finley revealed that he was deeply concerned about miscegenation or racial intermarriage. In the early years of the movement, he was able to attract powerful and prominent men to the cause. Some of these were Southerners who were not interested in abolition; they wanted to get rid of the free blacks, who, they believed, incited slaves to revolt.[35]

Lundy soon came to share the doubts of other abolitionists about the American Colonization Society, which he never joined, but he continued to believe that some free blacks ought to be offered the opportunity of leaving the prejudiced East Coast to settle in a more favorable land. To this end he became interested in exploring Haiti as a potential place for the resettlement of American blacks. Later, after this scheme fell through, he proposed establishing a colony in Texas.[36]

In 1824, Lundy moved his newspaper to Baltimore, Maryland, and in 1829 he hired a young New England newspaper man, William Lloyd Garrison. Garrison had become a disciple after reading *The Genius,* and after hearing Lundy speak in Boston in 1828. In Baltimore, Garrison met a number of middle-class blacks, including William Watkins, his son, William Watkins Jr., and Hezekiah Grice, who were opposed to colonization. Although it was several years later before he himself came out against the practice, their argument made an impression on the young journalist. In the pages of *The Genius,* Garrison opposed the slave trade in ever more stringent language. A piece he wrote attacking a New England shipowner who did business with a Baltimore slave trader resulted in a suit for libel against the fiery young journalist. Garrison was convicted and spent a month and a half in jail until a New York abolitionist, Arthur Tappan, paid his fine. He came out of jail more resolute than ever, and he decided to leave *The Genius,* after only one year, and found his own newspaper, the *Liberator.*[37]

While editing *The Genius,* Lundy made numerous trips to Philadelphia, attempting to rouse abolitionists to a more radical stand, and to garner financial support for his always needy newspaper.[38] He spoke to both Quaker and nondenominational audiences. Though a mild-mannered Quaker, he used forceful rhetoric in his denunciations of slavery. Slave owners, he asserted, were "too depraved to blush, and too wicked to repent." In an article in *The Genius* in 1823, he asserted that slaveholders were in the business of prostitution:

> Many slave holders are ipso facto the most disgraceful whoremongers upon earth; they make a *business* of raising bastards and selling them for money:—they keep poor miserable degraded females for this identical purpose; they compel them to submit to their abominable *avaricious*, and brutal lusts; they oppose the work of emancipation on this ground.[39]

Lundy's earnestness, his mild manner and yet powerful rhetoric had a profound effect on the young Purvis. Robert had grown up in an antislavery household, but his father's wealth and influence, and perhaps his own light skin, had spared him most of the indignities which he might have been expected to suffer. As Lundy described the horrors of slavery, and the moral obligation to end it, the young man was deeply stirred. Throughout his life, he looked back to the Lundy speech as a defining moment, and in his own speeches and letters often praised Lundy as "the antislavery pioneer."[40]

After first hearing Lundy speak, Robert Purvis made his own first antislavery speech sometime before his twentieth birthday, and began his lifelong commitment to the activism in the antislavery cause.

For the abolitionists, gaining the support of Robert Purvis was an extraordinary piece of good fortune. Here was an African-American, wealthy enough not to have to work for a living, and independent enough to be able to speak his mind without fear of reprisals. Handsome and well-spoken, Purvis could appear on any antislavery platform, and could support the movement financially in many ways. Antislavery advocates who wanted to practice interracial friendships could entertain him in their homes and introduce him to their guests. From his first exposure to the antislavery platform, to his death almost seventy years later, Robert Purvis was an important figure in the movement to end slavery in the United States and beyond.

CHAPTER 3

❦

Present at the Beginning

$\mathcal{A}$ more profound influence on the young Robert Purvis than that of Benjamin Lundy was James Forten (1766–1842), the wealthy black sailmaker who lived on Lombard Street. James was the son of Thomas Forten, a journeyman sailmaker and Margaret, who may have been a former slave. Young Forten attended the Free African School, founded by Anthony Benezet and conducted by Quakers at Willings Alley. Thomas Forten died in 1773, and James had to help support the family, working as a clerk in a grocery store. He was in Philadelphia when the Declaration of Independence was read and longed to help in the struggle for freedom. General George Washington, however, was not accepting blacks as soldiers. In 1781, Forten signed on as crew of a privateer, the *Royal Louis*, owned by merchant Francis Gurney. The first voyage was a success but on the second sailing the *Royal Louis* was captured by a British man-of-war, the *Amphion*, and its crew was sent to a prison ship, the *Jersey*, in New York harbor. Before this exchange could take place, and while he was still on the *Amphion*, James Forten befriended the young son of the captain. As a result, the captain offered James the opportunity to go with them to England as a companion to the younger boy, to be educated and raised as a gentleman. Forten refused, saying, "I have been taken prisoner for the liberties of my country, and never will prove traitor to her interests."[1]

After several terrible months aboard the prison ship, James Forten arranged his escape by hiding in the sea chest of a Continental officer who was being exchanged. At the last moment, though, he gave up his place for a fellow prisoner, Daniel Brewton, who was two years younger than he. As a result, the two became lifelong friends. After seven months, his name came up for release, and he made his way back to Philadelphia. He signed on for a voyage on a merchant ship, spent a year in England, and may have worked in a sail loft along the Thames River. Returning to Philadelphia in 1785, he entered into an apprenticeship with sailmaker Robert Bridges, and soon became foreman. When Bridges retired in 1798, he left the business in charge of James Forten.[2]

By managing the sail loft well, employing both black and white workers, and by investing his profits in real estate and money lending, Forten became a wealthy man. Continuing in the patriotic tradition, he volunteered to help build fortifications when the British threatened Philadelphia during the War of 1812. For the next thirty years of his life, while continuing his profitable business, he gave much of his time to public service for the black community.[3]

Robert Purvis and his brothers had grown up in and out of the Forten household. After their mother remarried, and spent time in New York City with her new husband, they may have come to regard the Fortens as their second home. The Forten daughters with whom they had played as children were now young women; it was natural that friendships ripened into something more. For Robert Purvis, the dark, beautiful, and talented Harriet Davy Forten, six months his senior, was increasingly appealing. Sometime in the spring of 1831, they became engaged.[4]

James Forten must have approved of Robert as a son-in-law. Not only had the young man inherited money, but he also was beginning to increase his wealth by buying, selling, and renting real estate properties, and lending money, a business which he was to conduct for the rest of his life. In addition, James found young Robert intellectually compatible. He shared many of James' viewpoints, was an articulate spokesman, and an accomplished writer. The two became close friends and colleagues, Forten feeling for Robert some of the warmth that he felt for his own sons.

On August 4, 1831, Robert became twenty-one and a few weeks later, on September 13, Robert and Harriet were married in an elaborate ceremony at the Forten home. The Right Reverend Bishop Henry Onderdonk of the Episcopal Church of New York officiated, since the Reverend J. M. Douglass, the minister of St. Thomas Episcopal Church, to which Harriet belonged, was prevented from attending because of a death in his family.[5]

According to all observers it was a good marriage, which lasted forty-four years, until Harriet's death in 1875. The two were partners in antislavery activities, and Harriet was a gracious hostess to Robert's many guests. He employed help so that Harriet was free to pursue her own activities, even though she had a large family of children. Harriet belonged, with her sisters, to the Black Female Literary Association, founded in September 1831, and later to the Gilbert Lyceum; they played an important role in the antislavery movement. Robert's lifelong commitment to the rights of women stemmed in part from his admiration of his talented wife.

Within a few months of the wedding, Harriet was pregnant, and it was time for the young couple to establish a home of their own. On June 15, 1832, Robert bought a two-story brick house and lot on the south side of Lombard Street, west of Ninth Street, from Thomas, Rachel, and Joseph Hutchinson for $3,050.[6] It was to be their home for the next twelve years.

From the beginning, Robert and Harriet used the house on Lombard Street as a center for entertaining abolitionist friends and holding antislavery meetings. In June 1832, they entertained William Lloyd Garrison, a frequent guest; in April 1833, they put up Arnold Buffum, a New England abolitionist. In December 1833, John Greenleaf Whittier visited the Purvises, and wrote a poem for Harriet's scrapbook, entitled "To the Daughters of James Forten," proclaiming his sense of kinship with them despite the difference in color.

> *Sisters! The proud and vain may pass you by*
> *With the rude taunt and cold malicious eye;*
> *Point the pale hand deridingly and slow*
> *In scorn's vile gesture at the darker brow' . . .*
> *. . . Fervent and pure let this frail tribute bear*
> *A brother's blessing and a brother's prayer.*

This poem was published in the *Liberator* in the fall of 1836, much to the annoyance of the Forten family, who considered it a private matter. Interviewed in 1890, an eighty-year-old Robert Purvis insisted that it had never previously been published.[7]

The influx of visitors to the Purvis home continued. In March 1835, George Thompson (1804–1878), the famous British abolitionist was a guest as well as George Benson, William Lloyd Garrison's brother-in-law. There was always room for one more at Harriet's table.[8]

Conversation at that table swirled often around the issue of colonization and the machinations of the American Colonization Society, now beginning to make an impact on the national debate on slavery. James Forten, Robert's father-in-law, was no stranger to the colonization movement. As a sailmaker, he had met a black shipowner, Paul Cuffe, from Westport, Massachusetts, whose ships traded up and down the coast. Cuffe was a Quaker who wanted to end the slave trade. This he thought might best be accomplished by developing commercial trade in agricultural and manufactured products between the United States, England, and Sierra Leone, the British colony on the West Coast of Africa. Cuffe believed this would be possible if a few prosperous African-Americans could settle in the colony and teach local people methods of farming, as well as establishing small mills for manufacturing.[9]

This scheme won the backing at first of many African-Americans, as well as the Quaker-dominated Pennsylvania Abolition Society. In Philadelphia, where the black elite had previously been opposed to the concept of colonization, Cuffe found support. James Forten became interested in engaging in the new trading arrangements. He helped Cuffe to organize a local African Institute to promote the scheme, and served for a time as its president.[10]

The organization of the American Colonization Society in 1816 had quickly brought an end to this support. Free African-Americans, especially working-class blacks, were quick to see the dangers in this plan, and their support for Cuffe vanished. In 1817, a large protest meeting was held in Mother Bethel Church in Philadelphia, chaired by James Forten; a committee of twelve was organized to coordinate opposition to the colonization society. In writing Cuffe about the meeting, Forten said: "Three thousand attended, and there was not one soul in favor of going to Africa." He did not mention that he himself had voiced his opposition, stating that his family had been Americans for 170 years; he was an American and entitled to full citizenship. Thereafter Forten and the Philadelphia abolitionists took the lead in opposing the American Colonization Society, fighting the efforts of the free blacks of New York City to assume the role of chief opponent to colonization.[11]

In January 1832, Purvis joined James Forten and another black abolitionist, William Whipper, to prepare a "remonstrance" against a Philadelphia group favoring colonization. Although the remonstrance is signed by all three men, its style suggests that it was written by Purvis. The remonstrance was occasioned by a group of so-called concerned citizens who had held a meeting at Upton's Tavern on Dock Street on November 23, 1831 to prepare a memorial for the Senate and House of Representatives or Assembly of Pennsylvania to ask that the U.S. Congress raise money for the emigration of a free colored population from the United States. In response, a large group of concerned black citizens met on January 4 to protest.[12]

The meeting at Upton's Tavern was very likely called by the Philadelphia Colonization Society. It was occasioned by the reaction of many

Northerners to the slave uprising of Nat Turner in Southampton, Virginia, which had struck terror in many hearts. The colonizationists based their argument on a recent report that a white woman was seized in Virginia; she had confessed to being the agent for a group of blacks in Philadelphia intent on stirring up slave rebellion. The woman, Purvis said, had refused to agree with this lie.[13]

Slave rebellions, Purvis and his colleagues argued, were not the result of the machinations of abolitionists but of slavery itself.

> We are sorry to hear of such scenes as that of the Southampton Tragedy; it proceeded from a natural cause; oppression, tyranny, and slavery always give birth to such events, and we can only say to Virginia, and the other slaveholding states, that so long as they continue to raise up Gabriels and Nats, just so long may they expect to see those scenes acted over and over again. So long as slaveholders and their apologists continue to apply the same remedy to abstract and foreign causes, so long the real cause will sleep in safety. Remove slavery, and the cause will cease—convert your enemies into friends, by rendering unto every man his due and then you may lie down in peace.[14]

As for the argument that sending free blacks to Africa would decrease the risk of slave uprisings, Purvis and his coauthors were scornful. Why attempt to create better conditions for uneducated African natives who were almost savages, while ridding the nation of freemen who were rapidly becoming educated and valuable citizens? As to the claim that the colonizationists were motivated by a desire to aid native Africans, and were willing to appropriate money to send free blacks to Africa to do so, why did they show so little interest in freeing the enslaved Africans in this country? And if the free blacks were a degrading influence here, why assume that they would make good rulers in Africa? Leave it to the consciences of free blacks as to whether they wish to emigrate to Africa "*Let us alone*; and if the spirit of *voluntary* emigration, becomes implanted in our hearts, we will in due time inform you."[15]

In this memorial, Purvis states some of the themes which he reiterated throughout his lifetime; his pride in being an American and a Pennsylvanian (since Pennsylvania had begun a gradual process of ridding itself of slavery in 1780), his belief that an appeal to reason would ultimately sway the general public, and his implacable opposition to colonization and to chattel slavery.

William Whipper, who may have been coauthor of the remonstrance, was a third influence on the young Robert Purvis. Born in Little Britain,

Lancaster County, Pennsylvania in 1804, Whipper was self-educated, and came to Philadelphia in 1828 to work as a steam scourer. He quickly rose to prominence in the black community, admired for his skills as a writer and an organizer. He shared with Purvis a patriotism for the United States and Pennsylvania, and a belief that color should not make a difference.[16]

In April 1832, Robert Purvis again assisted James Forten and William Whipper, this time in writing an appeal to the Pennsylvania Assembly to protest two pending laws, one written to "protect" Pennsylvanians from the immigration of additional free blacks, and the other to repeal the commonwealth's own liberal fugitive slave law and revert to the harsher federal law of 1793. This appeal also bears the stamp of Purvis's personal style. In arguing against the punitive legislation, the appeal cited once more the American penchant for liberty, Pennsylvania's leadership in abolishing slavery, the contribution of black citizens to the Commonwealth, the amount of taxes they paid, and their right to be treated equally, all these themes were to run through much of Purvis's consequent campaigning.[17]

> At the same time that your memorialists entertain the most perfect respect for any expression of sentiment emanating from so high a source as one of the legislative bodies of Pennsylvania, they cannot but lament, that at a moment when all mankind seems to be struggling for freedom, and endeavoring to throw off the shackles of political oppression, the constitutional authorities of this great state should entertain a resolution which has a tendency to abridge the liberties heretofore accorded to that race of men confessedly oppressed. Our country asserts for itself the glory of being the freest upon the surface of the globe. She wrested that freedom, while yet in her infancy, by force of arms, at the expense of infinite blood and treasure, from a gigantic and most powerful adversary. She proclaimed freedom to all mankind—and offered her soil as a refuge to the enslaved of all nations.[18]

This liberty was compromised, Purvis and his colleagues argued, by the existence of slavery. They were therefore proud that Pennsylvania was the first among states to renounce the institution. In the preamble to the Commonwealth statement in regard to slavery, adopted on March 1, 1780, it was stated: "It is not for us to enquire, why, in the creation of mankind, the inhabitants of the several parts of the earth were distinguished by a difference in feature or complexion—it is sufficient for us to know that all are the work of an Almighty hand." Why was this distinction now being made by the lawmakers of Pennsylvania? Why close the borders of Pennsylvania to persons whose only crime is to be other than white?[19]

William Whipper, Purvis's coauthor and mentor, had attended a convention of colored men called in September 1830 by the venerable Bishop Richard Allen. One purpose of this meeting was to aid the free blacks of Ohio, who were being forced out of the state by the decision of the legislature to enforce the Black Code, demanding that they pay a large bond if they chose to stay. Many of these blacks had decided to emigrate to Canada, and had appealed to free blacks in Philadelphia, New York, and elsewhere to raise money to aid them in this move. The delegates agreed to aid them. The convention was supposedly national, but was attended largely by Pennsylvanians, as the result of rivalry between New York and Philadelphia over leadership in the black community. One outcome was to establish a series of national black conventions.[20]

Robert Purvis had not attended the founding meeting, but he joined Whipper at the First Annual Convention of Colored Americans, held the following June at the Wesleyan Baptist Church in Philadelphia. This convention endorsed the settlement in Canada, urged delegates to oppose the American Colonization Society's efforts to limit the movement of free blacks, and promoted a drive for "*Education, Temperance and Economy*" among members of the black population.[21]

Present at the 1831 convention were several white friends of the abolition movement, including William Lloyd Garrison and Arthur Tappan. Garrison and Tappan proposed the establishment of a manual labor school in New Haven, Connecticut. Delegates stipulated that the new school should be supervised by a board in which African-Americans were in the majority; a number of delegates were appointed to oversee it. Robert Purvis was among several prominent Philadelphians placed on a committee to raise money. Unfortunately, the school did not materialize, owing to the hostility of the mayor and a number of prominent citizens of New Haven.[22]

In 1832, Garrison was again present at the Annual Convention, held in Philadelphia, and debated Ralph Randolph Gurley of the American Colonization Society who had asked to be present in an effort to win the organization's support for colonization. Gurley was certainly not successful in this, and the delegates were forced to rethink their continuing support for those blacks emigrating to Canada. A five-person committee was appointed to reexamine the Canadian question, with Whipper as one of the five. The committee could not agree, and a larger committee was appointed. Finally, a compromise wording was reached, recommending that money be raised to assist those who had already moved to Canada, where they were facing further prejudice. It was decided that a large tract of land should not be purchased for the sake of future emigrants.[23]

Present at this convention, the young Purvis was again assigned to the committee to raise money for the school in New Haven. The convention was made memorable for him by the presence of Garrison, whom he venerated, Gurley, whom he came to despise, and "a lady most friendly to the attainments of the rights of the people of color," very probably Lucretia Mott, a famous Quaker abolitionist, with whom his destiny was entwined.[24]

Following this convention, which went on record as supporting temperance and increasing educational and literary opportunities for black youth, Purvis joined with other Philadelphians in founding the Philadelphia Library for Colored Persons, and later served as vice president and corresponding secretary. This group met in the basement of St. Thomas's African Episcopal Church; Robert Purvis was a member.[25]

Purvis and Whipper were again delegates to the third annual meeting held in Philadelphia June 3–13, 1833. Purvis, now almost twenty-three, played a larger role in this meeting. He was appointed to the rules and regulations committee, and later to the post of corresponding secretary for the convention. He played a more active role in the deliberations of the meeting, seconding a motion to approve support of William Garrison's current visit to England to raise money for the manual labor college, and another to support the antislavery newspapers now proliferating. He also presented a motion of his own "that this Convention highly approve of the indefatigable labors of Miss Lydia White, in her establishment of a free labour store."[26]

At this meeting, the issue of emigration to Canada was once more discussed. In light of the fact that some of the blacks who had moved to Canada were experiencing discrimination, the convention minuted "that as there is not now, and probably never will be actual necessity for a large emigration of the present race of free coloured people, they therefore refrain from recommending any emigration whatever."[27]

The delegates went further to make a forceful statement against colonization, which sounds very much like the work of Whipper and Purvis:

> Resolved, that this convention discourage, by every means in their power, the colonization of our people, anywhere beyond the limits of this continent, and those who may be obliged to exchange a cultivated region for a howling wilderness, we would recommend to retire back into the western wilds, and fell the native forests of America, where the ploughshare of prejudice has as yet been unable to penetrate the soil.[28]

Robert Purvis's objection to colonization was further strengthened at the time of the third convention by reports from the colony established

by the American Colonization Society in Liberia. In the spring and summer of 1833, he received several letters from a Philadelphia black, originally a seaman, Joseph Dailey, who had gone to Liberia as a reporter for
a newspaper run by John R. Russwurm, a colonization supporter. Dailey,
however, took a dim view of the "Nigger Colony," as he called it. The
leadership was corrupt, he believed, the agricultural resources inadequate
to the number of colonists which the Society was dumping onto the land,
and the hospital full of the sick and dying, proving the climate was injurious. Because of these criticisms he found himself branded as "a character dangerous to the successful operations of the Society."[29]

Some months later the American Colonization Society refused to
honor a check drawn on its account by Dailey in order to pay the tuition
of his younger brother in New Haven. It was necessary for Robert Purvis
to intervene on Dailey's behalf. He wrote an icy letter to Ralph Randolph
Gurley, secretary of the Colonization Society, implying that the Society
was simply trying to get out of paying its just debts because of its deficits.
". . . the wonder naturally created by such a procedure, was soon dissipated
from my having understood that the funds of the Society were low . . ."
Purvis asked that the check be honored immediately.[30]

Robert Purvis continued to represent Joseph Dailey's interests in
the United States, and to speak out on his behalf against the American
Colonization Society. Some years later he wrote to the editor of the *Pennsylvania Freeman*, answering some allegations made by John Brooke Pin-
ney, corresponding secretary of the New York Colonization Society, based
on assertions made by John Russwurm, who had been temporary governor of Liberia in 1834, and had been embroiled with Dailey at that time.
Now he was bringing false charges against Dailey, who was not present to
defend himself.

> From Dailey's general good character, his firm adherence to abolitionist
> principles—his detestation of the "nefarious scheme"—and his having
> spurned the attempts of the American Colonization Society through its
> agent—R. R. Gurley—to win him over to the advocacy of its diabolical prin-
> ciples, [it] is quite sufficient for every "colored" man, and his true friends,
> to resist any impression against his character, from such a source as the ex-
> Governor of Liberia. In this belief—together with the fact that Mr. Dailey
> will soon be in this country, quite able and ready to meet every charge
> against him—I leave the matter.[31]

Robert Purvis's implacable hatred of colonization was deepened by
his reading of William Lloyd Garrison's "Thoughts on Colonization." It

was probably through the annual conventions that Robert Purvis first met William Lloyd Garrison, a third mentor who was to have a profound influence on his life. Garrison came to Philadelphia in 1830 to garner support for the newspaper, the *Liberator*, which he planned to found.

Both James Forten and Robert Purvis gave generously, and the *Liberator* was first published in January 1831. Garrison demanded in the publication the immediate and complete abolition of slavery. The two men also contributed to Garrison's expenses as he traveled about the country organizing antislavery societies. The New England Anti-Slavery Society was the first. In 1832, when Garrison issued a pamphlet, "Thoughts on Colonization," refuting the arguments of the American Colonization Society, both Forten and Purvis solicited subscriptions for copies and ordered many for their own use. Their support helped to keep the young journalist solvent.

In May 1832, William Lloyd Garrison wrote two letters to Robert Purvis, at first declining, then accepting the latter's invitation to stay with the Purvises when he came to Philadelphia to attend the annual colored convention in June. In his second letter, he announced that his pamphlet, "Thoughts on African Colonization" would go on sale the very next day. "I understand that I am very much indebted to you for your efforts, your very successful efforts, to procure subscribers for same."[32]

After the convention, Garrison wrote from Boston a letter of praise for their hospitality.

> The very generous and unremitted exertions made by yourself and your accomplished lady to promote my happiness and comfort during my residence in Philadelphia have left an indelible impression upon my memory, and opened in my heart a fountain of gratitude which only death can close.[33]

In the same letter, he outlined a proposal to travel throughout the free states for the purpose of forming antislavery societies. Arthur Tappan, the wealthy abolitionist, and Peter Williams, a black minister, both of New York, had approved the plan; the only difficulty, Garrison said, was procuring the necessary funds. He was also glad to report that Tappan had ordered one hundred copies of "Thoughts on Colonization," which Garrison called, "an extremely liberal subscription." He invited Robert and his brother Joseph to come to Boston for a visit.[34]

Garrison wrote again in December, congratulating Robert and Harriet on the birth of their son, William. "May he prove one of the best of his persecuted race." He then mentioned that "with much delicacy of feeling and reluctance" he had sent Purvis a circular asking for financial aid for the *Liberator*, which might otherwise go under. He reported that the appeal had been successful; and that "the extraordinary purchase of so large a number of copies of our "Thoughts" [on Colonization] in Philadelphia as were ordered by our friends Cassey, Forten and yourself, have given us material assistance."[35]

Garrison was briefly the guest of Robert and Harriet Purvis again in the spring of 1833 under unusual circumstances. Garrison had raised money for a trip to England to promote the *Liberator* and the antislavery cause. Shortly before he was due to sail, Garrison was indicted for libel. In the *Liberator*, he had written many articles in support of Prudence Crandall, a Connecticut schoolteacher whose decision to enroll a black student in her girls school met with violent protest. In response, Prudence had decided to enroll only black students, and was arrested and tried for enrolling out-of-state residents without consulting the town authorities. In his passionate defense of Prudence, Garrison had supposedly maligned the town clerk, Andrew T. Judson.[36] Arriving in New York to take passage, he found himself pursued by a sheriff. Lewis Tappan, brother of Arthur and also an abolitionist, sent Garrison on to Philadelphia with a letter to Purvis asking him to take Garrison immediately to Trenton by private carriage, and place him in the hands of a friend who would drive him to New Brunswick. Purvis described what happened next in a letter to abolitionist Rowland Johnson fifty-seven years later:

> ... and from thence Mr. Tappan had perfected arrangements by which Mr. Garrison would be placed on the ship which would be lying off at some convenient point near N. York—the precise details, I have forgotten.
>
> An incident, on my very hurried drive to Trenton—came very nearly ending in a fearful catastrophe in which your dear friend's life was endangered. Another time.[37]

The fearful catastrophe Purvis mentioned was a situation in which his horse had been startled, and came very close to pitching Garrison into the river. Purvis's recollection that Garrison was to be taken to a ship off New York was wrong, for Garrison evidently remained in hiding, staying in New York and New Haven, where he sat for his portrait commissioned by Purvis to be painted by Nathaniel Jocelyn, brother of the abolitionist minister, Simeon S. Jocelyn. In a letter to Robert Purvis from New York, just before sailing, Garrison said: "Mr. Jocelyn has completed what is described as a good likeness of the madman, Garrison." For many years thereafter, Garrison's portrait hung in the home of the Purvises.[38]

After a successful stay in England, Garrison returned to the United States, and came to Philadelphia in December 1833, to launch the American Anti- Slavery Society. Robert Purvis was present at the founding meeting at Adelphi Hall, and was one of three blacks to sign the Declaration of Sentiments. (The others were James G. Barbadoes of Boston, a coworker of Garrison, and James McCrummill, a well-to-do dentist.[39]) At this gathering, Robert Purvis rose to speak, saying he wished to utter "heartfelt thanks to the delegates who have convened for the deliverance of my people." Present at the founding meeting was the poet John G. Whittier, who wrote in his memoirs about the occasion:[40]

> A young man rose to speak whose appearance at once arrested my attention. I think I never saw a finer face and figure and his manner, words, and bearing were in keeping. "Who is he?" I asked one of the Pennsylvania delegates. "Robert Purvis, of this city, a colored man," was the answer.[41]

Purvis's own favorite memory of the gathering was the intervention of Lucretia Mott. When the declaration of principles was being read to the group, a woman rose to offer a grammatical change. In the sentence, "we may be personally defeated, but our principles never can be," she suggested that the last two words be deleted, to read, "but our principles, never." "Her beautiful face was all aglow," Purvis remembered almost sixty years later.[42]

According to a journalist present, Robert Purvis made a brief speech on the floor of the convention. Paraphrased, it was published in *The Abolitionist*:

> Robert Purvis of Pennsylvania said he was grateful to God for the day. He felt to pour out the speaking gratitude of his soul to the Convention. . . . The name of William Lloyd Garrison sounded sweet to his ear.[43]

Three years earlier (1830) Garrison had begun his denunciations of colonization, and had founded the *Liberator*. The church and the nation had been awakened. The effects of Garrison's campaign were to be seen in this convention.

> It is, indeed, a good thing to be here. My heart, Mr. President, is too full for my tongue. But whether I speak to them my feelings as they exist in my inmost soul or not, the friends of the colored American will be remembered. Yes, Sir, their exertions and memories will be cherished, when pyramids and monuments shall crumble. The flood of time, which is rapidly sweeping to

destruction that refuge of lies, the American Colonization Society, is bearing on the advocates of our cause to a glorious and blessed immortality.[44]

From that moment until 1870, when the American Anti-slavery Society was finally dissolved, Purvis worked tirelessly for its goals, serving at first as a member of the board of managers (1833–1840); vice president (1841–1865), and member of the executive committee (1865–1870). He not only supported the Society generously and tided it over when it was in financial straits, but also spoke at many of its annual gatherings. His friendship with Whittier and with Garrison lasted a lifetime, although he and Garrison were estranged for a time during and immediately after the Civil War because Garrison believed the organization should be discontinued. Purvis, however, sided with Wendell Phillips (1811–1884); they voted for the Society to continue.

Four days after the formation of the American Anti-Slavery Society, Harriet Purvis met with a group of women in a schoolroom of a Quaker schoolteacher, Catherine McDermott, to found the Philadelphia Female Anti-Slavery Society, an interracial group which played an important role in the subsequent history of the antislavery movement; it was a launching pad for the women's rights movement. Harriet's mother, Charlotte Forten, her sisters, Margaretta Forten and Sarah Forten, and her future sister-in-law, Mary Woods, were also founding members, along with Grace Douglass and Sarah McCrummill, all leading members of Philadelphia's black middle class. Harriet's niece, Charlotte Forten, later became a member. Harriet was a faithful participant in this group for many years, taking particular responsibility for the annual money raising antislavery fairs, and she attended as a delegate two of the national American Conventions of Anti-Slavery Women.[45]

At this founding meeting, none of the women present felt capable of acting as chairperson. Lucretia Mott, who had helped to call the meeting, had served in 1830 as clerk of Philadelphia Women's Yearly Meeting, an important position, but since Quaker decisions were (and are) made by consensus, or "the sense of the meeting," she had no familiarity with parliamentary procedures. As a result, the women asked James McCrummill to preside. They also heard remarks from two male delegates to the American Anti-Slavery Society, Samuel May and Nathaniel Southard.[46]

Following the organization of the American Anti-Slavery Society, Robert Purvis attended the annual meetings faithfully. In 1870, when the band of antislavery radicals dissolved, he remembered that he had missed only one session.[47] In April 1834, he joined the Philadelphia Young Men's

Anti-Slavery Society, and attended the national sessions of the AAS in New York as a delegate. Here he was named a manager. The following May 1836, he helped to form the Philadelphia Anti-Slavery Society before attending the annual meeting.[48] In 1837, he went to Harrisburg, as a delegate of the Philadelphia group, to help found the Pennsylvania Anti-Slavery Society, an organization to which he devoted a major portion of his life for many years.[49]

The Garrisonian antislavery campaign exactly suited Robert Purvis's beliefs and temperament. The fact that the Garrisonians prided themselves on being radical, made no compromises, and espoused complete racial equality (although not always practicing it) made them ideal comrades in his own struggle for justice and recognition. Later, when the Garrisonians began to insist upon equality for women, they touched a deep chord in Robert Purvis, who felt very strongly that women were entitled to equal respect. Through the AAS, Robert and Harriet developed deep and lifelong interracial friendships with James and Lucretia Mott, William and Helen Garrison (although this suffered a hiatus during a period of estrangement), Abby and James Gibbons, Sydney and Elizabeth Gay, Cyrus and Ruth Pierce, and many others. Robert Purvis never turned his back on the black community; indeed his deepest friendships were with the Casseys, the Fortens, with Grace Douglass and Robert Douglass, and their children, especially Sarah and Robert. However, his strong and growing belief that there was "but one race," was strengthened by the Garrisonians.

CHAPTER 4

❦

World Traveler

$\mathcal{D}$uring his trip to England in 1833, William Lloyd Garrison told some of the English abolitionists about the free black leaders in the American movement, among them, the rising young Robert Purvis. Sometime in the early months of 1834, he suggested to Robert that he visit Great Britain to follow up on Garrison's leads, continue to raise money for the *Liberator*, and fight the colonization movement.

That movement seemed to be gaining some ground in Great Britain, as its American advocates traveled in that country, seeking support and extolling the virtues of developing the colony of Liberia. There was need for a representative of the American Anti-Slavery Society to visit England to rebut the arguments of the colonizationists. And who better than the handsome and well-spoken Robert Purvis, who could afford to pay for such a trip from his own purse?

Robert may have hesitated for family reasons. His first son, William, was still a toddler and Harriet was again expecting a baby, due in the fall. However, she doubtless urged him to go. By the spring of 1834, he had agreed and Garrison wrote him letters of introduction to the English abolitionists. Purvis must see Daniel O'Connell, the Irish abolitionist, William Allen, a Quaker, and a scientist as well as a reformer, and George Thompson, an abolitionist who was contemplating a visit to the United States.[1]

England had recently freed its slaves in the West Indies and the Act of Emancipation was to become official on August 1, 1834. Robert Purvis wanted to be there to celebrate the day. He was also eager to persuade the British reformers of the iniquity of the colonization scheme, and to undo the work of Philadelphian Elliot Cresson, who was preaching the gospel of colonization to British audiences at that time.[2]

The first hurdle was obtaining a U.S. passport. Purvis turned for help to Horace Binney, the Philadelphia lawyer who had settled his father's estate. Binney went to Louis McLane, the Secretary of State under President Andrew Jackson, who refused to issue a passport because he understood that Purvis was "a colored man." Instead Binney obtained a "special passport" stating that Purvis was a free person of color born in the United States and in case of need was entitled to the protection of American officials abroad. Robert Purvis was incensed, and spoke of his anger to the Philadelphia reformer, Roberts Vaux, a member of the Pennsylvania Abolition Society. Vaux was a recent convert to the Colonization Society, but still retained ties to James Forten.[3] At any rate he was willing to help. Vaux wrote to McLane, saying that Robert Purvis was wealthy, lived like a gentleman and was nearly white in complexion. According to Robert Purvis's later recollection of the case, Andrew Jackson himself heard about the issue, flew into a rage, and ordered McLane to issue a proper passport, saying that no American citizen was to be denied a passport because of color while he was president of these United States. Robert Purvis may therefore have been the first man of color to receive a U.S. passport.[4]

However, Purvis's problems were not over yet. He booked passage on a packet on the Cope Line, a shipping firm owned by the Cope brothers, Philadelphia Quakers; they sailed their ships from Philadelphia to Liverpool during this time. A prominent Virginian, Bernard Carter, was planning to sail on the same ship. When Carter heard the story of the passport, and realized that he would be sailing with a colored man, he complained to the Cope brothers. Fearing they would lose much of their profitable Southern trade, the Copes attempted to appease Carter; meanwhile they begged Robert Purvis to give up his ticket. Purvis was at first outraged. To accept the Copes' appeal went against his principles. He believed this was shameful behavior for a Quaker firm. However, he discovered that he could reach England sooner if he took a ship from New York; he decided to sail on a vessel which landed in Liverpool several days in advance of the Cope packet. He waited in Liverpool, staying probably at the Adelphi Hotel, until the Cope ship arrived. After it had disembarked its passengers, he sought out the captain and learned the name of the man who had objected to sailing with him. The Copes had previously withheld this information. Sooner or later he intended to confront Bernard Carter.[5]

Meanwhile, Robert Purvis took the stage from Liverpool to Manchester, where he saw Joseph Sturge, a Quaker and corn merchant who had traveled in the West Indies to collect information on the condition of slaves and had led the fight for emancipation in Great Britain. From there Purvis traveled to Woodstock, Oxford, and finally London, where he took lodging at an inn and began looking up more of the men and women to whom he had letters of introduction.

From London he wrote to Garrison on July 13, apologizing for the delay in getting off a letter.[6]

> This pleasure I expected to have had soon after my arrival in this country; but such were the demonstrations of friendship which I received from my friends here, that I could never find the time to send you an epistle; and even at the moment, I am forced to write hastily and briefly.
>
> You must know, my dear friend, that I am regarded in this country as "Abolition property"—and you must also know, that there is a very "*particular* price" set upon such property, especially too, when the coloring of the building happens to fall below the instant and wavering shade of white, to the more substantial black or brown.[7]

He had seen George Thompson, who was about to embark for the United States, and others to whom Garrison had sent letters. He was busy attempting to undo the damage of Elliot Cresson, the advocate of colonization. In an attempt to prove that British abolitionist leaders supported colonization, Cresson had asserted that William Wilberforce,[8] the great abolitionist leader who had recently died, was not in his right mind when he signed a protest against the American Colonization Society. British abolitionists had vigorously denied this.

Perhaps Purvis's greatest experience in London was meeting the famous Irish advocate of abolition, Daniel O'Connell,[9] whom he encountered at the House of Commons:

> On my being presented to the Irish Patriot, as a *American Gentleman*, he declined taking my hand; but when he understood that I was not only identified with the Abolitionists, but with the proscribed and oppressed colored class in the United States, he grasped my hand, and warmly shaking it, remarked—"*Sir, I will never take the hand of an American, nor should any honest man in this country do so, without first knowing his principles in reference to American Slavery, and its ally, the American Colonization Society.*" In reply I remarked that it was asserted in America that he had caused his name to

be stricken off the Protest against the American Colonization Society: Mark his answer! "He who asserted that, Sir, asserted a *lie*, to the full extent and meaning of the term. I have heard," he continued, "that much was made of what I said in relation to the Americans—their Slavery, and their Colonization; but"—(turning to my friend, Rev. Mr. Scoble[10] to whom I was indebted for an introduction), "I shall express myself more fully and decidedly, in relation to these matters. Get you up a meeting for that purpose, and I will subscribe 5 [pounds] or more, to defray the expense." Such, verbatim, was the language of that fearless advocate of universal freedom. Now, will Cresson dare again to say, that DANIEL O'CONNELL erased his name from the British Protest?[11]

The impact of the well-spoken and ardent young Robert Purvis on the British abolitionists was immense. George Thompson wrote to him a few months later, saying that he believed that leadership in the struggle against slavery would fall by right to Purvis; he urged him "to weep, supplicate and labor" in the coming years for his race.[12]

For a month, Purvis continued to meet abolitionists and to lecture on the situation in the United States, and the iniquities of the colonization movement. In the course of that time, he met Sir Thomas Foxwell Buxton (1786–1845), leader of the antislavery forces, who also received him warmly. Finally leaving London, he traveled to Glasgow, where he spoke to a public meeting of the Glasgow Emancipation Society, and attended a committee meeting of the Ladies Anti-Slavery Society of Glasgow, where he delivered a letter from the Philadelphia Female Anti-Slavery Society. In responding to this letter the Glasgow Ladies said of Purvis: "He being a proof of the wickedness and absurdity of that prejudice which would limit moral worth, intelligence & the divine gifts, to any particular tinge of complexion."[13]

From Glasgow he went to Fife, where he visited some of his father's relatives, and discussed his father's estate. A problem had arisen over a large loan which William Purvis had made to John Purvis, son of his late brother Burridge, who had protested paying it. Harriet and William Miller and Harriet's living sons, Robert and Joseph, brought suit. Robert Purvis of South Carolina enlisted his Scots cousins in his defense. After the Philadelphia Robert Purvis had visited them and explained the situation, these relatives gave testimony in favor of the Philadelphia Robert and his brother, Joseph.[14]

Soon it was fall and time to sail for the United States. Purvis booked passage on a boat that sailed from Portsmouth. To his surprise, he discovered that Bernard Carter was also awaiting the same boat. Purvis's first impulse was to denounce the Southerner, but he realized that this would make the home trip awkward. Instead, he bided his time. Carter spoke to him, and finding him a Philadelphian with roots in the Deep South, like himself, befriended him and invited him to dine. Later, after they had boarded the ship and were en route to Philadelphia, Carter consulted him on some fine wines the South Carolinian was bringing home, as well as about a thoroughbred horse he was importing. Purvis was an abstainer, but he knew a lot about horses, and discussed them with Carter.[15]

The acquaintance progressed, and Carter invited Purvis to join him at dinner with other Southerners, and to dance with their ladies, one of whom was a South Carolinian. He was a good dancer and much sought after by these fellow passengers. On the last evening of the voyage, the captain gave his passengers a complimentary dinner. An Englishman toasted the President of the United States, and called upon the youngest American present to respond. Robert Purvis, who had just turned twenty-four, was given the honor. Normally Robert Purvis found little about his native land to toast, but he was still grateful to Andrew Jackson for intervening in his behalf in the passport matter. Using his growing oratorical skills, he therefore gave a toast praising Jackson, and the promise of liberty for all in the United States. He closed by toasting the King of England William IV. The Englishman jumped up and said that Purvis was the most splendid example of young American manhood he had ever seen. Carter rose to his feet to second the motion.[16]

They were by now in New York harbor, and after the dinner Purvis withdrew to his cabin and asked the steward to tell the captain's wife of his colored blood. According to Purvis the news shot around the ship like a fireball. The company despatched a German doctor to interview him and discover whether the allegation was true. "Yes, go back and tell the company it is true and I am proud of it," Purvis replied. The news was received with consternation by the Southerners, one of whom had said on the voyage that he considered the black man little removed from an animal. But it was highly amusing to the rest of the travelers. A judge was flat on his back, kicking his heels in the air with hilarity, according to Purvis's recollection.[17]

Back in Philadelphia, Purvis spoke at many antislavery meetings about his travels. Abby Hopper Gibbons, the daughter of famed abolitionist Isaac Hopper, went to hear him in November 1834 in company with James and Lucretia Mott; they found him entertaining and informative.[18]

Robert rejoiced in his reunion with Harriet, and celebrated the birth of his second son, Robert Jr. The hot Philadelphia summer had been hard on Harriet, and on the black community. In August, a major riot had occurred, occasioned by rivalry between two fire companies. On the night of August 8, a band of black youths attacked members of the Fairmount Engine Company and captured some of their equipment. The next night, in retaliation, a gang of white youths attacked a young son of James Forten, on the street. Somehow, Forten managed to escape. On Monday evening there was a confrontation between black and white youths at a tavern called the Flying Horses. Tuesday, August 12, a large gang of white men attacked black houses and churches in a systematic fashion. Despite efforts of the mayor of Philadelphia, John Swift, to calm the situation, there was further rioting on the night of August 13, in which one black man was killed, a number severely injured, and two black churches and many black dwellings attacked, sacked, and set on fire.[19]

In the aftermath of the riots, the mayor appointed a citizen's committee to look into the causes of the violence. James Mott was chosen to serve upon it. Lucretia Mott wrote to a friend about it:

> J & self have been down among our poor sufferers by the late riots and found much injury done to their property—say to the amot. of 5 or $6000—. Jas. is one of a committee of a town mg. called to investigate the subject & report the amot. of damages—they are to meet tomorrow evg. when it is hoped something will be raised for their relief.[20]

His own family had suffered no damage, but Purvis resolved to protect them from further harm by finding a country retreat. He consulted Joseph Cassey, a friend and a mentor in business matters. The Casseys also desired a summer retreat, and together they began looking for land in Bucks County. In January 1835, they purchased a house and ninety-seven acres in Bristol Township, for $10,000. Purvis was interested in farming, and though he hired a farm manager, he supervised the farm closely. In the coming years, he often listed himself as a farmer in his business transactions.[21]

Following the purchase of this original farm in Bristol township, Robert Purvis began to buy and sell properties in both Bristol township and Burlington County, New Jersey, entering into some of the transactions in partnership with Joseph Cassey and others alone. In 1836, he bought a farm of 136 acres from Joseph and John S. Green for $5,440. Two years later he sold this farm to Benjamin Valentine, and granted a mortgage to Valentine for $3,000. In 1838, Robert Purvis and Joseph Cassey sold their original farm to Amos Jeanes, for $12,000, making a profit of $2,000. They gave Jeanes a mortgage of $10,000. In December 1840, Joseph Cassey bought a farm in Willingborough Township, Burlington County, New Jersey and another in July 1841 for $5,000; Robert bought a tract of eighty-three acres in Eversham, Burlington County for $3,000.[22]

In January 1838, Joseph Purvis, Robert's younger brother, married Sarah Forten, Harriet's younger sister, thus cementing further the relationship between the two families. Joseph desired nothing so much as to be a farmer. In 1835, he bought a 205-acre farm in Bensalem, Bristol Township, for $13,500. In addition, he bought two smaller farms and rented them out. One of these was the farm Robert and Joseph Cassey had sold Benjamin Valentine. At first Joseph prospered, but later he became indebted and discouraged.[23]

Robert Purvis's real estate dealings were not confined to the country. In 1836, he bought a three-story brick house on Marshall Street, in the Northern Liberties section of Philadelphia for $6,125 from Benjamin Valentine; he planned to rent the property. In 1839, Robert sold his brother-in-law, Robert Forten, a two-story brick building on the south side of Lombard, near Ninth Street, very near Robert's own home, for $2,500. Robert had bought this property in 1832 for $2,200.[24]

Many of the properties he bought, he rented back to the previous owners. Thus, in January 1836, he bought a three-story brick building on Pine Street, between Fifth and Sixth Streets from Marie Carty for $1,000 and rented it back to her for $60 a month.[25] In partnership with Joseph Cassey in 1838, he bought a four-story brick building on the east side of Eleventh Street between Pine and Lombard. (Later he bought Joseph Cassey's share in this property.) In October 1839, he and Cassey bought a house and lot at Schuylkill Third and Ann Streets, near Locust, and the next year he bought Cassey's share of this property. The two partners also bought a three-story brick house on the south side of Walnut, westward from Schuylkill Third.[26]

In addition to all these properties, Robert bought and sold ground rents, an old real estate practice in which the buyer owns the right to rent the land to a tenant but does not own it. In some cases, he may have rented the lots to small businesses, while in others he held the land for speculation purposes. In October 1839 he bought three ground rents for properties in the Spring Garden section of Philadelphia, for the sums of $524, $716, and $595, and in December he sold the first of these ground rents for $716, a profit of $192. These rentals and sales, plus the interest he received on mortgages, kept augmenting his wealth.[27]

But though he spent increasing amounts of his time in business transactions, as befitted a young man of twenty-four, married and the father of two boys, Robert Purvis did not abate in his interest in the antislavery, anticolonization cause. Because of his trip to England, he had missed the 1834 meeting of the Colored Convention held in New York. But in 1835, he attended the annual convention held in Philadelphia in June, and played an active role, helping to shape the agenda and supporting or introducing a number of resolutions. One called for the formation of a committee to correspond with "gentlemen in Liberia who may have been deluded into going [there] by the American Colonization Society." Purvis was already corresponding with Joseph Dailey on the problems of the Liberian settlement. He welcomed the visit of George Thompson to the United States, and thanked Christian ministers who spoke out in favor of emancipation. He supported a resolution stating that it was the duty of every lover of freedom to abstain from slave products, and later a second resolution advising "our people" to produce beet sugar, rather than rely on slave-raised cane sugar. In solidarity with Garrison's nonresistance principles, he seconded several resolutions advanced by William Whipper: for example, that Philadelphia blacks be praised for their Christian forbearance during the race riots of 1834, and blacks should not aid the recapture of escaped slaves "but peacefully bear the punishment those inflict."[28]

A third resolution advanced by Whipper and seconded by Purvis, suggested that blacks hereafter eschew any racial designations:

> That we recommend as far as possible to our people to abandon the use of the word "colored" when either speaking or writing concerning themselves; and especially to remove the title of African from their institutions and the marbles of their churches.[29]

At the 1834 Convention, which Purvis missed, delegates had developed the concept of a new organization to promote moral reform within the black community, including a commitment to temperance, education, and nonviolence. The delegates drew up a statement of purpose and bylaws for the new organization, the American Moral Reform Society, and pledged themselves to lofty goals:

> Our object is to extend the principles of universal peace and good will to all mankind, by promoting sound morality, by the influence of education, temperance, economy, and all those virtues which alone can render man acceptable in the eyes of God and the civilized world.[30]

Much of the time of the 1835 Convention was taken up preparing for the new organization, the American Moral Reform Society. There was an effort to heal the breach between the rival groups of leaders from New York and Philadelphia. However, in 1836 there was no meeting of the Colored Convention. Instead, the American Moral Reform Society held its first meeting in Philadelphia in August 1836 with James Forten as chairman. The founders of the American Moral Reform Society pledged themselves to work for many of the same goals as those of the Colored Convention movement: education for blacks, including manual training schools; the establishment of literary societies; correspondence with those in Liberia; the support of the antislavery movement. They issued an Address to the American People, and one to the American Churches, sharply critical of the unwillingness of churches to take a positive stand against slavery and racial prejudice. Robert Purvis served on the committee to draft the letter.[31]

In the afternoon of the first day of deliberations, Purvis arose and made what was described as an "eloquent and stirring speech on the iniquitous system of American Slavery, which was listened to with deep interest." In the afternoon session, he presented four resolutions: (1) the Board of Directors of the new organization hire an agent or agents to lecture on Moral Reform; (2) members pledge themselves to raise $1,000 to forward the work of the American Moral Reform Society; (3) members pledge themselves to raise money to establish a Manual Training School "as soon as possible," and (4) the Board take measures to establish a monthly periodical. He also helped to prepare the "Address to the Christian Churches concerning the prejudice that exists against complexion."[32]

Although a few New York black leaders attended the initial meeting of the American Moral Reform Society, the commitment of the new group to Garrisonian principles—nonviolence, rights of women, attack on the churches as proslavery—was a significant factor in widening the gap. Most troubling of all was the effort to eradicate the use of racial language to practice color blindness. Some of the New Yorkers—and their allies in Philadelphia and Baltimore—felt that the Philadelphians were ashamed of, and tried to ignore, their racial background. Others believed that the reliance on white allies was false; ultimately the black community must rely on itself for leadership in the struggle for equal rights.[33]

Whipper, Purvis, and others who advanced the idea of color blindness were influenced by their association with Garrison and the American Anti-Slavery Society, members of which were eager to practice an early form of integration and to make no discrimination based wholly on "complexion." For members of the black elite, who felt fairly comfortable in white as well as black society, this point of view was welcome. They believed sincerely that more could be accomplished with the help of white allies than by blacks alone.

For Robert Purvis it was the first of many tests of his often stated belief: "In the matter of rights there is but one race, and that is the *human* race."[34] As a young and idealistic man, buoyed up by his reception in England, he believed it was only a question of time until this fact was established as universal truth. Later he would grow disillusioned with his white colleagues, and believe that only black men and women were capable of understanding the full brunt of prejudice, and only blacks could be relied upon to carry on the struggle. Yet he persisted to the end of his life in believing that the human race was one.

At the first annual meeting of the American Moral Reform Society held in Philadelphia the following August, Robert Purvis not only proposed a motion praising George Thompson for his "successful advocacy of the principles of human rights in both hemispheres," but also seconded a motion by William Whipper praising former president John Quincy Adams (1767–1848), for his defense of the right of petition irrespective of race. Whipper and Purvis also presented a resolution thanking "those women who are now pleading the cause of humanity, and devoting their time, talents, and industry to the cause of Universal Freedom." It was the first of many public statements made by Robert Purvis supporting the rights of women.[35]

Samuel Cornish, the New York editor of the *Colored American*, although opposed to the idea of ignoring color, attended the first few meetings of the American Moral Reform Society, and supported it in general terms in his paper. But when the group decided to publish its own periodical, *The National Reformer*, he took a different line. In March 1838, for example, he scolded the Philadelphia blacks for their insistence on eliminating racial terms:

> The good sense of some of our brethren in Philadelphia seems to have forsaken them. They are quarreling about trifles, while their enemies are robbing them of diamonds and of gold. Nothing can be more ridiculous nor ludicrous, than their contentions about NAMES—if they quarrel it should be about THINGS.[36]

Part of the anger directed against the American Moral Reform Society grew from the fact that it had effectively brought an end to the annual colored conventions. In the spring of 1840, David Ruggles, president of the New York Vigilance Society, issued a call to a new national convention to be held in New Haven in the summer while most of the leadership of the American Anti-Slavery Society would be in London. Robert Purvis had been working closely with Ruggles on Vigilance Society matters, and at first signed the call to the new convention. William Whipper did so also. Then, realizing that the call was to blacks only, they withdrew, stating that the American Moral Reform Society remained opposed to organizing philanthropic societies on a "complexional" basis. Separate schools, separate churches, separate societies were no longer required, the two argued, and the creation of separate institutions in which they had both participated had been done in error.[37]

> Let us boldly, fearlessly, and earnestly contend for the great principle of man's equality and leave to the pro-slavery advocates the hated task of dividing asunder human affections and ejecting their fellow human beings from the platform of common humanity.[38]

David Ruggles responded by pointing out that the oppressed must free themselves if their freedom was to be genuine.

> What would have been the condition of American liberty, "the great principle of man's equality," as taught by the Revolutionary Fathers of our country in their Declaration of Independence, had they hesitated to convene as oppressed Americans to consider and act in reference to the burdens under which they groaned? Their Convention was *"exclusive in its character,"* because they met as Americans, *oppressed* Americans.[39]

But Purvis believed strongly that enlisting whites in the campaign was not only right but also the only way to achieve full human rights, and he did not attend the convention. However, he admired Ruggles, who had organized in 1835 the first vigilance committee to aid escaping slaves (with which Purvis subsequently worked), and supported him when Ruggles was under attack by his committee for allegedly keeping poor financial records. Purvis wrote in 1841 in the *National Anti-Slavery Standard*: "the name and fame of David Ruggles are destined to outlive the base calumnies upon his noble character."[40]

For more than five years, Purvis played a leading role in the American Moral Reform Society, acting as corresponding secretary, and writing for its mouthpiece, the short-lived *National Reformer*, edited by his friend, William Whipper. The *Reformer* reported on the work of the Vigilance Society, praised the emancipation of the British West Indies, and reported on such Garrisonian initiatives as the New England Non-Resistance Society.[41]

There was also a Philadelphia City Moral Reform Society, organized on February, 12 1839. At its initial meeting, Robert Purvis was appointed to its committee on temperance and the economy. The latter reported the following month, urging those who had privileges not to despise, but to stretch out their hands to the laboring man. In December 1838, Purvis was asked to deliver an annual address for the Library Company, to which he belonged, and the organizers sought the use of St. Thomas African Episcopal Church. When the church agreed, as long as the subjects of colonization and abolition were not touched upon, the City Moral Reform Society was indignant. "Such, gentle reader, is the true history of the dictatorial assault on freed speech by the Vestry of St. Thomas," the editor proclaimed.[42]

In addition to its other goals, the American Moral Reform Society advocated the rights of women and admitted women to its sessions. Unfortunately, it did not draw white allies, as it hoped, and remained the subject of contention in the black community. It held its last convention in 1841. At this meeting, it expressed its opposition to colonization, called on the churches to fight prejudice, and reiterated its support of women's rights. By this time antiblack riots and antiblack legislation in Philadelphia and in Pennsylvania had made the need for unity in the black community more evident.[43]

The organization of the American Moral Reform Society proved disastrous to the colored convention movement. The split between the integrationists of Philadelphia and their more wary brothers in New York continued for many years. Not until 1843 did a national convention meet again, and meetings were sporadic until the 1850s. Philadelphians did not attend the national gatherings in any numbers until 1853, when a substantial delegation from Pennsylvania, including Robert Purvis, was present. By then the passage of the Fugitive Slave Act had galvanized the black community into the need for solidarity.[44]

Shortly after the organization meeting of the American Moral Reform Society in August 1836, word came that Thomas Shipley, president of the Pennsylvania Abolition Society, was ill, and in early September he died. Shipley had been one of the white allies on whom Purvis and others had relied. He had studied the laws carefully in regard to capture of fugitives, and many times had extricated free blacks from the hands of slave catchers. His continual advocacy of fairness to the black community had endeared him to many. Purvis wrote a short article for the *Liberator*, lamenting his death: "The tried, devoted, uncompromising, unwearied and unwavering friend of the oppressed colored man, has fallen!—indeed the heart of every colored man who knew him lies prostrate, bruised and bleeding."[45]

Members of the black community wanted to pay tribute to Shipley at a special ceremony at St. Thomas's African Episcopal Church, and Purvis was asked to prepare a funeral oration. Perhaps his stirring speech against slavery at the American Moral Reform Society was remembered. This was the first time that the young man, who was to become known for his silver-tongued oratory, was asked to speak. Purvis had just celebrated his twenty-sixth birthday, and he was undoubtedly flattered by the invitation. He prepared carefully, and the talk he gave on November 23 was long and well-reasoned, a justification for the antislavery movement as much as a testament to Thomas Shipley.[46]

He began by stating that Shipley had offered hope to "those oppressed, degraded and humbled in the dust." Now that hope appeared to be extinguished:

Let the southern kidnapper rejoice; let those fiends who stalk our streets, like ministers of hell, to prowl upon unsuspecting victims, console themselves, that now, with impunity, they can wage war against God and human rights; for in the darkness of the tomb sleeps that voice which so harassed their consciences, and thwarted their efforts. Happily, and alas, for such exultations, they are, they must be, but transitory; for the principles of Shipley, thanks to God, are rapidly diffusing themselves throughout the country; so, in firm expectation we are led to believe that the period is near at hand when, "neither in state or city, or town or hamlet, will be found a lingering trace of tyrant or a slave."[47]

Shipley was a Quaker, and his life had been based on the principles of truth and love, on which the Bible and all true religion is based. "What is the effect of these principles upon ourselves?" Purvis asked. "Have we become sanguinary? Do we believe that 'they who would be free, themselves must strike the blow?' Do we desire the achievement of our natural, God-given rights, through blood and carnage? No, Christian principles had mollified the warlike propensities of the flesh and given the black people confidence that God would in time bring justice to the oppressed."[48]

Returning to a favorite theme, Purvis spoke of the preamble to the 1780 Pennsylvania Act, outlawing slavery in the state, with its statement that God had given different complexions to different peoples but was the Creator of all. Did Pennsylvania regret that act? Look at the prosperity of her people, in contrast to the "deserted halls, dilapidated lands, and meagre populations" of the slave states. And look at what had happened to the black people themselves, who previously as slaves had known neither education nor religion. Yet despite "the green-eyed monster, prejudice," they had advanced rapidly in obtaining education, developing institutions such as churches, and providing for themselves. Soon "the men of colour, standing in the full confidence of the nation, prove that though skins are different, minds they have as pure, as spotless, and as highly intellectual as those of fairer complexions."[49]

The principles of Thomas Shipley had led directly to the creation of the American Anti-Slavery Society, Purvis said. Indeed Thomas Shipley and Benjamin Lundy were the pioneers of the movement that inspired the antislavery advocates. Shipley had been present at the founding meeting of the AAS in Philadelphia in 1833, and had signed the Declaration of Sentiments. This Society was now the forerunner in urging the immediate abolition of slavery and in fighting colonization, which was the name the enemies of the black people now gave to their pro-slavite sentiments. The AAS had grown in the past two-and-a-half years from twelve to six hundred members, published many newspapers, tracts and books, and had recently raised $50,000.

The successful organization of the antislavery movement had aroused the opposition, the slaveholders of the South and their ever-ready apologists in the North who called themselves "colonizationists," but were the "same malicious, determined haters of those whose skin is not colored like their own." "These," Purvis said, "were the men who get up mobs, who practice Lynch law to stop the current of Truth."[50]

The colonization advocates had at first tried to move public opinion by detracting the free blacks who opposed them. But recently they had turned to allurement and temptation, promising black leaders who would go to Africa all sorts of positions of power. Though they had been ready to give colored men the titles of governors, majors, colonels, and sheriffs, they had been unsuccessful in persuading the black community to accept their scheme. If they had met with approval, there would now be a series of new colonies: "Missionary Liberia, Temperance Palmas, Spiritualizing Bassa Cove, Quaker Edina, and a host of Pennsylvanias, New Yorks, Marshalls, Marylands, and last though not least, Port or Fort Cresson (in the language of him, whose name the latter place will immortalize), would be in most glorious and successful operation."[51]

"Colonizationists wanted to avoid the evil of interracial marriage," Purvis said. "There was no basis in fact for a fear that white people would marry those they so dislike."

> . . . it comes in bad odour from the South. Let them first put an end to their noonday licentiousness; let them first teach their sons to love and

respect the virtue of chastity, before they charge those upon whom no guilt of this kind can rest, with future prospective intermixture.[52]

In response to the argument that the antislavery agitation would lead to slave insurrection, Purvis was scornful. What, would slaves revolt upon being given their freedom? No, it was not human nature to return kindness with cruelty, and it was certainly not characteristic of the African and his descendants to act in this manner. It was antislavery principles alone which would avert a war of extermination.

Purvis concluded by saying he had limited himself to discussing the principles of Thomas Shipley, but would leave to a biographer the task of telling about his life.

> In summing up the amount of his labours, may we not say of him, that if ever there was a man who lived, breathed, and practically exhibited the truth and spirit of that Divine command which says, "Do unto others as you would have them do unto you," that man was Thomas Shipley.[53]

This speech was the longest and best Robert Purvis had given to date, outlining the major themes which he would address for many years to come: the advancement of the black man under freedom, the inquity of the colonization movement, the achievements of the antislavery movement, the belief that truth and justice were on the side of the oppressed. He also touched upon the principles of nonviolence which Garrison was promoting, and which Purvis then accepted.

Robert Purvis had always worshiped heroes: his father first of all, then Benjamin Lundy, James Forten, William Lloyd Garrison, George Thompson, Lucretia Mott, and Thomas Shipley. The speech gave expression to this hero worship, as well as his passion against racial prejudice. The black community in Philadelphia was impressed with Purvis's erudition and oratory, and from then on often chose him as a spokesperson. The larger antislavery community was equally impressed. Following this speech Purvis was ready to play a role on the national scene.

CHAPTER 5

❦

"We are Not Intruders Here"

$\mathcal{T}$homas Shipley had been one of several members of the Pennsylvania Abolition Society with whom the Philadelphia black community had worked harmoniously on antislavery issues, and such practical matters as the rescue of kidnapped blacks. But the organization of the American Anti-Slavery Society in 1833, with its call for immediate abolition, had attracted the white radicals as well as blacks to the new society. The Pennsylvania Abolition Society remained all white, and was growing not only more conservative, but also dwindling in membership.

In the fall of 1836, therefore, a number of Philadelphia black abolitionists joined with their white counterparts in organizing a statewide Pennsylvania Anti-Slavery Society, to be affiliated with the American Anti-Slavery Society. Among the signers of a petition calling for an organizing meeting were James Forten, his sons, and his son-in-law, Robert Purvis. When a convention was called in Harrisburg on January 31 and February 1–3, 1837, Robert Purvis accompanied his aging father-in-law as a delegate, along with James McCrummill, William Dorsey, and William Whipper. There were two hundred delegates in all, one-third of them from the western part of the state. The convention adopted a constitution and went on record as opposing the admission of Texas as a slave state, as condemning the Colonization movement, and as advocating the use of non-resistance in vindicating the rights of the oppressed.[1]

Although Robert Purvis was to play a prominent role in this organization in future years, his name does not appear in the minutes of this gathering. In general the Philadelphia delegates, both black and white, maintained a low profile, for they wanted to draw in antislavery advocates from around the state. In this they were unsuccessful, for the western abolitionists distrusted their eastern brethren. In 1839, the organization was split into eastern and western branches; however, the western branch dwindled. The westerners objected to mixing Garrisonian issues such as the admission of women, the advocacy of nonviolence, and a distrust of the political process into the antislavery movement.[2]

The purpose of the new antislavery society was to work for the emancipation of slaves in the South. But a few months after the organizing convention, abolitionists learned that blacks in Pennsylvania faced a new threat; their voting rights were being threatened. In theory, black Pennsylvanians could vote if they had lived for two years within the state and if they had paid county taxes. In practice, very few blacks were assessed, and very few voted, especially in the eastern portion of the state. Several attempts by radical reformers to arouse black voters to test their voting rights came to nothing.[3]

In the western parts of Pennsylvania, blacks had been accustomed to voting. In 1835, a black citizen, William Fogg of Luzerne County, went to the polls to vote; he was turned away. He brought suit in the County Court of Common Pleas, which upheld his right as a freeman and a taxpayer. Political opponents of black suffrage appealed the case to the Pennsylvania State Supreme Court, which overturned the ruling in July 1837; the ruling stated that under the state constitution of 1790, the black man had no right of suffrage.[4]

In May 1837, Pennsylvania lawmakers gathered in Harrisburg for a Reform Convention, to rewrite portions of the State Constitution which had become outdated. One object was to lower the property requirement for voting, thus admitting more working men into the voting pool. This laudable democratic impulse, however, encountered racial prejudice. If the property requirement was lowered, it would make more blacks eligible to vote. Though a few Pennsylvania lawmakers supported preserving the franchise for blacks, most opposed it, fearing that blacks, particularly in Philadelphia County, might actually dominate in some districts. They were influenced also by the fact that other states had recently disenfranchised blacks, based on the same reasoning.

The black community had a few friends among the delegates. One was Thomas Earle, a Philadelphia Quaker lawyer, and a member of the American Anti-Slavery Society. On the first day of the sessions, he proposed that the Constitution be amended to penalize anyone . . . "who shall by mob violence or otherwise interfere with the right of freedom of speech, of the press, and of public discussion . . . and that the Legislature shall provide by law for the compensation of all persons . . . who shall be injured in any mob or riot." This was clearly a reference to recent race riots in Philadelphia.[5]

Most of the delegates felt otherwise. Within days of the opening of the Convention, Benjamin Martin, a delegate from Philadelphia County, offered a fatal resolution: "Resolved, that the committee to whom is referred the third article of the constitution be instructed to enquire into the expediency of so altering the first section of said article that all white male citizens who have arrived at the age of twenty-one years and upwards, and being liable to pay tax, shall enjoy the rights of electors."[6]

Word of this attempt to remove their voting rights spread quickly in the black community. Philadelphia blacks gathered in June to appoint a committee to prepare a memorial to be delivered in person to the Convention. Soon thereafter the Convention recessed without any decision about the black franchise. However, the issue had been raised and was widely discussed throughout the summer and early fall. This had the effect of stimulating some black voters to demand their right to vote. A number voted in a Bucks County election in the fall; Democrats claimed they had lost as a result.[7]

When the convention reconvened in October 1838, this time meeting in Philadelphia, sides were tightly drawn. James Biddle, a Philadelphia delegate, brought forth a memorial from the Religious Society of Friends, sympathetic to the blacks, and Thomas Earle, who had argued vigorously for black suffrage throughout the Convention, seconded it.[8] This caused a heated debate. Some delegates worried that giving the blacks voting rights would attract more blacks to the state; others thought it would bring the anger of the white working-class men to a boiling point. By the time the convention closed on February 22, the section of the new constitution denying blacks the right to vote was included in the final document.

Hope for reversal of this harsh decision now rested with Pennsylvania voters, who could refuse to ratify the new constitution in the fall elections. The Pennsylvania Abolition Society, which had watched the progress of the new restrictions with growing concern, undertook to make a survey of the black community in Philadelphia, hoping to demonstrate its respectability, its levels of education, and its support of black churches. Benjamin Bacon and Charles W. Gardner conducted the census.[9]

At a meeting of black leaders at St. Paul's Lutheran Church, a seven man committee was appointed to prepare a memorial to the voters.[10]

Robert Purvis was asked to chair this committee, and the resulting document, *The Appeal of Forty Thousand Citizens Threatened with Disfranchisement to the People of Pennsylvania,*[11] is widely regarded as his handiwork.

Purvis began the appeal by questioning that the voters of Pennsylvania had elected the delegates to restrict suffrage: "Was it really the business of the convention?" he asked, "to deny that all men are born equally free by making political rights depend upon the skin in which a man is born? Or to divide what our fathers bled to unite, to wit, TAXATION and REPRESENTATION?"[12]

This, Purvis argued, was a matter which concerned all Pennsylvanians: "It is the safeguard of the strongest that he lives under a government which is obliged to respect the voice of the weakest. When you have taken from an individual his right to vote, you have made the government, in regard to him, a mere despotism; and you have taken a step toward making it a despotism to all."[13]

Behind the effort to disenfranchise blacks were the advocates of colonization, Purvis wrote. Their scheme of sending blacks back to Africa, cloaked as it was in the language of benevolence, was abhorrent to loyal blacks:

> We love our native country, much as it has wronged us; and in the peaceable exercise of our inalienable rights, we will cling to it. The immortal Franklin, and his fellow laborers in the cause of humanity, have bound us to our homes here with chains of gratitude. We are PENNSYLVANIANS, and we hope to see the day when Pennsylvania will have reason to be proud of us, as we believe she has now none to be ashamed. Will you starve our patriotism? Will you cast our hearts out of the treasury of the commonwealth? Do you count our enmity better than our friendship?[14]

Purvis then returned to the state constitution of 1790, in which the word "white" was first used to qualify those entitled to civil rights, and then withdrawn, perhaps due to the lobbying of the Pennsylvania Abolition Society under its president, Benjamin Franklin. The recent State Supreme Court ruling in the case of *Fogg v. Hobbs* was in error, Purvis believed, for the judgment was based on the recollection of some lawyers that a case against black voting had been ruled upon in 1795. But there was no record of such a case, and the evidence was therefore hearsay. It was therefore to be hoped that State Supreme Court would soon retract its unjust ruling.

As to the argument made before the Convention that blacks were an inferior race and therefore did not deserve suffrage, Purvis was indignant:

As to the charge of idleness, we fling it back indignantly. Whose brows have sweat for our livelihood but our own? As to vice, if it disqualifies us for civil liberty, why not apply the same rule to the whites, so far as they are vicious? Will you punish the innocent for the crimes of the guilty? The execution of the laws is in the hands of the whites. If we are bad citizens let them apply the proper remedies. We do not ask the right of suffrage for the inmates of our jails or penitentiaries, but for those who honestly and industriously contribute to bear the burdens of the State. As to inferiority to the whites, if indeed we are guilty of it, either by nature or education, we trust our enjoyment of the rights of freemen will on that account be considered the less dangerous. If we are incompetent to fill the offices of State, it will be the fault of the whites only if we are suffered to disgrace them. We are in too feeble a minority to cherish a mischievous ambition. Fair protection is all that we aspire to.[15]

Citing the findings of the census conducted by the Pennsylvania Abolition Society, Purvis noted that the black population of Philadelphia numbered 18,708 persons. They owned real and personal property of $1,350,000, paid taxes in 1837 of $3,252.83, and house, water, and ground rents of $166,963.50. The rents they paid, the goods they bought, and the labor they afforded white employers all added to the wealth of the city. Yet among those who depended upon city charities, administered by the Guardians of the Poor, only twenty-two persons out of a total of 549 were black.[16]

Black citizens took care of their own, Purvis insisted. Mutual relief societies established by blacks spent more than $7,000 a year caring for the black poor. To support their religious interests and the education of their children, blacks in Philadelphia, Pittsburgh, York, West Chester, and Columbia supported altogether twenty-two churches, forty-eight clergymen, twenty-six day schools, twenty Sabbath schools, one hundred twenty-five Sabbath schoolteachers, four literary societies, two public libraries, consisting of about eight hundred volumes, besides 8,333 volumes in private libraries, two tract societies, two Bible societies, and seven temperance societies.[17]

Purvis then launched into what was to become his favorite topic: the contribution of blacks to the founding of the nation, and to its struggles for freedom. Citing the testimony of congressmen from Rhode Island, New York, Pennsylvania, Georgia, and South Carolina, he spoke of black men who fought during the Revolutionary War. (He did not mention Crispus Attucks who was killed in the 1770 Boston Massacre, a prelude to the Revolutionary War.) He spoke of those who had endured the "horrors of the Jersey Prison Ship" (among whom was his father-in-law, James Forten).[18]

At Mobile, Alabama, General Andrew Jackson had praised the bravery of black troops during the War of 1812. The mayor of Philadelphia had lauded the courage of black men in nursing the sick during the Yellow Fever epidemic of 1793, an enterprise in which two black pioneers, Absalom Jones and Richard Allen, had played a role.[19]

He next touched on the sensitive question of miscegenation. Blacks did not seek such alliances, and the territories of the Commonwealth were ample enough that blacks and whites did not need to live in proximity.

> Besides, we are not intruders here, nor were our ancestors. Surely you ought to bear as unrepiningly the evil consequences of your father's guilt, as those of our father's misfortune. Nothing promoted racial mixing as much as the degradation of our blacks by white rulers. Give us that fair and honorable ground which self-respect requires to stand on, and the dreaded amalgamation, if it takes place at all, shall be by your own fault, as indeed it always has been.[20]

He spoke of slavery, and the Fugitive Slave Act of 1793, which authorized the claimant to seize his human property without a warrant, to drag the slave before any magistrate of the slave holder's choosing, and by "proving" by whatever means that the man or woman was his slave, return him or her to slavery, without a trial by jury. While the slave catchers were now more active than ever, the Reform Convention had refused to provide for a jury trial in these cases. He begged his readers to imagine their own wives and children trembling at the approach of every stranger, lest their husbands and fathers should be dragged into a slavery "worse than Algerine—worse than death!"[21]

Perhaps the real object of the Convention had been to drive black citizens from the state. But if so, this was doomed to failure. Let others desert the basic principles of Pennsylvania, blacks would maintain them to the last man.

> Pennsylvania's fields, valleys, mountains, and rivers; her canals, railroads, forests, and mines; her domestic altars, and her public religious and benevolent institutions; her Penn and Franklin, her Rush, Rawle, Wistar and Vaux;[22] her consecrated past and her brilliant future, are as dear to us as they can be to you. Firm upon our old Pennsylvania BILL OF RIGHTS, and trusting in a God of Truth and Justice, we lay our claim before you, with the warning that no amendments of the present Constitution can compensate for the loss of its foundation principle of equal rights, nor for the conversion into enemies of 40,000 friends.[23]

The Appeal was widely read and praised in the abolitionist press, but it made no difference to the outcome. Robert Purvis had been shocked by the apathy of most white citizens in response to the Convention of 1838. Despite his appeal, and those of a few white allies, the public was unmoved, and the new Constitution was enacted in October 1838. Purvis never forgot the insult to his manhood that this disenfranchisement perpetuated. His father had been welcomed to the vote on becoming a U.S. citizen; Purvis himself could have voted if he had chosen to ignore his ties to the black race. But because of that identification, he was refused the franchise, while other men, far less educated and less wealthy than he, were free to exercise it. Not until 1870, when he at last regained the right to vote, was he free of the bitter feelings this legislation caused.

Despite the apathy he had observed, even among white reformers, Purvis had not lost faith in the need to work with white allies on current issues. When a group of blacks in Pittsburgh organized a conference to push for voting rights, he did not attend because it excluded whites. He was disheartened; not for another ten years did he attempt once more to gain the vote.

He was not ready to give up on Philadelphia, however. When the *Charleston Courier* published an article which claimed to be written by a black man, a former Charleston resident, who had moved to Philadelphia and regretted his decision to leave his "sweet home," Robert Purvis and Daniel Payne, a minister of the African Methodist Episcopal Church, organized a meeting of former Charlestonians now living in Philadelphia, to prepare a protest against the "libelous attacks." Contrary to the charges of the writer, they said, it was possible for southern blacks to "improve their condition" in the North. As for the charge that there was more depravity in the North than the South, the writers asked if the man in question had worn blindfolds when walking in the streets of Charleston? And as to his assertion that white people shunned their black counterparts, Payne and Purvis pointed to the philanthropists who aided the blacks, and to the colleges and seminaries where blacks and whites attended and mixed in the classrooms.[24]

"In respect to the 'sweet home' to which the gentleman says we are desirous to return, we assert that no home is sweet to us, but the house of freedom," the protestors declared.[25]

Despite the protestations of the former Charlestonians, however, Philadelphia was experiencing growing violence against the black community. Economic depression caused blacks, and white immigrants, many of them Irish, to compete for a shrinking job pool. Many of the new white working-class families were moving into areas surrounding incorporated

Philadelphia: Moyamensing, the Northern Liberties, Southwark, and Spring Garden, where Philadelphia police had little control. Sometimes they rented houses owned by blacks, and resented paying rent to such landlords. In some areas, blacks and whites frequented the same taverns, with resulting brawls.

Following the riots of 1834, tensions continued to simmer between blacks and whites, breaking out in yet another race riot in the summer of 1835, this time set off when a deranged black man attacked his employer. A mob of youths began attacking black homes and churches as before. When they set fire to several buildings, a fire company arrived attempting to put out the flames, but the firemen themselves were attacked. Finally a group of white citizens intervened in an effort to keep the whole city from burning.[26]

During the 1834 riot, many blacks had fled across the river to New Jersey. This happened also in 1835, but a group of black men armed themselves, and prepared to resist further attacks. Inevitably, a group of white rioters responded, and only quick action by the mayor prevented a major confrontation.[27]

The Philadelphia newspapers covering the event uniformly urged blacks to remain indoors, to be meek and well-behaved, not to respond to confrontation. In a description of the riot published in the *Liberator* a correspondent lamented: "We look in vain for a holy indignation at the base attempt on our lives and properties and a vindication of our rights, as a deeply injured and unoffending people." The correspondent was likely Robert Purvis, whose devotion to nonresistance was being deeply challenged by the white violence directed at his people.[28]

Frightened by the violence against blacks, white organizations and white churches began to close their doors to abolitionist meetings, fearful of what might happen to their property. Though most Quakers were sympathetic to the abolition of slavery, they were fearful of the radicalism of the Garrisonians, and one by one they prohibited antislavery gatherings in their meetinghouses. By 1836, the reformers had formed a new organization, the Pennsylvania Hall Association, dedicated to raising money for the construction of a new auditorium where such meetings could be held. Daniel Neall, a dentist, was its chairman and Samuel Webb served as treasurer. James Mott served as a board member and Lucretia Mott helped with fund-raising. By selling stock shares at $20 apiece, the group was able to raise $40,000 for the new building.[29]

The Hall was to be located on the Corner of Sixth between Mulberry and Sassafras. Construction began in the summer of 1837; it was completed in the spring of 1838. The resulting structure was handsome.

Its pillared facade resembled a Greek temple. Its first floor contained a small auditorium, committee rooms, offices, and a free produce store; the second floor consisted of a large auditorium capable of seating three thousand, with galleries above. The hall was lit with gas and there were ventilators in the ceiling to permit a flow of fresh air. The interior was decorated in blue and white, the chairs upholstered in blue plush and the sofas in blue damask.[30]

One of the organizations which would use the new building was the American Convention of Anti-Slavery Women. In May 1837, this group had assembled for the first time in New York City's Third Free Church, on the corner of Houston and Thompson Streets. Harriet Purvis was unable to attend; her third son, Joseph, had been born in February. Many of her colleagues from the Philadelphia Female Anti-Slavery Society were there, however, including her friend Sarah Mapps Douglass, and Sarah's mother, Grace Douglass, who was elected a vice president. In addition to those from Pennsylvania, there were delegates from New Hampshire, Massachusetts, Rhode Island, New York, and Ohio.[31]

The 1837 Convention passed without commotion and was notable for the leadership of Angelina and Sarah Grimké, two sisters from Charleston, South Carolina. They had moved to Philadelphia to get away from the racism of their home state, had joined the Society of Friends, and were now serving as agents of the American Anti-Slavery Society.[32]

The American Convention of Anti-Slavery Women was one of several organizations planning to hold an annual convention when the Hall opened its doors on Monday, May 14, 1838. Others included the Pennsylvania Anti-Slavery Society, a Requited Labor Society, and the Philadelphia Lyceum. Philadelphia filled up with visitors for the occasion. William Lloyd Garrison came down from Boston, accompanied by Maria Weston Chapman, a member of the New England Anti-Slavery Society and editor of the *Liberty Bell*, a yearly publication of antislavery women. With Maria Chapman, Abby Kelley of Lynn, Massachusetts came—she was just beginning to be known as an antislavery orator. John Greenleaf Whittier was present not only to attend the convention, but also to begin his duties as editor of the *Pennsylvania Freeman*, a publication of the Pennsylvania Anti-Slavery Society. Angelina and Sarah Grimké were staying with their sister, Anna Grimké Frost, at her home on Spruce Street, for Angelina was preparing to marry antislavery orator, Theodore Weld, in her sister's front parlor.[33]

The opening exercises on May 14 were attended with much pomp. John Quincy Adams, ex-president of the United States and Thaddeus

Stevens, noted antislavery lawyer and member of the Pennsylvania Assembly, sent regrets and good wishes; John Greenleaf Whittier read a poem he had written for the occasion, and David Paul Brown, a Philadelphia lawyer, gave a keynote address:

> Here, in the very center of fifteen millions of charted freemen, here in Pennsylvania, the brightest star in the republican constellation, where first freedom was proclaimed, and in 1780 Slavery abolished, as priest of this day's sacrifices, I solemnly dedicate this temple to liberty.[34]

The afternoon was given over to the Philadelphia Lyceum, and on the first evening Arnold Buffum, an abolitionist from Rhode Island, spoke on temperance. On Tuesday morning the Anti-Slavery Women held the first session of their convention, and agreed on resolutions calling for boycotting the products of slave labor, and for the end of slavery in the District of Columbia. They could not agree, however, on a pressing question which was dividing the antislavery ranks, the right of women to speak to mixed or "promiscuous" audiences. It was settled finally that on the third day of the meetings, an unofficial meeting would be held in which some women would speak without the sanction of the Convention.[35]

Meanwhile the meetings continued. While the women were meeting, Lewis Gunn gave a talk on freedom of speech, and Charles Burleigh on "Indian Wrongs." Then William Lloyd Garrison was called to the platform. He immediately attacked the managers of the hall for the fact that not a single black person was seated on the platform.

> Why is this? It cannot be because there is no one present, who, on the score of intellectual and moral worth is entitled to such respectful treatment. Is it, then, the result of accident or design? I fear this exclusion may be traced to a wicked prejudice, or to a fear of giving public offense.[36]

Garrison also attacked David Paul Brown for advocating gradual, not immediate, abolition; he went on to excoriate the Colonization Society, naming names. According to later reports, he may also have claimed that George Washington was a slaveholder and therefore a "man stealer and a tyrant."[37]

Word of Garrison's outburst spread quickly throughout the city, along with reports of blacks and whites meeting together in what was called "amalgamation of the races." Rumors spread about blacks and whites mingling, even, a black and white wedding. Overnight, placards went up throughout the city calling attention to the meetings, which were being conducted for "the avowed purpose of effecting the immediate emancipation of slavery throughout the United States" and urging "citizens who entertain a proper respect for the right of property and the preservation of the Constitution to interfere, forcibly if they must, and demand the immediate dispersion of said convention."[38]

A mob began gathering outside Pennsylvania Hall the next day. It took courage for the abolitionists to pass through the crowd in order to enter the hall. Despite angry mutterings, however, it was relatively peaceful during the day while the Pennsylvania Anti-Slavery Society held its meeting, and the final ceremonies for opening the hall were completed.[39]

In the evening, the women held their unofficial meeting at which both men and women were allowed to speak. By now a large and ugly mob had gathered around the building. William Lloyd Garrison opened the ceremonies with a speech which brought an outburst from the mob; some members broke into the hall. Maria Weston Chapman of Boston spoke next, quieting the mob, although a few brickbats were thrown. Then Angelina Grimké Weld spoke. Her marriage to Theodore Weld the day before had been attended by both blacks and whites. This event started the rumors about an "amalgamation" wedding. Angelina had been giving eloquent antislavery lectures all winter, and now she spoke from her heart:

> I have seen it! I have seen it! I know the horrors that can never be described. I was brought up under its wing. I witnessed for years its demoralizing influences and its destructiveness to human happiness. I have never seen a happy slave. I have seen him dance in his chains, it is true, but he was not happy. There is a wide difference between happiness and mirth. Man can not enjoy happiness while his manhood is destroyed.[40]

A shower of stones followed her speech. Abby Kelley spoke next, giving her maiden speech to a promiscuous audience; it was "the still small voice within" that called her to speak:

> The parable of the Lazarus and the rich man we may well bring home to ourselves. The North is the rich man. Now he is clothed in purple and fine linen, and fares sumptuously every day. Yonder, yonder at a little distance is the gate where lies the Lazarus of the South, full of sores and desiring to be fed the crumbs that fall from our luxurious table. Look! See him where he lies! Ought we not to raise him up and is there no one in this Hall who sees nothing for himself to do?[41]

Then Lucretia Mott took the podium to explain that this had not been an official session of the Anti-Slavery Convention of American Women because some of its members considered it improper for women to speak to mixed audiences. "Let us hope that such false notions of delicacy and propriety will not long obtain in this enlightened country," she concluded drily.[42]

The sessions concluded, the participants passed through the angry mob without much damage, although some of the blacks were pummeled. The next morning, Thursday, an even larger mob assembled, and the delegates continued to meet. They were uneasy, for they were concerned about the mob congregating outside. There was a talk on free produce and requited labor, both subjects in which Robert and Harriet Purvis were interested, and some concluding sessions of the American Convention of Anti-Slavery Women. Alarmed by the threatening aspect of things, Daniel Neall and some other officials of the Hall visited Mayor Swift and asked for police protection. The mayor told the men that the situation was the fault of the abolitionists for behaving in a provocative fashion; he was sure if black women would stop attending the sessions, the mob would disperse. Asked to give this message to the women holding their concluding meeting, Lucretia Mott delivered it but said she did not agree with it; she hoped that the women would not be put off by "little appearance of danger." Then she arranged for the women to leave the Hall two by two, a black and a white woman arm in arm.[43]

All day the mayor hesitated to take action. Then at sundown he addressed the mob, saying that the managers had given him the key to the Hall and there would be no meetings that night. He appealed to the mob to disperse peacefully, then he left the scene. Shortly thereafter, the leaders of the mob broke into the building, collected all the furniture and draperies, and set them on fire. Fearing for his newspaper, John Greenleaf Whittier disguised himself in a doctor's coat and managed to reach his office and rescue the precious pages, but almost everything else within the Hall soon went up in smoke. The fire companies that arrived sprayed the adjoining buildings, but let the Hall burn to the ground.[44]

Not content with this destruction, the mob set off toward the Mott's house on Ninth Street, but were diverted by a friend who shouted, "On to the Motts!" He led the crowd in the wrong direction. Instead, the mob turned to the south and attacked the First African Presbyterian Church as well as the Shelter for Colored Orphans. Finally they were restrained by the police; Mayor Swift had at last decided upon action.

In the early hours of the riot, the mob sought to find William Lloyd Garrison. Robert Purvis was asked to get him out of the city, and he complied. Many years later he wrote about it to his friend, Rowland Johnson:

I have not time to write you at length this morning, but will reply to query, knowing I am competent to do so—Pennsylvania Hall, was not destroyed in 1835—it was in the month of May 1838 that the devilish deed was done—our friends Garrison & Wright were especially obnoxious to the mobocrats and their lives considered to be in great peril—About midnight—several young men, one of whom I recollect was a son of the late Dr. Joseph Parrish sought me, for the purpose of taking our friend Garrison from the city, to my country residence, on the Neshamony [*sic*] in Bucks Co., twenty miles from the city—after a few hours rest at my home, and a hasty breakfast—we drove Mr. G. to "Cornwells Station" from wh. he took passage for N. York.[45]

Robert had escorted Harriet to the meetings. Some months later he attended the trial which the managers of the Hall had brought for damages. The county of Philadelphia defended itself by trying to prove that the abolitionists had caused the trouble by promoting the intermingling of blacks and whites, especially between the sexes. At the trial it was alleged that in one instance, a black woman was seen to arrive at the Hall, and she was handed down from her carriage by a white man, who escorted her to the building. The witness described in detail the time of the arrival of the carriage, and the clothes of the two principals. Robert Purvis wrote to his friend, British abolitionist Joseph Sturge, about the event:

In regard to my examination before the Jury in the Pennsylvania Hall case, I have to say, that it was both a painful and ludicrous affair. At one time the ful[l]ness of an almost bursting heart was ready to pour forth in bitter denunciation—then the miserable absurdity of the thing, rushing into my mind, would excite my risible propensities. You know the county endeavored to defend itself against the award of damages, by proving that the abolitionists were the cause of the destruction of the building, in promoting promiscuous intermingling, indoors and out, of blacks and whites, thereby exciting public feeling, &. A witness, whose name I now forget, in proof of this point stated, that upon a certain day, hour &., a "negress" approached the hall in a carriage, when a white man assisted her in getting out, offered his arm, which was instantly accepted, and he escorted her to the saloon of the building! In this statement he was collected, careful, and solemn—minutely describing the dress, appearance of the parties, as well as the carriage, exact time, &c.—the clerks appointed for the purpose taking down every word, and the venerable jurors looking credulous and horror-stricken. Upon being called to rebut the testimony of the county's witness, I, in truth and simplicity, confirmed his testimony in every particular! ! The attorney on our behalf, David Paul Brown Esq., a gentleman, scholar, and philanthropist, in a tone of irony peculiarly severe, demanded "whether I had the unblushing impudence, in broad day-light to offer my arm to my wife?" I replied that, in deep affectation of the criminality involved, that the only palliation I could offer, for conduct so outrageous was, that it was unwittingly done, it seemed so natural. This, as you might well suppose, produced some merriment at the expense of the witness for the county, and of all others, whose gullibility and prejudice had given credit to what would have been considered, had I been what is called a white man, an awful story.[46]

The litigation against the city for the destruction of Pennsylvania Hall lasted nine years, and went to the state supreme court. The managers of the Hall were able to collect only $27,942.77 including interest, far less than the Hall had cost. Not until 1864 were the Hall managers able to close their books and dissolve.[47]

The day after the Hall was burned, the Anti-Slavery Convention of American Women met for a final session in Sarah Pugh's schoolhouse. Here they pledged themselves to meet again in Philadelphia the following year. Rather than give way to the ugly prejudice that had marred this year's sessions, they promised to expand their social relations with their black friends.

Thoroughly alarmed by the events of Pennsylvania Hall, some of the more conservative abolitionists resolved to end any appearance of interracial mingling. Dr. Joseph Parrish, president of the Pennsylvania Abolition Society, hearing about the women's decision, came to visit Lucretia Mott with the plea that this pledge be stricken from the minutes. If the cost of reprinting was an issue, he would gladly pay for it. When the women refused, he called together a group of "respectable colored people" at the home of Robert Douglass, husband of Grace Douglass, and advised them not to accept interracial invitations when offered to them, and to issue a disclaimer, saying they had no desire for interracial contact.[48]

The reaction of the timid only strengthened the determination of the Garrisonians to practice interracial friendships. A few days later, Lucretia Mott held an "amalgamation tea" with Grace and Sarah Douglass and Charlotte and Margaretta Forten as guests, and shortly thereafter, she drove out to Bucks County with James and Miller McKim to spend the weekend visiting Robert and Harriet Purvis on the farm they shared with Joseph and Amy Cassey. The Motts also called on Joseph and Sarah

Purvis, who lived on a nearby farm. "We were entertained handsomely at both places. Robert has 3 pretty children," Lucretia wrote her brother-in-law, David Wright.[49]

The following year, when the Anti-Slavery Convention of American Women sought a hall in which to hold their annual gathering, none could be found except the Pennsylvania Riding School. Shortly before the meeting was to be held, the new mayor of Philadelphia, Isaac Roach, approached Lucretia Mott and asked that they avoid "unnecessary walking with colored people." Mott rejected his suggestions, and his halfhearted offer of protection, and told him the women would protect themselves, and that it was a "fixed principle with us to make no distinction on the basis of color." The meetings, in which Harriet Purvis and her sisters took part, passed without incident.[50]

The burning of Pennsylvania Hall had served to deepen tensions within the American Anti-Slavery Society, between followers of Garrison, who believed they must include issues of sex as well as race in their campaign, and their more conservative fellows, led by clergymen, who believed that it weakened the antislavery campaign to introduce other issues. Garrison's organization of the New England Non-Resistance Society in the fall of 1838 made matters worse. At the May 1839 meeting of the American Anti-Slavery Society, held in New York at the Chatham Street Chapel, the issue of accepting women into membership was raised and battled over throughout the sessions. Toward the end of the first day, the delegates voted 184 to 141 to admit women. Robert Purvis, present as a delegate and elected to the board of managers, was one of those who voted in the affirmative.[51]

CHAPTER 6

To Aid the Fleeing Slave

The climate of violence which had settled over Philadelphia in the 1830s made it more difficult to aid the fugitive slaves who, from time to time, came over the Maryland border. Slave catchers felt freer to move about, and to bring questionable cases before magistrates, now that public opinion appeared to be on their side.

The problem of protecting runaways from slave catchers was a complicated one. In 1820, at the instigation of the Pennsylvania Abolition Society, the Commonwealth of Pennsylvania passed "An Act to Protect Free Negroes and to Prevent Kidnaping [sic]." This law was designed to modify the federal Fugitive Slave Law of 1793, by putting the power to try fugitive cases in the hands of county judges; the law made it a felony for anyone to capture an alleged fugitive slave unless he had a warrant from a judge. Maryland, however, protested, and in 1826 Pennsylvania modified its law to state that the slave owners could obtain a warrant from any member of the minor judiciary. The right of trial by jury, for which blacks had been arguing for more than thirty years, was denied them.[1]

Robert Purvis had always been sensitive to the needs of fleeing slaves, perhaps remembering tales he had heard in Charleston, and certainly aware of slave captures which happened regularly in the City of Philadelphia. His house on Lombard Street contained a hidden basement room, under his children's schoolroom, reached by a trap door, where he could conceal slaves in an emergency. At one time he had so many refugees in his house that the constables became suspicious. Purvis waited until night, then transported all his visitors aboard a small ferry that traveled up and down the Delaware River. An hour before the scheduled time of departure, it sailed away, leaving the regular passengers stranded, but taking the blacks to New Jersey and freedom.[2]

In the summer of 1836, four slave brothers named Costly escaped from their home in Liberty, Frederick County, Maryland, and found their way to Purvis's house in Philadelphia. Their master, Sabrick Sollers, was actually their father. He had promised to give them their freedom when he died, but his white son, Thomas Sollers, was not willing to obey his father's wish. [3]

After a few nights, Purvis proposed that he take the brothers to his farm in Bensalem. One brother, Thomas, said he wished to remain in the city, but Purvis took the other three to his Bucks County farm. Here he employed one brother, Basil, on his own land, and found jobs for the other two, William and Charles, with nearby farmers. All four had changed their last name to Dorsey.[4]

Basil was married to a free black woman, Mary, and the couple had two children. With the help of Mary's brother, Robert Purvis was able to arrange to have this family brought to Philadelphia to rejoin their husband and father; he put them up in his house in the city, before taking them to Bucks County for the reunion. All went well for about a year. Then Mary's brother quarreled with Basil, and to avenge himself he wrote to Sollers and offered to help him recapture the Dorsey brothers. Sollers hurriedly hired a slave catcher and some helpers to accompany him to Philadelphia. These men soon caught Thomas in Philadelphia and carried him off to Baltimore; they intended to ship him to the New Orleans slave market. Friends of Thomas, however, raised $1,000 and bought his freedom. He returned to Philadelphia as a free man and became a well-known caterer.[5]

Soon after they captured Thomas, the slave owner and his accomplices set out for Bucks County; they arrived on Purvis's farm just before sunset one evening in late July. Basil was plowing a distant field; he did not notice the men as they deployed. They surprised him. He put up a fight, swinging and kicking, but the men were too many for him, and he was soon subdued. A neighbor's son who had been watching ran to tell Robert Purvis that Basil had been captured and was being taken to Bristol.[6]

Purvis had just returned from Philadelphia and was eating his supper when the boy arrived. On hearing the news, he saddled his horse and rode to Bristol, where Basil was just being jailed. A large crowd had gathered to watch the struggling Basil. Purvis spoke to them, telling them the man was being returned to slavery against his will. Thomas Sollers, the slaveholder, was present, and Purvis was able to talk with him. The slaveholder appeared reasonable, and the two men agreed to meet in Bristol at seven the following morning, in order to ride to Doylestown to appear before the local judge. Here Sollers hoped to prove his right to recapture his slaves. Purvis next hurried home to see if Basil's two brothers had also been taken. He arrived at his farm just as a posse of slave catchers appeared, and Charles Dorsey came out of the house holding a double-barreled shotgun. The men from Maryland retreated; Purvis was able to drive Charles and William to the nearby farm of his brother, Joseph Purvis. Later that night, after it was completely dark, Joseph drove the fugitives more than forty miles to a friend's farm in New Jersey, where they were able to hide until they could find a way to Canada and freedom.[7]

Purvis slept a few hours, then got up at dawn to ride to Bristol. A short way down the lane, he met a woman who told him that the slaveholder and his party had started at five for Doylestown, and that Basil had shouted to her as they passed to notify Purvis. Purvis returned to his house and arranged for a farmworker to drive Mary and the children to Doylestown. Then he harnessed up a trotting horse, and traveling swiftly, was able to pass the Maryland party while they were eating breakfast in a roadside tavern; he reached Doylestown in advance of the slavecatchers. Here he looked up a local abolitionist, William Johnson, who found him a lawyer, Thomas E. Ross, to appear in Basil's behalf. By the time the Maryland party arrived, Mary, Basil's wife, and the children were also in Doylestown.[8]

When the court opened, Basil said he had free papers which were being held by a friend in Columbia, Pennsylvania. The judge was influenced by the sight of Basil's pretty wife and young children. He decided to postpone the trial for two weeks, giving Basil time to recover the papers.

Basil did not have free papers, and Purvis thought the case was hopeless. He began to plan a campaign to organize the local blacks to rescue Basil from the authorities, if the trial should go against him. He also considered buying the slave, but Sollers kept raising the price. Finally, he decided to go to Philadelphia and consult with the abolitionist lawyer, David Paul Brown, about the case. Brown was interested, and agreed to defend Basil at no charge.[9]

On August 1, 1837, the trial began before Judge Fox, with Basil's wife and children again present. The Marylanders had not brought their own lawyer; they hired a very inexperienced one, A. M. Griffith. David Brown asked Griffith to prove that slavery actually was legal in Maryland. Griffith requested a brief recess and soon returned with a book published by Virgil Maxey, Esq. containing a compilation of the laws of Maryland. Judge Fox ruled that the book could not be considered as authority, for it did not appear to be published by any authority of Maryland; he dismissed the case, telling the slaveowner he could get a warrant for Basil's arrest from another magistrate.[10]

Basil did not seem to understand his good fortune until Robert Purvis drew him from his seat and hurried him out of the courthouse to a waiting buggy. While the slaveholder was looking for a magistrate, Purvis drove Basil at a fast clip to his mother's house on Seventh Street in Philadelphia. Harriet Miller hid the escaped slave overnight, and the next day Purvis drove him to New York, and placed him in the hands of Joshua Leavitt, the editor of an antislavery paper, *The Emancipator*, who took Basil to his farm in Connecticut. Later Basil went to Northampton, Massachusetts where he worked for George Benson, Garrison's brother-in-law.[11]

The Dorsey brothers' case was one of many in which David Paul Brown defended fugitives. In gratitude to Brown for this assistance, Purvis and his colleagues decided to give him a testimonial gift. In 1841, in a ceremony at Mother Bethel Church, Purvis presented Brown with two silver pitchers engraved with kneeling slaves. Purvis gave a short speech, thanking Brown in the name of "an oppressed portion of your fellow citizens of this city," for the services he had rendered without money in advocating the rights and liberties of the oppressed—"God grant unto you, Sir, unmeasured blessings here and the reward of the Christian philanthropist in the untold joys of a glorious eternity."[12]

It was an opinion Robert Purvis would revise later.

The experience of the Dorsey brothers caused Robert Purvis and other leaders of the black community to believe that Philadelphia needed a Vigilant Committee, similar to that organized by David Ruggles in New York in 1835. In early August, a month after Basil Dorsey's release, they met to organize the Vigilant Association of Philadelphia, with the primary aim of "creating a fund to aid colored persons in distress." To join, members were asked to pay twenty-five cents and pledge to contribute seventy-five cents annually, and to elect, by ballot, an acting committee. At its first session, this Vigilant Committee chose James McCrummill as president, Jacob White as secretary, and James Needham as treasurer. White was also asked to serve as paid agent for the group.[13]

The work of this committee was necessarily kept a secret, but its fund-raising was public. A month after its formation, the organization submitted a letter to the *National Enquirer and Constitutional Advocate of Universal Liberty*, thanking the women who had assisted them in raising funds. In April 1838, it held an open meeting which was covered by the *National Enquirer*, now renamed the *Pennsylvania Freeman*.[14] In July, they announced, through the *Freeman*, the formation of an auxiliary, the Female Vigilant

Association, with Elizabeth White as president and Hetty Reckless as secretary. This group immediately set to work raising money, holding a West Indian Emancipation Day public meeting and a December Fair.[15] There was also a Young Men's Vigilant Society, which supported the organization, and marched in the August 1 parades honoring the liberation of the blacks in the Virgin Islands.[16]

In May 1839, the Vigilant Association held a reorganization meeting, changed its name to the Vigilant Committee and elected its founder, Robert Purvis, as president, and Edwin Coates, a Quaker abolitionist, as vice president. Jacob White, who had been serving as secretary, was relieved of the job in order to devote more time to his work as agent, at an annual salary of $250.[17]

Under Purvis's leadership the work of the committee increased. White undertook to screen those who claimed they were fugitives, placed runaways in private homes, primarily in the black community in Philadelphia but sometimes in the country, provided them with clothes, medical care, and legal counsel, and paid their transportation when they were ready to be sent to David Ruggles, executive secretary of the New York Committee of Vigilance in New York. In six months' time, from June to December 1839, the committee sent fifty-one fugitives on their way North.[18]

The records of the Vigilant Committee, saved over the years, were presented to the Historical Society of Philadelphia in 1933 by Leon Gardiner. Though covering only a short period of the life of this group, they give a vivid picture of the day-to-day work of the agent.

> No.s 2 & 3, June 27. Two men. One sent to the Committee by William Whipper, Columbia, from Vir, light complexion, an interesting young man, sent to Morrisville, from thence to N.Y. for Canada; the other was employed some few weeks at Fallsington at Mr Chas Hoags, since left for Canada. The expense attending these two cases was $4.83.

> No.s 4 & 5, July 3rd. Two cases formerly from Vir. Lived with Warner, been here about 10 years. One rather lighter complexion than the other. Brothers, Henry and Isaiah sent to C. Hoag, Falsington, to go thence to Canada. Expenses incurred $3.82.

> No. 6, July 6th. One case. Man from Vir. reported by S. H. Gloucester at Patterson, Wood St. Schuylkill 6th and 7th Str. Sent to Vigilant Committee of N.Y. Note to Wm P. Johnson, expenses $3.25.

> No. 7. July 10th. Man sent to E. Coates by C. Wise, from N. Orleans. Sent to N.Y.V. Committee. This man was stout made, rather light complexion, intelligent, has several acquaintances here. One coloured man named Cambwell, expenses, $2.00.[19]

There were a few imposters. White recorded case No. 49 on December, 4, 1849, as that of a man called Samuel Williams from Columbia, an imposter. "This man was brought to Edwin Coates, and feigned himself deaf & dumb, but not succeeding to his satisfaction, he made a second call representing himself as a slave. He was, however, detected and finally acknowledged the fraud," White wrote. "But from the statement made by him, believing him in want, we gave 20 cts to help him on his way and furnished him with some food, 20 cts."[20]

Though the amounts spent were small, money for this enterprise was always in short supply. By 1840, the committee found it necessary to drop the salary of its secretary and agent, Jacob White, and elect an acting committee of three men to aid the runaways. Most of the work of this acting committee fell to Robert Purvis. Meetings of the committee were held at his house on Ninth Street. Toward the end of 1840, all the white members were off the committee. Instead, Robert Purvis persuaded his brother-in-law James Forten Jr., and the Reverend Daniel A. Payne of the African Methodist Episcopal Church, his fellow South Carolinian, to serve.[21]

This appears to be a reversal of the policy of "color blindness" which Robert Purvis continued to pursue through the American Moral Reform Society. It was probably a decision based on expediency rather than principle; since most of the blacks were hidden in the black community, it made more sense that a black committee, with headquarters at Purvis's home on Ninth Street, took care of the fugitives.

A meeting held on April 25, 1841, at Robert Purvis's house on Lombard Street can be considered as typical. This gathering was attended by Purvis, chairman, Charles Gardiner, Daniel A. Payne, James Needham, Robert Forten Jr., and J. C. White. A donation of $10 had been received from "Mrs. Mott" (perhaps from the Philadelphia Female Anti-Slavery Society). Robert Purvis reported that eleven cases had been attended to since the last meeting of the Committee, the expenses were "eighteen dollars and 50 cents." The committee had collected eighteen dollars, and Purvis was willing to contribute the fifty cents.[22]

> Messrs Purvis, Gardiner, & Payne were appointed to make all the arrangements for a soiree to be held at such time & place as they may designate for the benefit of the Committee.[23]

The resulting soiree was held in May, and was attended by many of the leading lights of the antislavery movement including the venerable James Forten, William Lloyd Garrison, Charles C. Burleigh, and Nathaniel P. Rogers. At seventy-five and ailing, James Forten was unable to speak, but

James Forten Jr. gave a speech and Robert Forten sang "The Pilgrim Fathers." The proceeds amounted to $42.45.[24]

The number of fugitives aided rose regularly during the life of the Vigilant Committee. From 1839 through 1842, the cases of runaways served by the Committee were reported to the Philadelphia Female Anti-Slavery Society by Hetty Reckless, who was a member of both the Female Society and the Female Vigilant Society. The purpose of these reports was to enlist the enthusiasm of the members of the Female Society in fund-raising. According to the minutes of this organization, from June to December 1839, the committee sent forty-six fugitives to freedom—from June 23 to September 2, 1841, the number was thirty-two and from September 2 to October 11, seventeen. In 1842, it helped forty-six refugees between January and June and from June to September, 117. From September 1842 to March, 1843 an additional 140 were aided. In all these records, it is clear that more fugitives left in the summer than the winter. In February 1843, it was noted that three were waiting to leave as soon as the ice broke up.[25]

Interviewed at the age of eighty-five by Wilbur Siebert, the first historian of the Underground Railroad, Robert Purvis estimated that throughout its lifetime the Vigilant Committee sent North one fugitive a day. If this figure is true, it represents a larger number than was handled by the later Vigilance Committee, organized in 1852 by Purvis but operated largely by William Still (1821–1902), clerk in the office of the Pennsylvania Anti-Slavery Society. The figures in the Minutes Book of the Vigilant Committee and of the Female Anti-Slavery Society are the earliest accounts of an organized Underground Railroad in the Maryland, Delaware, Pennsylvania area. Unfortunately, Purvis destroyed the remaining records at the time of the passage of the Fugitive Slave Law, lest they endanger escaped slaves still living in the United States, and those who had aided them in their flight. Although in his time he was sometimes called "the President of the Underground Railroad," (the *New York Times* gave him this appellation at the time of his death), his fame in this regard has been eclipsed.[26] When William Still wrote his book *The Underground Railroad* in 1872, he made scant reference to the earlier Vigilant Committee.[27]

Purvis also recalled late in life that he had been assisted in his work by two market women in Baltimore, one of whom was black; they helped to forward escaping slaves to his home. These women had managed to obtain certificates of freedom which they gave to slaves seeking to escape. These "passports" were then returned, and used over and over. The son of slave owners in New Bern, North Carolina also served as an agent, and sometimes traveled in the free states with a retinue of body servants, hoping they would fall into the hands of vigilant abolitionists. Two sea captains, who hauled wood from New Bern to Philadelphia, were willing to take hidden passengers. Many passengers were forwarded, according to Robert Purvis, by Thomas Garrett and Samuel Burris, both of Delaware.[28]

Probably the most famous runaway whom Purvis assisted was Harriet Brent Jacobs, a slave who spent seven years hidden in the attic of her grandmother's house in Edenton, North Carolina, in order to escape the efforts of her master to make her his concubine. Years after her escape she wrote a book, *Incidents in the Life of a Slave Girl, Written by Herself*, which became well-known among slave narratives. Purvis wrote to his friend, journalist Sydney Gay, about the case in 1858, sixteen years after her escape. He got a few of his facts wrong.

> I have lost the name, and all trace of the woman of whom you enquire. She went from this to N.Y. to meet her lover (a white man). She was a beautiful creature, quadroon in blood, *just enough* of Negro admixture to preserve her beauty from the premature ugliness of whites in this country—by the bankruptcy of her Master she was seized and sold publickly-bought by a "Negro Trader"—and was to be taken to the N. Orleans-Market. She managed by the Aid of her Mistress—to secret herself for a few days—but being pressed so closely by her pursuers—and giving up all hope of escape—she went to her Mother's—an old emancipated slave—who lived in the suburbs of the town (Newbern, N.C.) supposing of course she w'ld soon be *taken* from there—days, days—weeks—months—years passed and no search was made there for her. In the loft of her Mother's hut—a place of a few feet in dimensions—this poor creature was confined for *seven years*. A small opening—with a shutter nearly closed—admitted a little light and air. It was at this little window—or opening—that her little boy—who had been purchased with another child by their father & emancipated—clambered and quietly and stealthily looked in upon his mother—as he said-every day—Finally at the end of seven years—friends were found—in whom they could confide—and she was brought in a vessel to Phila. Her long Confinement had so effected [sic] her in feelings that she repeatedly expressed to me—a desire to return to the "little dark place"—as she called it—in which she had been so long immured—Hers was a truthful representation of Byron's "Prisoner of Chillon"—When he declares—upon being set free—
>
> > *"My Very Chains and I grew friends—*
> > *So much a long communion tends*
> > *To make us what we are:—even I*
> > *Regained my freedom with a sigh."*[29]

Purvis's increasing preoccupation with aiding fugitives in their flight North did not interfere with his continuing involvement in the Pennsylvania Anti-Slavery Society and the American Anti-Slavery Society. In both these organizations, he had become a spokesperson for the admission of women. When the Pennsylvania group held a special meeting in Coatesville in the fall of 1838, he was among the delegates who voted for the admission of women on an equal basis; he was able to welcome his wife Harriet as a member. In 1840, he traveled to New York to take part in the annual meeting of the American Anti-Slavery Society.[30]

Since the rancorous meeting of the national society in 1839, when women were admitted to membership, sides had been sharply drawn between those who supported the Garrisonian approach—admit women, advocate nonresistance, allow freedom of speech—and the more conservative members who felt the antislavery message was being diluted by side issues; they believed in political action. On the first day of the meetings, May 12, Abby Kelley was nominated to the business committee, and elected by a vote of 557 in favor, 451 opposed.[31] Robert Purvis, present as a delegate from the Pennsylvania Anti-Slavery Society, was one of those voting for Abby, a fact he referred to forty-eight years later when he spoke to the International Council of Women:

> I can not claim, as my friend Douglass can,[32] to have been a member of the first Woman's Rights Convention at Seneca Falls; but I owe it to myself to say that anterior, some few years at least, to the matter to which Mrs. Blackwell[33] has referred in the test vote touching the appointment of Abby Kelley, subsequently Abby Kelley Foster,[34] I stand rightly upon the record in that vote which I gave that time. I had before committed myself to the belief that whatever was morally right for a man, was equally so for a woman.[35]

Following Abby's appointment to the committee, a large number of delegates withdrew to form the American and Foreign Anti-Slavery Society, taking with them most of the publications and assets of the old organization. The remaining Garrisonians pledged themselves to raise $10,000 in order to fund a new periodical, the *National Anti-Slavery Standard.*[36] From this time on the lines between the two groups were tightly drawn. Robert Purvis stayed with the Garrisonians, although he was shortly to break with their allegiance to nonresistance.

Shortly after the New York meetings, American abolitionists of both persuasions gathered in London for the World Anti-Slavery Convention. Both the Pennsylvania and Massachusetts Anti-Slavery Societies sent women as delegates. These were refused seats on the basis of their gender. Lucretia Mott, friend and colleague of the Purvises, made a protest so vigorous that she attracted many admirers. One of these was Elizabeth Cady Stanton, present at the meetings as the young bride of Henry B. Stanton, a lawyer and representative of the "New Organization." The young woman was so impressed that she took Lucretia Mott as her mentor, and later organized with her the famous Seneca Falls Woman's Rights Convention to which Purvis referred.[37]

Robert Purvis was also preoccupied at this time by another matter. In the summer of 1839, a group of African slaves being transported to Cuba for sale on a slave ship, the "Amistad," rose up against their captors, killed the captain and several members of the crew, and ordered the remaining sailors to take them back to Africa. The white steersman sailed east by day, according to the orders of the Africans' leader, a young Mendi chief named, in Cuba, Joseph Cinque. But at night, when he thought the Africans would not notice, he turned the boat north. Not understanding celestial navigation, Cinque was unable to detect this change of course, although he thought it odd that they remained often in sight of land. Finally, the boat entered Long Island Sound, where it was eventually captured by a merchant ship and brought into harbor at New Haven, Connecticut. The captain claimed the ship as a prize of war. The U.S. Government also claimed it. Spain sued for the return of both the vessel and the slaves. The authorities decided to keep the Africans in jail while the court made a decision about what to do with them.[38]

A newly formed antislavery group, the American Missionary Association, supported the cause of the Africans who claimed their freedom, and provided them with lawyers. In 1841 the case reached the Supreme Court, where former president John Quincy Adams won liberty for the Africans.[39]

As the story of the bravery of the Africans became known, Cinque was hailed as a hero to many American blacks. Robert Purvis decided to commission Nathaniel Jocelyn, the New Haven artist who had painted Garrison, to do a portrait of Cinque.[40]

Robert Purvis showed his newly acquired portrait to John Sartain (1808–1897), a Philadelphia artist, who suggested that the painting be submitted to the Artist Fund Society for its annual exhibition. Several other artists had seen the work and pronounced it excellent. Nathaniel Jocelyn was invited to become an honorary member of the Society. But when the work was submitted, it was rejected, with a letter to Purvis from John Nagle, secretary, saying, "it being contrary to usage to display works of that character, believing that under the excitement of the times, it might prove injurious to the proprietors and the institution."[41]

Incensed, Purvis took the portrait to his home, where it was his most treasured possession for many years. John Sartain, angry at the rejection of the painting, did an engraving from the portrait which was sold for one dollar to benefit the defense fund for the Amistad rebels. Jocelyn withdrew from the Society, and Henry C. Wright, a fiery abolitionist, wrote a denunciation of the Society's action:[42]

> Why then was the portrait rejected? The plain English of it is, Cinque is a NEGRO. This is a Negro hating and a Negro stealing nation. A Slave-holding people—The Negro-haters of the north, and the Negro-stealers of the south will not tolerate a portrait of a Negro in a picture gallery. And such a Negro! His dauntless look, as it appears on canvass, would make the souls of slaveholders quake. His portrait would be a standing anti-slavery lecture to slaveholders and their apologists.[43]

The rejection of the portrait of Cinque was a milestone in Robert Purvis's life. The fact that neither his wealth nor his reasoned appeal to universal human rights could do anything to redirect the mindless prejudice he kept encountering was a wound that simmered in his soul. In 1892, when he was an old man, he willed the painting to the New Haven Colony Historical Society, rather than the Philadelphia Museum of Art, or the Historical Society of Pennsylvania, both of which would have been happy by then to receive it.[44]

At the time of the Cinque trial, Robert Purvis was forty-one years old. He was the father of four children, a daughter, Harriet, having been born in 1839. He was president of the Vigilant Committee, and a rising star in the antislavery movement. And he was rich, for he continued to invest the capital originally left him by his father in businesses and in real estate. He continued to buy and sell properties despite the economy turndown following the Panic of 1837, which was causing distress to many businesses, including that of his father-in-law, James Forten.

In February 1840, for instance, Robert Purvis bought a four-story building and lot on the corner of Lombard and Fothergill Streets, for $5,500, and sold it four months later.[45] In March, he bought from Joseph Cassey a lot and a three-story brick building on the northeast corner of Schuylkill and Third, and Ann Streets.[46] In July, he bought at public auction a three- story building and lot on the south side of Powell near Fifth Street; he paid $1,675 for it.[47] In July, he bought from Joseph Cassey half of a three-story brick building and lot on the south side of Walnut, from Schuylkill and Third, a property they had bought together in 1839.[48] In August, he sold Cassey a half share of a four-story brick building and a lot on the east side of Eleventh Street, between Pine and Lombard, which they had bought together in 1838.[49]

In January 1841, he sold the property at Schuylkill and Third which he had bought a half share of from Joseph Cassey.[50] In March, he bought a lot on the south side of Lombard, between Eighth and Ninth Streets (near his home), and received a second adjoining lot from a sheriffs sale.[51] Two weeks later he sold the new buildings for the payment of taxes due on the property, and a rent of $70 a year.[52] On April 28, he bought a rental property on Marshall Street for $1,875.[53] On July 8, he sold a brick building and lot on the south side of Walnut Street for $4,000. This property had been bought two years earlier by Purvis and Cassey, who later sold his share to Purvis.[54] A week later, apparently using money from this sale, he bought eighty-three acres in Evesham Township, Burlington County, where Joseph Cassey had bought property the year before.[55] During this period he also bought and sold several ground rents. In July 1842, he bought a four-story brick house and "back buildings" on the north side of Lombard for $3,100.[56]

Purvis also lent money from time to time to owners of small businesses, and even to members of his extended family. By 1841, he was a wealthy man, paying what was a large amount of taxes in his day. In the fall of that year, when the state levied an extra tax in order to meet its indebtedness, he wrote a letter to the *Philadelphia Public Ledger*, protesting this as taxation without representation, and referring bitterly to the disfranchisement of forty thousand black men.[57]

Black citizens already paid property taxes which more than covered the amount the state spent on the education of their children and the care of their poor, Purvis asserted. But the state was appealing to the patriotism of blacks, while it denied them the right to vote. "Any vagabond foreigner, who by swearing allegiance to a country, of whose laws and institutions he may be totally ignorant, assumes a position above even our revolutionary fathers, whose scars bear an honorable testimony to their bravery and patriotism in those days "which tried the souls of men," and which secured independence for this country, and freedom for a *portion* of its inhabitants."

"The fundamental principle of the government of the United States is taxation and representation," Purvis wrote. Britain's violation of this principle caused the Revolutionary War. The first blood to flow was that of an American of African descent. Should taxes be extorted from a people who were denied the exercise of feelings of patriotism?[58]

> Then how hypocritical would any implied acknowledgment of the existence of those feelings appear to any one acquainted with human nature! How infamously tyrannical to extort payment for that we *are not allowed to possess!* Can we feel any interest in the honor of a state which has disgracefully and unjustly dishonored us? Would not resistance by us to this unjust tax, based upon and demanded from the *patriotism* of the people, be in obedience to the principles of justice and right? Let the depredatory arm of the Commonwealth, through its officers, seize our goods or even our persons—the sacrifice will be made upon the altar of humanity. Let that suffice.[59]

The antiblack elements in the Philadelphia public reacted swiftly to his letter; the night of its publication his house was surrounded by an angry mob. Robert Purvis was afraid for the safety of his family. Fortunately for the Purvis household, but unfortunately for others, the rumor was spread that there were a large number of armed and dangerous men in the Purvis house, and the mob turned aside, and vented its anger by burning a black church in the vicinity.[60]

CHAPTER 7

❦

A Time of Loss

$\mathcal{T}$hroughout these tumultuous early years Robert Purvis had the support and friendship of his father-in-law, James Forten, to strengthen his resolve. He loved and admired the civic-minded and patriotic sailmaker. Forten in turn regarded him as a son, in many ways as close as his own sons.

Tragedy struck the Forten family in 1840. In May, Robert Forten Jr. and his wife Mary Virginia lost a baby boy. Two months later Mary herself died, leaving a three-year-old daughter, Charlotte, to be raised by her grandmother. Robert and Mary had been neighbors of Robert and Harriet Purvis, but now the heartbroken Robert Forten moved back to his parents' home.[1]

Mary Virginia Forten had been a pious woman, and on her deathbed she spoke of her faith, and her desire that all members of her extended family should share in the blessings of religion. Her words on this occasion were published in the *Colored American*. At one point she spoke to a member of the family, very likely Robert Purvis. Taking his hand, she said, "You are moral and good but you need religion, you need the grace of God. O seek it!"[2]

His sister-in-law's words well-described Robert Purvis's view of religion at this time in his life. His ties with St. Thomas Episcopal Church were apparently loose; his name does not appear in the vestry records, nor is there any evidence that he had his children baptized at that church. After the episode in which the vestry of St. Thomas prohibited Purvis from mentioning the colonization movement or the antislavery movement in a speech to be given in the church, Robert and Harriet relinquished their pew, claiming that the church was pro-slavery! Asked to state his religious beliefs in this period of his life, Robert Purvis was prone to say that he believed in the fatherhood of God, the brotherhood of Man, and Christianity in action. Though he came to have many ties with the Religious Society of Friends, he never joined a meeting, for he was disturbed by the obvious racial prejudice of some Quakers. With Garrison and Lucretia Mott, he decried dogma of all kinds. Only in his old age did he speak of his belief that those who worked to end slavery were divinely led.[3]

Following the death of Mary Virginia, the Forten family began to worry about the health of James. Early in 1841, it became apparent that the seventy-five year old veteran suffered from asthma and congestive heart failure. Although Forten had been turning over his sail loft to the management of his sons, his experience was still needed at a time when credit was tight, and growing racial prejudice in the white community made it less likely that white businessmen would assist the younger Fortens, as their earlier counterparts had assisted James. It was in this climate that Robert Purvis lent the firm, at various times, over $10,000.[4]

James Forten had written his will in 1836, naming Purvis as an executor, along with Forten's wife, Charlotte, and his daughter, Margaretta. In this will, Forten stipulated that upon their marriage his daughters were to retain an equal share of his estate, in order to circumvent the married women's property law. Forten also arranged to turn over his house and lot to Robert Purvis and to James Forten, Jr. on condition they either allow Charlotte to occupy it, or pay her whatever rents they collected.[5]

Up until the last, Purvis worked with James on issues close to both their hearts. Colonization continued to be advocated by many Philadelphians. When the American Colonization Society tried to attract black supporters by suggesting that all vessels taking blacks to Africa be manned by black sailors, who would subsequently become owners of the vessel, Purvis helped to organize and spoke at an anticolonization rally held in St. Paul's Lutheran Church on January 7, 1839. He doubtless sought James Forten's advice in planning the 1839, 1840, and 1841 meetings of the American Moral Reform Society in Philadelphia, an organization in which he, William Whipper, and Daniel Payne were now the guiding leaders. And he reported to his father-in-law on the national meetings of the American Anti-Slavery Society which he attended, including his crucial vote in 1840 on electing Abby Kelley Foster to the business committee.[6]

By January 1842, it was clear that Forten's end was near. He said goodbye to old friends, and met with Daniel Alexander Payne as a spiritual advisor, and with William Douglass, of St. Thomas African Episcopal Church, his priest and friend. On the night of Tuesday, March 1, he said goodbye to his family, gathered at his bedside. To Robert Purvis he said: "I love you so much that I could take you to my bosom and carry you with me to heaven." He also charged Robert Purvis, "Never forget the plight of the suffering slaves." He lingered on, not able to speak, until the morning of March 4, when he died.[7]

The extended Forten family, including Robert and Harriet Purvis, were deeply grieved by Forten's death. They were not alone. Forten had made a major contribution to Philadelphia in countless ways. More than three thousand persons, many of them white, attended his funeral on March 6, held at St. Thomas African Episcopal Church. Writing to Irish Quaker friends, the Webbs, Lucretia Mott described the event:

> We yesterday attended the funeral of Jas Forten. You will see an accot. of his death in the *Standard*—an obituary written probably by Mary Grew. It was a real amalgamation funeral—hundreds of white people & thousands of colored.[8]

The obituary in the *Standard* was actually written by James Miller McKim, a member of the Pennsylvania Anti-Slavery Society. At first Lucretia Mott thought it was inferior to the one that Mary Grew had prepared, but she later felt it was ". . . good and true. So was H. C. Wright's announcing his death."[9]

In the *National Anti-Slavery Standard*, Miller McKim had written:

> The vast concourse of people, of all classes and complexions, numbering from three to five thousand, that followed his remains to the grave, bore testimony to the estimation in which he was universally held. Our wealthiest and most influential citizens joined in the procession; and complexional distinctions and prejudices seemed forgotten in the desire to pay the last tribute of respect to the departed to the memory of worth.[10]

And, writing in the *Liberator*, Henry C. Wright also commented on the integrated nature of the crowd:

> That noble MAN is dead. The courteous and warm-hearted *friend*—the generous and ever-watchful philanthropist—the beloved and affectionate father—the friend of God and man—has passed to his rest in heaven, in the 76th year of his age. I have this moment returned from his funeral. Thousands came to see his body, and to follow it to the grave. . . . He gained a victory over a nation arrayed against him; for around his dead body, *complexion* was forgotten. Many of our most beloved and respected citizens were present, to testify their respect for the deceased, and their sympathy for his afflicted family.[11]

The day after Forten's funeral, Stephen Smith presided at a memorial service held at the First African Presbyterian Church of Philadelphia. On April 27, there was a service at the Second African Presbyterian Church; Stephen Gloucester offered the eulogy. In between, Robert Purvis had his opportunity to speak at a service held at Mother Bethel Church on March 30. This speech, one of Robert Purvis's best, was often quoted in the Philadelphia community.[12]

Purvis began by describing his father-in-law as a *great* good man. Proof of his goodness was the interracial triumph of his funeral procession. "It is *enough*, it is enough that in his death he accomplished a victory so glorious over the ghastly and hideous features of a skin-hating aristocracy."[13]

Purvis next told the story of the life of James Forten, his early education, his enlistment on a privateer, his capture, his patriotic refusal of an offer to be educated in England, and his dreadful experiences on a British prison ship, the *Jersey*. He described Forten's unselfishness in helping another young prisoner to escape, in place of himself. This prisoner was Daniel Brewton, now in charge of the Lazaretto, the quarantine ship in the Philadelphia harbor. He spoke of recently witnessing a deathbed reunion between the dying Forten and Brewton; Brewton left in tears.[14] He told of Forten's later release, his return to Philadelphia, and his subsequent voyage in 1784 on the *Commerce*, with his new brother-in law, William Dunbar. Upon reaching London, he learned of the struggle against slavery and the efforts against it headed up by Granville Sharp. Since no letters survive from this period in Forten's life, biographers and historians have relied on this account by Purvis to describe the early life of this important figure.[15]

Continuing in a biographical vein, Purvis spoke of Forten's apprenticeship to sailmaker Robert Bridges, and his rapid advance in the company. Upon Bridges' retirement in 1798, Forten took over the sail loft. His reputation for capability and industry caused white businessmen to help him as he built up the business. It was during his long and active life as a business man that he developed a widely admired reputation.

> —so courteous, polished, and gentlemanly in his manners; so intelligent, social, and interesting; so honest, just and true in his dealings; so kind and benevolent in his actions; so noble and lofty in his bearing—that none knew him but to admire; to speak of him but in praise. He lived but to cherish those noble properties of his soul, and those exalted principles of action which ever prompted him to deeds of benevolence, patriotism, and honor.[16]

Purvis spoke of Forten's benevolence, not only expressed in support of many organizations and individuals, but also in personal acts of courage, such as his rescue at different times of some seven individuals from drowning in the Delaware River; he was given an honorary certificate by the Humane Society of Philadelphia for bravery. And he lauded Forten's patriotism, citing his refusal to accept a pension for his service in the Revolutionary War—"I was a volunteer, sir,"—and his actions during the War of 1812. He labored, along with his apprentices and journeymen, in elevating breastworks along the west bank of the Delaware River. James Forten's feelings for his country had been so strong that members of his family would express surprise, to which he would respond "that he had drawn the spirit of her free institutions from his mother's breast, and that he had fought for her independence." His patriotism had led him to fear for this country when she continued to discriminate against her people of darker skin. He had often quoted Thomas Jefferson: "I tremble for my country when I reflect that God is just, and this his justice will not sleep forever."[17]

The action of the Pennsylvania Reform Convention of 1838 in disenfranchising blacks had appalled James Forten. Because he was born in Pennsylvania, with ancestors who were residents for as long as 170 years, and because he paid large amounts of taxes, and made voluntary contributions to many of the city's finest institutions, he considered the action of the state legislature a gesture of insensitivity and ingratitude. He was equally upset by the refusal of the legislature to amend the Fugitive Slave Law of 1793, "which authorizes the claimant of any fugitive slave to seize his victim without a warrant from any magistrate, and allows him to drag him before any magistrate of a county, city, or town corporate, where such seizure has been made, and, upon proving by oral testimony or affidavits to the satisfaction of such magistrate that the man is his slave, gives him the right to take him to interminable bondage."[18]

Purvis described the organization of the American Colonization Society, and Forten's part in pulling together the gathering at Mother Bethel Church which denounced the new organization and stated the determination of those gathered to remain in their native land. Parts of the Declaration of the assembled group had been written by Forten himself, Purvis stated:

> *Resolved,* That we never will separate ourselves voluntarily from the slave population in this country. They are our brethren by the ties of consanguinity, of suffering, and of wrong; and we feel that there is more virtue in suffering privations with them than fancied advantages for a season.[19]

He went on to describe Forten's support for William Lloyd Garrison, and for the principles Garrison espoused, including his belief in the equality of women, and the importance of a free expression of ideas, and the freeing of minds from the shackles of dogma. He spoke of his long association with St. Thomas Episcopal Church, of which he was the last surviving founder. However, he added: "He ever valued the spirit of Christianity, as exemplified in the characters of men, as being of infinitely more importance than a mere unity in doctrinal views and creeds." [20]

As a business man, Purvis said Forten had been consistently honest and fair, never misrepresenting or deceiving his customers. A believer in temperance, he had forbidden intoxicating liquors in his sail loft. He was a member and the Presiding Officer of the American Moral Reform Society, and stood for all things moral and uplifting.

> He was a model, not as some flippant scribbler asserts, for what is called "colored men" but for all men. His example will ever be worthy of emulation, his virtues never forgotten in the community in which he lived; and let us, while we enkindle a proper ardor of feeling in imitating his goodness and benevolence, while we deplore our great loss—for, "as a man, we ne'er shall look upon his like again"—be consoled in the thought that though his body has returned to the dust from whence it came, his immortal spirit is where we all again can meet. [21]

Sorrowful events continued to plague the Forten family. Grace Douglass, a cherished friend of the family, with whom James Forten had operated a school for black children, died March 9 just five days after James Forten. The younger Fortens and the Purvises had grown up with the Douglass children, Sarah, Robert, James, Charles, and William, and had known Grace as a strong influence in the black community. A founding member of the Philadelphia Female Anti-Slavery Society, she had also helped to forge interracial friendships in fractured Philadelphia. The Fortens and Purvises mourned her loss.

Yet another death followed. Mary Isabella, Harriet's younger sister, had been in poor health for some time. On July 16, she succumbed to tuberculosis. Robert Purvis wrote a fond tribute to his sister-in-law which appeared in the *National Anti-Slavery Standard*:

> And in brighter and more enduring worlds will shine those virtues which here beautified and made attractive the character of Mary, youngest daughter of the late James Forten. To finished mental culture, combining the graces of a spotless heart, she moved in the circle of her acquaintance,

admired and loved. But Death, ever unsparing and insatiate, in the morning of her day, in the springtime of her hopes, marked her for his own. She died. But the "grim monster" had no terrors for her, her faith grounded upon the merits of Christ's redeeming blood, was sufficient. In perfect resignation she submitted to the Divine will. [22]

In the midst of all their mourning, the Forten family had to deal with the matter of settling James Forten's complicated estate. Although he had died a comparatively wealthy man, owning a number of properties, Forten had borrowed money and had debts to settle. He had loaned large sums to various shipowners and merchants he had worked with through the years; these loans needed to be called in to settle the estate. Unfortunately, Philadelphia was in the grip of a depression, and many of those who owed the Forten estate were unable to pay. [23]

Forten had chosen as his executors his wife, Charlotte, his oldest daughter, Margaretta, and his favorite son-in-law, Robert Purvis. Forten had borrowed from Robert, and in order to settle the estate, Robert Purvis found it necessary to sue the Forten brothers, Robert and James, who had inherited the business, as well as their creditors. His suits were successful, but the firm was now near bankruptcy and unable to pay. Robert in turn was sued by one of James's creditors; he was successful in winning the law case and he avoided damages. In 1844, the brothers sold the sail loft, and James Forten Jr. left for New York and disappeared from the family records. Robert stayed in Philadelphia and eventually remarried, choosing as his second wife a wealthy widow, Mary Hanscome, from Charleston, South Carolina, with a background similar to Robert Purvis's. In fact, it is probable that Robert Purvis introduced them. With the help of his wife's estate, Robert Forten bought a farm in Warminister, but after some years the couple moved to Canada, settling first in Toronto, then in London, Ontario. Still unsettled, they moved to England in 1859, but Robert returned alone to the United States during the Civil War. [24]

Following the death of James Forten, Robert Purvis was accorded the slightly dubious honor of being elected to the Pennsylvania Abolition Society. From its inception in 1775, and its reorganization in 1787, the Abolition Society had remained staunchly white, despite its concern with black issues. In this it differed from the American Anti-Slavery Society, which was integrated from the beginning. Perhaps the honors paid Forten at his death jolted the Society into action. At any rate, they decided in 1842 to elect the light-skinned and aristocratic Purvis as their first black member. Offsetting this radical step, the

Society at the same time elected Benjamin Coates, a Philadelphia merchant who favored colonization.[25]

During the unhappy months of her father's illness and death, Harriet Davy Forten Purvis was pregnant with her fifth child. On April 4, 1842, Charles Burleigh Purvis was born. Harriet had the assistance of an English governess in caring for the smaller children, and in tutoring the older ones in a room set aside for this purpose, the schoolroom, in the house on Lombard Street. Still, the burden of caring for five children was heavy. Robert did what he could to lighten the load, hiring additional domestic help, and adjusting his schedule whenever possible to be of support to Harriet. He was moved by his love for his wife and also his principled belief in the equality of women.

Harriet had been one of a small group of women who organized the interracial Philadelphia Female Anti-Slavery Society on December 9, 1833, just five days after the founding of the American Anti-Slavery Society. For many years she served as a faithful member of this body, along with her older sister, Margaretta, who often served on the board of directors, and her younger sister, Sarah. Harriet was frequently a delegate to the Free Produce Conventions, and she was always appointed to the committee to organize the Anti-Slavery Fairs which occurred each year at Christmas time, which raised money for the antislavery cause.[26]

In addition, Harriet was sometimes a delegate from the Philadelphia Female Anti-Slavery Society to the Anti-Slavery Convention of American Women. In 1837, when the first successful convention was held in New York, she was pregnant with her third son, Joseph, and did not attend. However, she was present at the Second Annual Convention, held in Philadelphia in 1838, and attended the rump session held in Sarah Pugh's schoolhouse on Water Street, where the delegates pledged themselves to work more vigorously at expanding their interracial contacts. She was also a delegate to the Third Annual Convention, held in Philadelphia in 1839, in a riding stable because no group in Philadelphia would allow the women to use its hall.[27]

The Philadelphia Female Anti-Slavery Society also served as a watchdog for obvious cases of racial discrimination. At a meeting on June 15, 1841, they noticed with dismay that children from the black Sunday schools had been refused participation in an exhibition of Sunday schools held in Independence Square. The women agreed to publish a remonstrance against this outrage in the *Public Ledger*. A year later they reported triumphantly that at a second such exhibition, the colored Sunday schools were allowed to take part.[28]

An advocate of the Free Produce Movement, Harriet was also active in the Colored Free Produce Association and shopped regularly in Free Produce Stores, such as that run by Lydia White, the woman whom Purvis had praised at the colored convention. Robert and Harriet supported the Colored Free Produce Association,[29] buying only goods that had not been raised or manufactured through slave labor. These goods sold were often more expensive and of poorer quality than those to be obtained on the open market. The Free Produce stores were barely able to break even. For a household to use only Free Produce products meant considerable sacrifice, not only in money, which the Purvises could afford, but also in time, which came more dearly in this busy household. Nevertheless, the Purvises maintained this testimony for many years. Working together in these and others ways for the antislavery movement cemented their marriage throughout the years.

Whenever possible, Harriet accompanied Robert on his trips to attend antislavery meetings. Thus in May 1840 she went with him to Harrisburg for a meeting of the Pennsylvania Anti-Slavery Society, and then to New York for the eventful meeting of the American Anti-Slavery Society, where the group split over the election of a woman to a committee.[30] They attended the annual meetings regularly, and in 1846, Robert was made a vice president of the organization. In 1855, Harriet was named to a committee to report to the officers of the Society during the coming year.[31]

Harriet also kept up her membership in the various literary associations for African-American women in which her sister, Sarah Forten Purvis, a poet, was active. These included the Female Literary Association, the Female Minervian Association and the Edgeworth Literary Association. Members of these associations often published their work in the antislavery newspapers, such as the *Liberator*, but always under assumed names. It is not possible to identify any of the poems that Harriet wrote at this time, but she was always an interested reader.[32]

With both Robert and Harriet active, and an increasing number of children to care for, life at the Purvis house on Lombard Street was busy, but happy, and it might have continued to be so, had it not been for the growing violence of the times. The angry mobs that gathered in the summers of 1834 and 1835 had swept close to their home, and in 1838 had attacked Mother Bethel Church, just three blocks away. Often the Purvis house was selected for special attention; when it was suspected that Robert Purvis was harboring fugitives, and in 1841, when he published a letter in the local press deploring his being heavily taxed while denied the vote.

In the hot summer of 1842, tensions against the black community mounted among Philadelphia workers. The depression that had begun with the withdrawal of federal funds from state banks in 1841 was at its deepest, and unemployment was rife, at a time when fresh waves of Irish working-class men and their families were arriving. They were fleeing "the Troubles," over the denial of Home Rule, and mounting famine.

In addition, the black community had alienated the working-class neighborhoods by the crusade against alcohol, mounted by middle-class and wealthy blacks through the American Moral Reform Society and the black churches. In 1842, the reformers erected a small hall in the working-class neighborhood of Moyamensing where alcoholics were invited to confess their sins and make a fresh start. The Philadelphia Female Anti-Slavery Society warmly applauded this effort, and pledged $10 a month to support The Retreat, as it was called. However, this retreat proved a provocation.[33]

Further heightening tensions, rumors that a national convention of black leaders was to be held in Philadelphia circulated in the summer of 1842. On August 1, the anniversary of the establishment of freedom in the British West Indies, the black community had planned celebrations, as usual. The leaders of the temperance group decided upon a parade in which a number of reformed alcoholics would march through the streets near the working-class area. Several black leaders perceived this as provocative, and tried in vain to dissuade the marchers.[34] The march was nevertheless held as planned, and all went well until the marchers passed Fifth and Shippen Streets. Here the onlookers attacked, provoked, they claimed, by the incendiary banner carried by the Young Men's Vigilant Committee. The marchers responded in kind. The mob began attacking buildings owned by blacks along Lombard Street and intervening alleys. Further inciting the rioters, blacks fired on the mob. The mayor arrived and attempted to intervene, but the riot continued. By evening, the mob had set fire to two black buildings, the Second Presbyterian Church and Smith's Beneficial Hall. As in the case of Pennsylvania Hall, the fire companies did nothing to save the buildings.[35]

On the first day of rioting the mob was mixed, but on the second day it became predominantly Irish, and increasingly ugly. Many black homes were set on fire and many residents fled the city. There was little or no intervention by the constabulary. Only by calling in the militia was the mayor able to end the violence.[36]

Robert Purvis had been speaking on antislavery in Norristown on the day the rioting began. Coming home, he was met by the English governess of his children who pleaded with him not to go home because the

mob had surrounded his house and intended to kill him. Purvis nevertheless rushed home where he found his terrified wife and children; they
were safe. He sent them and the servants upstairs, and took a seat on the
stairs, with his rifle across his knees; Purvis was prepared to kill anyone
who attacked his family. It was for Purvis a final break with the Garrisonian theory of nonresistance.[37]

That first night, the fires at the Second Presbyterian Church and
Smith Hall drew off the attention of the crowd. The next day, however,
the mob was back, in an even uglier mood. After a time, a courageous
Catholic priest, Father Patrick Moriarity, intervened and rebuked the rioters.[38] Later they returned and Sheriff Lewis Morris came by the house
to say that he could no longer guarantee protection. Purvis then sent his
family to their country place in Bensalem.[39]

But while he and his beloved family were saved, Purvis's spirits were
dashed. When his friend and fellow abolitionist, Henry Wright, wrote to
him for details of the riot, hoping to use them in England to promote
abolitionist sentiment, Purvis wrote back that he was too discouraged to
answer properly. The brutality and murderous spirit of the mob was bad
enough, but what had really hurt him was "the apathy and *inhumanity* of
the *whole* community."

But I am even now, in every way disqualified for making proper answers
to your interrogations in reference to one of the most ferocious and
bloody spirited mobs, that ever cursed a *Christian*(?) community. I know
not where I should begin, nor how, or when to end in a detail of the wan-
tonness, brutality, and murderous spirit, of the actors, in the late riots,
nor of the apathy and *inhumanity* of the *whole* community—in regard to
the matter—Press, Church, Magistrate, Clergymen and Devils are against
us—The measure of our sufferings is full—"man's inhumanity to man, indeed makes countless millions mourn"—From the most painful and
minute investigation, in the feelings, views and acts of the community—in
regard to us—I am convinced of our utter and complete nothingness in
public estimation—I feel that my life and those tendrils of my heart,
dearer than life to me, would find no change in death, but a *glorious* rid-
dance of a life, weighed down and cursed by a despotism whose sway
makes Hell on Earth—We the *tormented*, our persecutors the tormentors—
But I stop; I am sick—miserably sick—everything around me is as dark as
the grave–Here & there the bright countenance of true friend is to be
seen, *save that*—nothing is redeeming, nothing hopeful, despair black as
the face of Death hangs over us—And the bloody *will* is in the heart of the
community to destroy us.[40]

After the second night of rioting, Purvis joined his family at their country home at Bensalem. Always before the farm had functioned as a pleasant escape from the heat of the city. Now, however, Harriet and Robert began to weigh the possibility of moving permanently to the country, thus saving their children from the constant danger of mob attack, and the humiliation of being discriminated against because of the color of their skin. Robert's faith that there was just one race, the human race, was severely tried, not so much by the rioters, as by the apathy of the white community, including, he felt, many of his white antislavery colleagues.[41]

CHAPTER 8

Gentleman Farmer

$\mathscr{D}$espite the rashness that his colleagues detected in his speeches, Robert Purvis was always deliberate in matters pertaining to property. Though he and Harriet undoubtedly debated the decision to leave the city, and looked at various country and suburban communities, it was not until a year after the riots of 1842 that they made a move. In September 1843, Robert bought a "mansion house" and a tract of 104 acres from Cyrus Pierce for $13,000. The farm, consisting of two large lots separated by a road, was in Byberry, a rural area in Philadelphia County, twelve miles north of the city. To help pay for this purchase, he sold a four-story house on the north side of Lombard to Pierce, a house and lot on the south side of Lombard to Sarah and Mary Widdifield, and a house and lot on Pine, to Joseph Donath. It was at this time, too, that he sued his Forten brothers-in-law for money he had lent the Forten estate.[1]

The Cyrus Pierce farm that the Purvises bought was situated on the corner of the Byberry and the Thorton Roads across from Byberry Friends Meetinghouse, erected in 1808, and the Byberry Friends School, which dated from the 1700s. A portion of the land lay across the road, behind the Meetinghouse. Robert Purvis farmed the section west of Byberry Road, and leased, then gradually sold off the acres to the east. In 1873, he sold one acre to the Byberry Friends Meetinghouse, to enlarge its burial ground.[2]

The Purvis's new neighbors were farming families who had lived in the area for generations. Robert and Harriet were, in effect, desegregating the neighborhood, and despite their best efforts to fit in, there was feeling against them among some of the neighbors for many years to come.[3]

Robert and Harriet and their children moved to Byberry in 1844. This move marked a major milestone in the family's life. While Robert Purvis remained deeply identified with the struggle against slavery and for equality, his lifestyle became more that of a country squire than a wealthy Philadelphia black. He never apologized for this move, believing his first obligation was to his family, but he was increasingly touchy about his status as the only black among whites. When his children were grown, he returned to the city, and the endless task of defining a black man's place in a white world.

Robert and Harriet's new home in Byberry Township, called Harmony Hall, had been built in 1770 by William Walmsley. It was three stories tall, with an open stairway to the third floor, and a hall extending the width of the house. A parlor, a living room, a dining room, and an old-fashioned kitchen with a pump and a high Dutch dresser occupied the first floor. A porch surrounded half the house, and there was a cellar with outside steps. Soon after arriving, Robert ordered the construction of a special room in the basement for concealing runaway slaves.[4]

To reach the house, one entered between two large gateposts, and came first to a two-story carriage house. Beyond the house was a large barn with a cupola and an ice house, also with a cupola. On the grounds were orchards of apple, cherry and plum trees, and kitchen gardens. Beyond were the stables, grazing fields, and acres of farmland.[5]

When she first arrived at Harmony Hall, Harriet had a brand new baby, Henry, to care for. Nevertheless, with Robert's help she managed to furnish her new home pleasantly with a view to entertaining. She owned a large set of sterling silver, and fine china, some bearing antislavery messages. Two pictures, which the Purvises prized, the portrait of Cinque, the black Mendi leader of the capture of the *Amistad*, and the other of William Lloyd Garrison hung in the large dining room. The Garrison portrait was taken down only once, when at the request of Maria Chapman, it was crated and sent to Boston, to appear in the publication, the *Liberty Bell*, and to be shown at the Boston Anti-Slavery Fair.[6]

At Harmony Hall, the Purvises constantly entertained. The leading abolitionists of the day were among their guests, as well as members of the extensive Forten-Purvis clan, friends from the city, as well as (less conspicuously) escaping slaves. Sallie Holley, an antislavery lecturer, who visited in the 1850s, described the atmosphere:

> Mr. Purvis is a coloured man, but so light that no stranger would suspect it. His wife is very lady-like in manners and conversation; something of the

ease and blandness of a southern lady. The style of living here is quite un-
commonly rich and elegant. Upon my arrival I was ushered into a beautiful room where there was a large wood fire blazing most delightfully in an
open fireplace. It was so charming to me after my twenty miles' ride
through the mud and the cold.[7]

William Lloyd Garrison, a frequent visitor, wrote to his wife about
having lunch at Harmony Hall, and enjoying ice cream and fresh straw-
berries. James and Lucretia Mott came often. Abby Kelley Foster stopped
by in 1849 to plead for money to save the *Anti-Slavery Bugle*, a Ohio newspaper she had helped to found. Purvis gave her $100. Elizabeth Cady
Stanton and Susan B. Anthony were entertained at Harmony Hall.
Aaron Powell wrote of his visit there.[8]

He was a genial host. In connection with my earliest visits to Philadelphia,
many years ago, I was most kindly welcomed by him and by his family in
their hospitable rural home of the period, at Byberry, a refuge and shelter
also for many a fugitive from slavery, en route to Canada.[9]

Purvis was thirty-four when he moved to Byberry. By buying, selling,
and renting real estate, making loans and underwriting mortgages, he
had more than doubled the money left him by his father. Though he continued to buy and sell real estate, after 1844 it was at a reduced pace, however, he continued to give generously to the antislavery cause. Yet, he died
a very rich man.[10]

At Byberry, he settled down to the life of a gentleman farmer. Both
he and Harriet became interested in raising prize vegetables, flowers, and
livestock; they won many blue ribbons at local country fairs. Robert's lifelong love of fine horses blossomed at Byberry; he raised a number of thor-
oughbreds. He became interested in the breeding of livestock, and wrote
an article for a local paper, expressing his belief that it was better to con-
centrate on local stock than on importing cattle from abroad. Although
he had won a number of prizes for his imported stock, he was not satis-
fied, for he observed the tendency of imported stock to deteriorate.[11]

Would it not be better for us, in trying to improve our stock, to make our
selections for the purpose without regard to the animal's origin? In milch
cows, for example, ought we not to chose the finest-looking animal and
best milker we can find, whether native, imported or "mixed" and ought
we not to see that the offspring are the product of a sire chosen on the
same principle? Is it not likely, and does not experience, as far as it has

been made, show that the tendency of this sort of breeding is to continual improvement of the stock? I would ask the same question in regard to hogs, fowl, horses, sheep, and all other kinds of animals. In other words, ought we not to make more account of our native breeds, and seek by judicious crossing and care in all other respects, to attain the end which we have not yet reached in the matter of stock-raising?[12]

This, he said, was the way that England had improved her varieties. Americans should do the same. The finest flavored pear in the world, he thought, was the Seckel, the finest raspberry the Brinkle, the best apple the Newtown pippin, all native to Philadelphia.

Why can't we therefore, on the same principle, raise native cattle of corresponding excellence? Why can't our farm-yards be made to do as well as our gardens and orchards? If England comes to us for our apples and peaches and our sowing and mowing machines, why can't she be made to come to us for our native animals?—a favorite breed, for example, of the milch cow, or some other animal, in the rearing of which she now is so much our superior? It strikes me that if we would attain such advancement as we aspire to, we ought to try what virtue there is in our native breeds.[13]

It is possible that Robert Purvis was also thinking of preserving the American "stock" whether Caucasian or African-American, rather than bringing in the many immigrants who were beginning to flood the American soil. This attitude stemmed not so much from prejudice against the newcomers, but from his distress that these new arrivals were granted privileges which he, as a man of color, was denied.

According to the Federal Agricultural Census of 1850, Robert Purvis had forty-six acres under cultivation, a total cash value to his farm of $6,000, with $300 worth of farm machinery. His lifestock, consisting of five horses, four milch cows, and four pigs, was valued at $800. He was raising 220 bushels of wheat, 400 bushels of corn, 250 bushels of potatoes, forty tons of hay, and 500 pounds of butter; he had slaughtered $150 worth of animals. By the 1860 census, he had forty-nine acres under cultivation, and a farm valued at $15,000 with $800 worth of farm machinery and $2,000 worth of animals, including seven horses.[14]

Despite all his success as a farmer, Robert Purvis continued to encounter discrimination. In 1846 members of the Bensalem Horse Company, a local association of livestock breeders, made an effort to have him expelled. And in 1853, although he had won first prize in the past three exhibits, the Philadelphia Chicken Fanciers refused to receive Purvis's chickens.[15]

Purvis told one of his guests, Sallie Holley, about a typical episode, which Sallie retold in her memoirs.

> During the poultry exhibition, or "Hen Convention" as it is called on the spot, a gentleman came near Mr. Purvis's exhibit, and as he was admiring them and remarking on their rare beauty, he said to Mr. Purvis (not knowing him), "And these belong to that black nigger down in Byberry." Mr. P. replied "Why friend, you put it in rather strong language, but you can judge for yourself—I am that man." The other man turned and went away.[16]

Almost directly across from Harmony Hall was the Byberry Friends Meeting House. Because of this proximity, and because some of the Purvis's colleagues were Quakers, it has been assumed that they attended, perhaps joined the meeting. This, however, was not the case.[17] Not only were some of his Quaker neighbors resentful of his buying a farm in their midst, but Purvis was painfully aware that other blacks had been denied membership in the Religious Society of Friends. The Quakers had decided at their yearly meeting of 1796 to permit black members, though few if any joined at this time. Increasingly, public prejudice against blacks had seeped into the Society of Friends in the nineteenth century, and the Friends tended to segregate blacks to special benches when they attended Quaker meetings. Grace Douglass, who had been raised as a Quaker, had been discouraged when she considered applying for membership in the Arch Street Meeting, she was asked to sit on a separate bench. A proud man like Robert Purvis was not prepared to risk such a rebuff.[18]

Purvis would also have been aware of the divided Quaker attitudes toward antislavery. While a number of Quakers were active in the antislavery movement during this time, the meetings discouraged members from participating in organizations, such as the American Anti-Slavery Society, which was made up of persons from other denominations. It was a period of withdrawal for Quakers, and they were urged to work against slavery within their meetings, but not to join with "the world's people." It was also feared that the agitation surrounding the antislavery movement would ultimately lead to bloodshed. Some Quakers were disowned for being too active in the antislavery cause. Even a Friend as prominent as Lucretia Mott was threatened with expulsion.[19]

Some years after the Purvises moved to Byberry, they joined a number of antislavery Friends who were tired of restrictions on their activities imposed by their individual meetings. They issued a call for the development of a new yearly meeting, to be called the "Yearly Meeting of Progressive

Friends" at Longwood. Robert and Harriet signed the call and attended the first gathering; and several other of the yearly gatherings, Robert serving on the antislavery committee. There was no official membership in this group and evidently Robert kept up his ties with the Progressive Friends. Many years later his second wife, Tacie Townsend Purvis, was buried in the burial ground across from the Progressive Friends Meeting House.[20]

To provide a place in Byberry where antislavery matters could be openly discussed, Robert Purvis attended an auction in May 1845 and bought a four-acre lot across the road from Harmony Hall for $500. It was located adjacent to the meeting house;on this lot he built an edifice, that he called "Byberry Hall," to be used as a center for debate and discussion of social and educational issues, including abolition. In 1847, he sold the land surrounding the hall to trustees of the hall for the nominal sum of $50. He helped to organize a Philosophical Society, which met in the Hall, and he gave a series of lectures on such subjects as education and the "intellectual condition of the colored race."[21]

The need for Byberry Hall was made clear in November 1847 when anti-slavery advocate Rowland Johnson spoke in Byberry Meeting. He was interrupted by a member who suggested that he should more appropriately make his remarks in Byberry Hall, or "Free Hall," as he called it. Another member, however, cautioned patience and Johnson was able to finish his speech without other incident.[22]

One of the groups that met regularly at the Hall was the Bensalem Horse Traders, which had threatened Purvis with expulsion. They desisted, however, when several of his friends and admirers attacked them in the press. One of these was Miller McKim, who asked why the horse traders wished to expel him.

and for why, think ye reader? Why, everlasting contempt upon their guilty heads, because say they he is a colored man! We endorse all that the *Freeman* says of our friend Purvis—he is a gentleman in every sense of the word, and could possibly have no superior in that association. . . . Still, we are told, that his color made him objectionable; which allegation we deny since it is with difficulty, such is the fairness of his complexion, that any one, unacquainted with him, could, without being informed of the fact, tell that he is a colored man at all. [23]

If he did not become a Quaker, Robert Purvis decided at this stage in his life that he was no longer an Episcopalian. In October 1848, Frederick Douglass published an article in his paper, the *North Star*, charging that three black churches in Philadelphia barred their doors to antislavery lectures.[24] One was St. Thomas African Episcopal Church. Frederick Douglass believed that its misguided minister, William Douglass, was afraid of mob violence, but Purvis was more blunt. He remembered being denied the opportunity to speak on antislavery subjects at the church. In December, he wrote a letter to the *North Star*, saying that he had received ten dollars for relinquishing his right and title to a certain pew in St. Thomas African Episcopal church (which he had subscribed to in 1830), because he now regarded that church as pro-slavery. Instead he would give his ten dollars to "the suffering slave."[25]

In leaving St. Thomas' Church, Robert Purvis was taking part in the movement launched by William Lloyd Garrison for abolitionists to separate themselves or "to come out" from any church or political body that had slaveholders as members. The "Come-outers," as they were called, often withdrew from conservative churches and even Quaker Meetings which refused to allow either antislavery meetings on their premises, or permit their members to participate in antislavery political campaigns. The Philadelphia Female Anti-Slavery Society pledged itself to "no union with political or ecclesiastical organizations that had union with slaveholders," and would not permit Thomas Cavender, a member of the political Liberty Committee, to sell his goods at the Anti-Slavery Fair. Later Mary Earle, wife of Thomas Earle, a supporter of the Liberty Party, resigned from the PFAS in protest.[26]

The greatest problem that the Purvises encountered in Byberry pertained to the education of their children. With the birth in 1849 of a daughter, Georgianna, named for Harriet's friend, Georgianna Bruce, (an African-American woman from Philadelphia who attended antislavery meetings with her), Harriet and Robert now had eight children to educate. The Purvises continued to employ a governess and to set aside one room in their house as a schoolroom. But they also sent several of their children to the Byberry Friends School across from their property.[27]

The first building to house Byberry School was built in 1720; a second in 1789, and the present structure, a two-story building, in 1823. At its peak, the school consisted of eight grades, all educated in one small room. Each child paid $2 a month, and supplied his/her own tablets, slates, and pens. It proved hard to find qualified teachers to tend the school, and there were hiatuses during which it was closed. Sometimes the teacher found it necessary to concentrate on the youngest pupils, and allow the older ones to fend for themselves. During the winter months, due to the fact that it was difficult to heat the schoolroom, school was often dismissed because of heavy snows. In the spring, there was scant attendance, for most of the older children were needed on the farm to help with plowing and planting.[28]

Among the many men and women who taught at Byberry School, the best-known was John Comly, a devout Quaker who led the Hicksite or liberal branch of the Religious Society of Friends when that body separated into two branches, Hicksite and Orthodox, in 1827, due to a controversy over authority. Comly, closely related to Purvis's immediate neighbors, wrote a number of textbooks which were used in the school, including English Grammar, 1803, Spelling Book, 1806; Primer, 1807; and Spelling and Reading Book, 1842.[29]

Byberry School claims that it always accepted children regardless of race, but it is probable that the Purvis children were the only children of color who attended. School records are not available for most of the years the Purvises attended, but there is a notation that Georgianna Purvis attended the school. And Charles Purvis wrote to the Old Pupils Association in 1906 that "my five brothers and two sisters and myself were among the attenders."[30]

> My mind frequently reverts to my boyhood days, so pleasantly spent in Byberry. It is over fifty years since I attended the little school located in the yard of the Friends meetinghouse. My first teacher was Mr. Ivins, who used to find pleasure in arousing me from my delightful slumber by squeezing water from a sponge into my ear. My next teacher was Jane Hillborn, a dignified lady for whom I entertained great respect though I was a mere boy—There was no ostentation, no parade, but a quiet installation of those sentiments that have made us a people and a nation what we are.[31]

Unfortunately, it was necessary for the Purvis children to attend the public schools after they had outgrown Byberry Friends; here they experienced severe discrimination. In 1848, two public schoolteachers humiliated two of the Purvis children; they asked them to sit together and apart from the other children. Robert Purvis brought a suit against them, with the support of many of his neighbors. In a letter to the *Pennsylvania Freeman*, he spoke bitterly of the outcome:

> In reply to many queries about the position of affairs in regard to the Byberry public schools, its directors, && I will inform our friends that the Grand Jury refused to find true bills against Charles Knight and Jacob Sides (teachers)—confining their judgment merely to the assault upon the boys, which truly in one sense was merely nominal,[32] as the boys sustained

no personal injury. Yet the flagrant and high-handed outrage upon their rights, and that of their guardians, would seem to have demanded a different result. But alas! The dastard spirit of pro-slavery only strikes the oppressed and their friends. This by no means ends the matter—a *mandamus* from the Supreme Court will doubtless be issued, and the right, justice, and constitutionality of the school law will be settled, we opine, in a manner adverse to the wishes of Knight and his Philadelphia backers, for here I would say that *all* who truly give character to this township, on the score of moral, intellectual, and pecuniary worth, are opposed to this palpable violation of law and justice, and at farthest it needs but the period of time when the righteous indignation of the honest and true hearts of the township, shall express through the ballot box their opinion of the *worthiness* of those directors who have so unanimously perverted the object of their trust, and cravenly bowed the knee to the bloody Moloch of oppression.[33]

In 1853, Philadelphia County set up separate schools for blacks, and the Purvis children were excluded from the public schools. Under a law passed by the Pennsylvania Assembly the following year, if a school district could provide a separate school, they were not required to admit black children into the public school. Moreover the black schools were required to stay open only four months of the year. When Purvis objected to a school board director, who happened to be a Quaker, about this exclusion, he was told that the segregated school was good enough for his children.

I was informed by a *pious* Quaker director, with sanctifying grace, imparting, doubtless, an unctuous glow to his *saintly* prejudices, that a school in the village of Mechanicsville was appropriated for "*thine.*" The miserable shanty, with all its appurtenances, on the very line of the township, to which this *benighted* follower of George Fox alluded, is, as you know, the most flimsy and ridiculous sham which any tool of a skin-hating aristocracy have resorted to, to cover or protect his servility.[34]

Under these circumstances. Purvis decided he could no longer, in good conscience, pay his school tax. In a letter to the tax collector which was published in the *Liberator,* Purvis said that paying such a tax would grossly insult his feelings as a man, a parent, and a citizen.

I am perfectly aware that all that makes up the character and worth of the citizens of this township look upon the proscription and exclusion of my children from the Public School as illegal, and unjustifiable usurpation of my right. I have borne this outrage ever since the innovation upon the usual practice of admitting *all* the children of the Township into the Public Schools, and at considerable expense, have been obliged to obtain the services of private teachers to instruct my children, while my school tax is greater, with a single exception, than that of any other citizen of the township.[35]

To pay this tax voluntarily would be cowardly, Purvis said, and he felt conscientiously impelled to resist it. He ended by assuring the tax collector of his warm personal feelings for the man, who was just doing his job.

Purvis's letter and his threat to no longer pay his school tax, were effective. The school board voted to no longer exclude black children from the public schools. In 1856, Charles, Henry, and Granville Purvis attended the Benjamin Rush Public School. Purvis was credited in abolitionist circles as having desegregated the township schools. Ironically, when the former school for blacks at Mechanicsville was rebuilt some years later, it was renamed the Forten School in honor of Harriet Forten Purvis.[36]

As the children grew older, the Purvises sent them away to suitable boarding schools and colleges. In 1850, the three older Purvis sons, William, Robert, and Joseph, attended Central College in McGrawsville, New York, founded by the American Baptist Missionary Society in 1849 and financed in part by abolitionist Gerritt Smith. This college was the first to hire black faculty members as well as admit black students. Charles Reason, a teacher at the Institute for Colored Youth in Philadelphia, taught there for several years.[37]

In July 1850, Harriet Purvis accompanied Lucretia Mott to Central College, where the Quaker minister had agreed to be the commencement speaker on July 4. It was a chance for Harriet to see her sons. Mott made a fiery speech, denouncing the notion of innate human depravity, which shocked some of the Baptists. Charles Reason, whom Mott described as "a black professor of belle lettres," came to her defense.[38]

In 1855, Hattie Purvis attended the Eagleswood Boarding School run by Angelina and Theodore Grimké Weld as part of an intentional community, the Raritan Bay Union, near Perth Amboy, New Jersey. Here, Ellen Wright, daughter of Martha Coffin Wright and niece of Lucretia Coffin Mott, was her classmate. The two formed a friendship which was to last a lifetime.[39]

Though Robert Purvis may have had the backing of at least some of his Byberry neighbors in protesting the segregated schools, he lost this goodwill in 1856 when he opposed the move of Byberry residents to separate the township from Philadelphia and attach it to Bucks County. In 1809, the farmers of Byberry had attempted to separate themselves from

Philadelphia County, by proposing a new county made up of portions of Bucks, Philadelphia, and Montgomery Counties. In 1831, this change was again proposed without success. In 1854, Byberry citizens were dismayed when their township was incorporated into the city of Philadelphia under the Consolidation Act. In 1856, a vigorous attempt was made to lobby Harrisburg for the creation of a new county. Purvis, with the interests of the Philadelphia black community at heart, fought vigorously against this effort to separate off the rich suburban area of Byberry from the city. His was the winning side, but his reputation as a troublesome outsider was only increased by his participation.[40]

Despite their loyalty to Philadelphia, the Purvis family continued to receive racial snubs from the city as well. In 1848, an exhibit of wax statuary in the Assembly Buildings in Philadelphia was opened to the "colored" for only one day a week, a situation which Robert Purvis joined with others in protesting in the pages of the *Pennsylvania Freeman*, under the headline "Violent Spasm of Color Phobia." In 1853, his son, Robert Jr. escorted two young women of color, Sarah Remond from Salem and Annie Wood, younger sister of his former sister-in-law Mary Virginia Wood Forten, on a trip to the city. They tried to attend an exhibit at the Chinese Museum in Philadelphia sponsored by the Franklin Institute; they were turned away solely because of their color. The Purvises sued unsuccessfully in alderman's court.[41]

This insult followed the decision of the Agricultural Fair to exclude colored exhibitors. Martha Coffin Wright, sister of Lucretia Coffin Mott, who was in Philadelphia at the time, wrote to her husband, David, about it:

> He felt the insult keenly as from his refined sensitive nature he must, and in consequence of these repeated insults has serious thoughts of selling out and going to England. You have seen the account of his son Robert's being requested to leave the Franklin Institute Exhibition because Miss Remond was with him, his own color being too light for suspicion—Mr. Purvis spoke feelingly of it here, and said he was very sorry that his son did not insist on his right to remain—he said to him, when he came home so excited and told him of it, "Why didn't you die rather than submit to this insult?"[42]

Although living twelve miles north of the city, the Purvises continued to keep in close touch with their families and the social and political life of Philadelphia. To reach the city from Byberry, one could ride horseback, drive a buggy, or take a boat on the Delaware River, from the Andalusia landing. It was an arduous journey but both Robert and Harriet traveled back and forth, to attend lectures and art exhibitions, to participate in civic responsibilities, and to visit their families.

Harriet's mother, Charlotte Forten, lived on for many years in the house on Lombard Street, with her daughter, Margaretta, and her grand-daughter Charlotte, attending antislavery meetings, knitting, and reading. To stretch the money left from James Forten's estates, she bought and sold ground rents in the neighborhood. Harriet was a dutiful daughter, and visited as often as possible.[43]

Robert's mother, Harriet Judah Miller, continued to live in the house on Seventh Street which her husband, William Miller, had bought for her with the money left her by William Purvis, Jr. She and William Miller received money from time to time from William Purvis, Sr.'s estate, administered by Thomas Fletcher. In December 1845, William Miller died, leaving the house to Harriet, and the rest of his estate to various Miller relatives in New York. Following Miller's death, Harriet sent for a niece from Charleston, Sarah Judah Vickers, to live with her. The Purvises and their children often also visited this household.[44]

Among their civic responsibilities, none were more important to Robert and Harriet than the antislavery societies. This was a period of Harriet's greatest responsibility for the Anti-Slavery Fairs. Her letters, appealing for support for these fairs, appeared regularly in the *Pennsylvania Freeman* and *The National Anti-Slavery Standard*. She worked on organizing the fairs with Anna Mott Hopper, oldest daughter of Lucretia and James Mott, further cementing her relationship with this family. Harriet also sewed articles to sell at the antislavery fairs. One of Lucretia Mott's favorite possessions was a large workbag embroidered in red, green, and yellow which Harriet Purvis made for the Fair in the 1850s.[45]

These fairs, held each December, were no trifling affairs. In 1854, the annual sale made a profit of $2192.38, an amazing sum for the times.[46] Antislavery women gathered in sewing circles in Philadelphia, and in many of the surrounding communities, to prepare items to be sold at the annual fairs. Similar groups in New York and New England sent goods to be sold. From Great Britain antislavery women sent items, with the stipulation that half of the proceeds should be sent to the Free Produce Society. In 1851, the list of contributing groups included: Bristol, Neshaminy, Byberry, Marlborough, Kennett Square, Kimberton, Schuylkill, Darby, Norristown, Germantown, Yardley, New York, Staten Island, Providence, Rhode Island, Canterbury, Connecticut, Nantucket, Boston, Massachusetts, and Bristol, England.[47]

For his part, Robert was increasingly active with the Pennsylvania Anti-Slavery Society. The anti-black prejudice which had sparked the riots and driven the Purvises from the city, had not abated. Although the PAS-S supported Home Rule for Ireland as part of its platform of human rights, their motives were suspected by the Irish. In 1843, a Dr. Moriarity charged that the abolitionists were attempting to introduce antislavery into the Repeal Association in an attempt to discredit it, and that they had been behind the burning of a convent in Maryland. The response to these and other charges, signed by the officers of the Board of the Pennsylvania Anti-Slavery Society, was apparently written by Purvis in his typically emphatic style.[48]

> In answer, we deny that we have ever felt any other feelings than those of abhorrence for that act, and of desire that the sufferers by it should be promptly compensated; and we know of no member of the American Anti-Slavery Society possessed of different feelings; nor have we the least belief that any member of that Society, or its branches, participated in that outrage.[49]

Following the 1840 split in antislavery ranks, the PAS-S was divided for five years between those who backed Garrison, those who questioned the many reforms he attached to his anti-slavery campaign, and his opposition to political action, his "no-government" stance. Thomas Earle, for example, favored political action. More of the women than the men were Garrisonians.[50]

In 1844, Miller McKim, agent of the Pennsylvania Anti-Slavery Society was accused in the pages of the *Liberty Herald* of "denying solicitations to inviting any of your political friends, although he knew some of them would gladly have come." Purvis, who had accompanied Miller on a trip to Boston, was quite sure they had invited a number of those supporting political action, including Ellis Loring and Samuel Sewall, members of the Board of the Massachusetts Anti-Slavery Society. He attributed the attack to Thomas Cavender, Lucretia Mott's son-in-law, who had chosen to affiliate with the New Organization. "I hope, my dear friend, you will not be discouraged by these miserable attempts to injure you but the nature of those who live [illegible] sect and party—more than truth—We shall believe you faithful to the slave and rights if [it] were at all necessary or possible to make you more so, as these new bigots to party & sect—pour out their shame upon you."[51]

In 1845, at an annual meeting of the Pennsylvania Anti-Slavery Society, held in Kennett Square, the Garrisonians won the day. Robert Purvis was elected president, and would be reelected for four successive terms. His wife, Harriet, served as his secretary. The Society continued during this period to respond to criticism, to gather petitions against slavery, to assist runaways, to support *The Liberator* and the *National Anti-Slavery Standard*, the newspaper established by the American Anti-Slavery Society after the split of 1840. They urged the use of Free Produce, which the Purvis family continued to practice, and they kept up the battle for black suffrage. In 1847, the Society lobbied for a bill in the Pennsylvania legislature, the Anti-Kidnaping Bill, which would make it illegal to use force to bring a runaway before a judge; it rescinded the law requiring a black person to live in Pennsylvania for six months before claiming his/her freedom.[52]

During his term of office, Robert Purvis was frequently absent from the weekly meetings of the executive committee of the Pennsylvania Anti-Slavery Society, which met at the home of the Motts, and which James Mott chaired. This was due probably to the distance he had to travel to reach the city. But he was present for the annual meetings, and he often represented the group at national conferences. While he was president, the organization made two personnel decisions which were of note: in 1845, the first year of his presidency, the Society employed Frederick Douglass along with Cyrus Burleigh as antislavery lecturers. And in 1847, they hired William Still, a free black from New Jersey, to serve as clerk and janitor in the antislavery office run by Miller McKim at 107 North Fifth Street.[53] In December 1848, Robert Purvis attended a black state convention held in Harrisburg, Pennsylvania, where a second appeal to the voters of Pennsylvania was prepared by a committee of six, Purvis among them. One cannot be sure, but the writing is certainly in his style. Referring to the rise of republicanism in France and elsewhere in the past year, as well as the United States victory in the war with Mexico, petitioners asked once more for suffrage in Pennsylvania.[54]

> We have been witnesses to those soul stirring appeals in behalf of republicanism, in foreign lands; and the conviction forces itself upon our minds that however much you may admire and extol the progress of free principles in other states, that of your own dearest Pennsylvania must occupy the highest seat in your affections. . . .
>
> . . . It is now left for you to decide whether Pennsylvania shall be less fortunate. Must the arduous labours of your great men fail to be con-

summated, while those of their confederates have been crowned with triumphant success?[55]

The convention also appealed to their fellow blacks to support the petition. Again Purvis was one of the authors, if not the sole author, of the appeal. In it he admitted for the first time that prejudice against color was behind the disenfranchisement:

> So they disenfranchised us by extinguishing justice—disqualifying merit, assuming condition as their reason, and complexion as the standard. . . . Condition was but the pretext—the capital on which to furnish arguments—a passport to power, and that point being gained, they were determined to disfranchise us, as a body, on account of complexion; they did not need reasons, because they were prepared to vote on the ground of prejudices. And if their power had been co-extensive with their wills, many of them would not only have disenfranchised us, but the poor of every nation, and whole political parties that were opposed to them in the bargain.[56]

Striking a new note of militancy, Purvis and his fellow authors called for blacks to demand suffrage as a moral duty:

> Slaves have learned to lick the dust, and stifle the voice of free inquiry; but we are not slaves—our right to natural liberty, and a qualified citizenship, is guaranteed to us by the Constitution. Full, civil, and political liberty is regarded by the ablest writers on government as the only true safeguard to individual liberty—so that their presence is vindicated by necessity.[57]

Robert Purvis was a hero at this convention. Many years later in 1848, Isaiah C. Wears, a twenty-four-year-old youth, remembered the occasion; he was surprised that Purvis so readily and ably represented the blacks, although he was identified with the Garrisonians, who objected to voting at all. They claimed it validated a government made illegal by its acceptance of slavery. Wears did not realize that Purvis had advocated for black suffrage many times before, and did not go along with Garrison any longer in either nonresistance, or in avoiding government office.[58]

The 1848 convention was significant in marking a change in the thinking of Robert Purvis in regard to race. In years past, he and William Whipper had refused to speak of race as an issue, maintaining always that there was but one race, the human race. Many things had happened to weaken his convictions on this point, and now he was clear that blacks needed one another in demanding their rights.

The Vigilant Committee became less active in this period, due primarily to Purvis's departure from the city, but the old comrades worked together whenever there were fugitives to be aided. One of the most spectacular cases of the period was that of Henry Brown, a slave from Richmond, Virginia, who arranged in 1849 to have himself placed in a crate and delivered to the office of the Pennsylvania Anti-Slavery Society in Philadelphia, where James Miller McKim as agent, and William Still as clerk and janitor, released him. He was known forever afterwards as Henry Box Brown.[59]

CHAPTER 9

"This Wicked Law"

$\mathcal{T}$he passage of the Fugitive Slave Act in September 1850 came as a blow to all abolitionists, but especially those of color, who believed that their countrymen would eventually see that justice and fairness demanded an end to slavery. Instead, the nation as a whole seemed committed to safeguarding the rights of the slave owners. The fact that ordinary citizens might be deputized to assist in the recovery of slaves or face severe penalties, seemed designed to drive a wedge between law-abiding abolitionists, and those willing to break the law and commit other acts of civil disobedience.

For Robert Purvis it seemed the end of all his hopes. Shortly after the passage of the Act, he persuaded his Byberry neighbors to join him in a fiery protest written at Byberry Hall. The group stated their belief that Congress neither had power to raise money to support a band of kidnappers, a right to deprive any persons of the right of trial by jury, nor constitutional power to suspend the writ of habeas corpus; and that every law officer was morally obligated to resign his office rather than enforce such a law. In that light, the meeting commended the action of Colonel Kane in resigning his office as a commissioner since the passage of the law.[1]

The group of thirty-four residents of Byberry, many of them Quakers, then pledged themselves to civil disobedience:

> Resolved, that we utterly disregard the monstrous and inhuman requirements of said bill, viewing them as subversive of the principles of Christianity—the Laws of God and our common humanity—and will not be deterred, come what may to our *"reputation, property or lives,"* by its unrighteous penalties, from the exercise of that higher law which commands,

"That whatsoever ye would that men should do unto you, do ye even unto them"; and we will as heretofore open our doors for the reception and protection of every flying bond man, who may make his escape from the prison-house of bondage.[2]

After discussion with his family, Purvis decided to destroy all the records of the old Vigilant Committee, which he had kept personally, lest his house be raided and previously resettled slaves placed in danger. Except for some cases recorded by the Philadelphia Female Anti-Slavery Society, some scattered newspaper items, and a book of of minutes at the Historical Society of Pennsylvania, the records of this earliest of Underground Railroads in Pennsylvania were thus lost. Historians of the Underground Railroad have had to rely on a few scattered sources, and Purvis's own recollections when he was an old man.[3]

At the annual meeting of the Pennsylvania Anti-Slavery Society in West Chester on October 17, 1850, Purvis gave an impassioned speech against the Act, saying, "should any wretch enter my dwelling, any pale-faced spectre among ye, to execute this law on me or mine, I'll seek his life, I'll shed his blood."[4]

A few days later, Purvis met with a group of blacks at the Brick Wesley African Methodist Episcopal Church in Philadelphia to denounce the new act and declare their resolution to disobey it:

> Resolved, that while we have heretofore yielded obedience to the laws of our country, however hard some of them have borne upon us, we deem this law so wicked, so atrocious, so utterly at variance with the principles of the Constitution; so subversive of the objects of all law, the protection of the lives, liberty, and prosperity of the governed; so repugnant to the highest attributes of God, justice and mercy; and so horribly cruel in its clearly expressed mode of operation, that we deem it our sacred duty, a duty we owe to ourselves, our wives, our children, and to our common nature, as well as to the panting fugitive from oppression, to resist this law at any cost and at all hazards; and we hereby pledge ourselves, our fortunes and our sacred honor to do so.[5]

In the spring, following the passage of the Fugitive Slave Law, the Purvis family endured a devastating tragedy. Their son Joseph, a brilliant student, enrolled in Central College, contracted meningitis, and, after an illness of seven weeks, he died on May 8, 1851, just short of his fifteenth birthday. He was buried at the college; the authorities prohibited his being brought home because of the quarantine.[6] Robert and Harriet mourned deeply. Many tributes were written about him, and the loss of his potential, among them a letter in *Frederick Douglass's Paper:*

> Young Purvis was a youth of noblest make. Generous, high-minded, and thoroughly energetic, he impressed himself strongly upon all who came within his reach. Brilliant in talents, accomplished as he would have been in scholarship, clear in his conceptions of the right and true. He would have been, if he had lived, not one of those who are like unto "dumb driven cattle" but "a hero in the strife." Slavery never had an enemy more uncompromising nor the cause of freedom in one so young, a friend more faithful and untiring.[7]

Dying at the same time was a young woman student, Anna Pierce, a Byberry neighbor, daughter of abolitionists. Another neighbor, herself a graduate of Central College, Tacie Townsend, wrote a poem dedicated to Joseph, blaming his illness and death on his determination to succeed for the sake of his race. She called it "The Martyr Student."

> *For the midnight's lonely vigils,*
> *For the student's holy dream,*
> *For the brave soul martyr dying*
> *No proud monument is seen.*
> *Still within the hearts that watched him,*
> *Hour by hour and day by day,*
> *Like some holy thought he'll linger*
> *Nevermore to pass away.*[8]

Fortunately, perhaps, the press of events distracted the Purvises somewhat from their grief. In September 1851 a Maryland slaveowner, Edward Gorsuch, came to Pennsylvania to hunt down some escaped slaves in the little town of Christiana, where a black leader, William Parker, had organized the blacks for mutual defense. A member of the old Vigilant Committee learned of the arrival of the Maryland party in Philadelphia, and was able to send a messenger, Samuel Williams, to notify the blacks of Christiana. William Parker then brought the slaves to his home, a tenant house on the farm of Levi Pownall, and rallied local blacks to the slaves' defense. In the course of the action the slave owner was killed and his son wounded. Parker and several others escaped to Canada, but many blacks were rounded up and captured indiscriminately. The United States government, desiring to make an example of this case, brought suit for treason against thirty-eight persons, including three local Quaker farmers who had refused to obey the order of the sheriff to cooperate in arresting the blacks.[9]

The prisoners had been captured on a mild September day, but were held until late in November for trial. The women of the Philadelphia Female Anti-Slavery Society worked hard to supply them with warm clothes. They also knit matching caps and woolen scarfs for all the prisoners. On the day of the trial, the sight of the black prisoners marching in identical costumes amused the audience and confused the prosecution, since it was very difficult for them to identify each prisoner. For these and other reasons, the authorities were unable to prove their case, and the accused eventually released.[10]

The Christiana riots brought to the fore a debate among the Garrisonian abolitionists. Prior to this time most had been committed to the use of nonresistance in the antislavery struggle. Now, however, some began to question whether the blacks could be expected to obtain their freedom without the use of force in self-defense.

Robert Purvis had supported nonresistance in his speech at Thomas Shipley's memorial service. But he had unhesitatingly not only armed himself to defend his family at the time of the Philadelphia race riots, but he also had declared himself ready to defend his family after the passage of the Fugitive Slave Act. The Christiana riots were a clear example, he thought, of the need for violence if used in self-defense. At the October meeting of the Pennsylvania Anti-Slavery Society following the events, he said that the colored man in defending himself had only been true to himself, his family, true to liberty, true to God. He was glad, he said, that the first battle for liberty had been fought. Lucretia Mott, a strong supporter of nonresistance, disagreed, and the two argued heatedly over the subject. It was perhaps at this meeting that Robert Purvis called Lucretia Mott, "the most belligerent nonresistant he had ever known." Fortunately, the two remained devoted allies despite this difference of opinion.[11]

The Christiana riots made it clear that a vigilance committee was again needed. The old Vigilant Committee was largely inactive, so a new General Vigilance Committee was organized in December 1852, with Robert Purvis as chairman of the General Committee, and William Still as agent of the Acting Committee. Since Still worked for the Pennsylvania Anti-Slavery Society as clerk and janitor in the office, the two groups were closely tied. William Forten, James Forten's youngest son, became a member of the new group, first emerging into leadership when he helped to raise money for the defense of those imprisoned after the riots. The General Vigilance Committee is credited for having forwarded about eight hundred fugitives between 1852 and 1860. Although Purvis attended meetings, and often sheltered runaways in his home in Byberry, and interceded for them in the courts, the day-to-day operation of this second vigilance committee fell to Still.[12]

The passage of the Fugitive Slave Act had brought the concept of colonization once more to the fore. A few of the militant black leaders, dismayed by events, and believing that the black man or woman would never be fairly treated in the United States, had swung over to emigration in recent years, including the influential Henry Highland Garnet. Purvis feared that colonization would continue to win new converts. In January 1851, Robert Purvis wrote to Miller McKim suggesting that new action was needed quickly. Why not send a delegation to the World Convention being held in Exeter Hall, London, England, where the slaveholders would be present in force, and exhibit such fugitives as Pennington, Garnet, Wells Brown, Box Brown, and the Crafts in order to make clear to worldwide abolitionists just what injustices the Fugitive Slave Act entailed?[13]

> The history of each, and all of those would electrify the choice gatherings from all the nations, which would doubtless attend. If England could be aroused to a sense of duty by a single pamphlet from the pen of a woman, and moved to the disenthrallment of nearly a million human beings from "Slavery's Chains,"why may we not hope for a more glorious result to millions, by the combined power of the world, put forth in the language of entreaty, indignation and demand? However flatteringly we may note the successes of Anti-Slavery efforts in this country, have we progressed in view of the greatness of our cause and the spirit of the age in which we live? In physical and mental advancement, who disbelieves anything? What new discovery breaks in upon us to be denied or ridiculed? In many enterprises for the moral improvement of the world the means and successes have followed so closely that surprise seeks no explanation, but excites new desire and new expectations. Can we not make some *dash* upon the World and strike *home* to the *American heart* by that awakened world's power, in the name of *Justice, Humanity, and God,* for the overthrow of Slavery, the destruction of Prejudice and fair, equal just recognition of man's rights without regard to condition or the color of the skin, which one common God and Father has given him?[14]

When Harriet Beecher Stowe's *Uncle Tom's Cabin* was published in March 1852, Purvis was deeply disappointed to find her advocating colonization in her last chapter. He wrote to Gerrit Smith, with whom he differed on the question of political action, to praise a public letter the latter had written attacking colonization.[15]

In the spring of 1852, Robert Purvis joined in the call to black Philadelphians to rally against an act in the Pennsylvania legislature asking for an appropriation to "assist free people of color to emigrate to the Republic of Liberia." A mass meeting was held at the Philadelphia Institute on April 16, 1852. Robert Purvis spoke "with great power and eloquence," asking the legislature to withhold such an appropriation.[16]

Only once did Robert Purvis waver in his decision to resist the siren call of colonization. In 1853, he experienced the action of the school board in segregating his children, the insult to his son and companions when they were denied entrance to the Franklin Institute, and his own ejection from the Poultry Society. It was too much, and for a short while he and Harriet considered moving to England, and thus fulfilling his father's original intention. "If you had staid longer in Eng(land) . . . you might perhaps have seen us over there," Harriet Purvis told Sarah Pugh, a member of the Philadelphia Female Anti-Slavery Society. "For ourselves we might endure to the end—as we have suffered so long—but for our children it is a question whether we ought not to seek another home."[17]

Under the Fugitive Slave Act, problems with escaping slaves proliferated. In the fall of 1853, several deputies made a brutal attack upon a black man named William Thomas in the city of Wilkes Barre, claiming he was a former slave. The Pennsylvania Abolition Society hired a lawyer and retained witnesses to prove a case against the deputies, but rumors spread in the Philadelphia black community that the Society was not doing enough. A mass meeting was called to discuss this allegation. Passmore Williamson, a member of PAS, told of the work being done on the case, and Stephen Smith, a wealthy black merchant, said that money would be raised in the black community to assist. Purvis defended the PAS (of which he was a member) and argued passionately against divisions between the groups, lest they further weaken the cause.[18]

In 1855, Philadelphia abolitionists were involved in a spectacular slave rescue. Jane Johnson, a North Carolina slave, along with her two young boys, was brought to Philadelphia by her master en route to Nicaragua, where he was to become U.S. Ambassador. While staying at the Bloodgood Hotel, she told a black bellboy that she wanted her freedom. The boy took the message to William Still at the Anti-Slavery office on Fifth Street. Two members of the Vigilance Committee, William Still and Passmore Williamson, hurried to the hotel, and, finding her gone, followed her to the ferry dock just as her master was about to take her across the Delaware River to catch a train for New York City. They told her that they believed she could claim freedom, because she was brought to Philadelphia as a slave. While Jane hesitated, her master tried to restrain her. Five black porters on the ferry protected her from him. Jane said that she chose freedom, and went with William Still to a waiting carriage. The driver took her and her children to a safe hiding place, with a black family. [19]

The angry slave owner sued, charging them and several others with riot and with kidnaping his slave against her will. The judge ordered Passmore Williamson to bring Jane to the courthouse for a preliminary hearing. Jane was being housed in the free black community and Passmore literally did not know where she was. But when he refused to produce her, the judge sentenced him to one hundred days in jail for contempt of court. William Still, and the five porters who had come to Jane's rescue on the ferry, were charged with riot and assault.[20]

Passmore Williamson was well known in Philadelphia, and many people were indignant about his imprisonment. The case heightened public interest in the antislavery cause. Robert Purvis helped the Vigilance Committee hire lawyers to defend their members as well as to gain Jane's freedom. These lawyers thought it would help if Jane herself were to appear in court to state that she had not been coerced, but had chosen of her own free will to stay. Lucretia Mott and three other women of the Female Anti-Slavery Society accompanied Jane to the courtroom. In court, Jane stood up and in a clear voice testified that she had chosen freedom of her own accord. After her appearance, the women conducted Jane to a certain street corner where a carriage picked her up and hurried her out of town, safe from the slave catchers.[21]

As a result of Jane's testimony, William Still and three of the porters were found not guilty; two, however, served a one-week sentence. Purvis attended the trial. He was angry about Passmore Williamson's detention, and he prepared a protest to be issued in the name of the Vigilance Committee. He also publicly and heatedly advocated that Judge Kane be impeached for his unjust sentencing of Passmore.[22]

A national Colored Convention was being held in Philadelphia at the time of Passmore Williamson's imprisonment. After the long hiatus caused by dissension over the Moral Reform Society, the colored convention movement had been reinstated in 1853 with a convention held in Rochester, New York. Robert Purvis signed the call to the convention, but evidently did not attend. In 1855, however, he was present, and was named the chair of a committee to visit Passmore Williamson in Moyamensing Prison and express to him the gratitude of the delegates.[23]

Mr. Purvis . . . reported verbally that the Committee had waited upon Mr. Williamson, and tendered him the resolutions of sympathy; that Mr. Williamson received the resolutions, and tendered his best wishes to the Convention, and assured them that no matter what the consequences may be, he will not sacrifice a single principle upon the altar of slavery. The Committee have only to fear that Mr. Williamson's health will suffer from his long confinement.[24]

The convention was otherwise made memorable by the decision of the assembled delegates to admit Mary Ann Shadd Cary of Canada as a corresponding delegate, thus allowing for the first time the participation of a woman.[25]

By 1854, Purvis overcame the various disappointments which had been burdening him, and was again his old passionate, committed self. Garrison invited him to speak at the twentieth anniversary of the founding of the American Anti-Slavery Association, held in May in New York City. He could choose his own topic: "Colonization, colorphobia, the claims of the colored population to freedom and equality in land of their birth." When Purvis accepted the invitation, Garrison told him to "Blaze away."[26]

Instead Purvis offered an upbeat resolution:

Resolved, That the contrast between the present aspect of the anti-Slavery cause, now, and as it presented itself twenty-three years ago, is in the highest degree cheering—that the change which has taken place in public sentiment on the subject of the colored man's rights, as evinced in the tone of the newspaper press, and in the character of the current literature of the day, is such as not only to inspire the friends of the cause with the liveliest satisfaction, but to produce in the minds of all careful observers the conviction that a mighty revolution is going steadily on in this country, that will result, and that at no distant day, in the utter overthrow of American slavery, and the restoration to the colored man of the rights of which he has been so long robbed.[27]

Purvis illustrated his optimistic statement with the change of public opinion to oppose two New York politicians, John Mitchel and Thomas Francis Meagher, who had been leading the attack on the black community. Since Purvis had led a movement among Philadelphia blacks to demand Home Rule for Ireland, he was particularly bitter about the opposition of these Irish patriots. He also spoke of Stephen Arnold Douglass, who had recently introduced into the senate the Kansas–Nebraska Bill calling for "squatter sovereignty" in the new territories. Purvis called him "a man who would offer up to the blood Moloch of Slavery, the un-polluted and virgin soil of a territory larger than the original thirteen States." (The Kansas–Nebraska Bill passed the House three days later.)

> Mr. President: It is hard to bear up against the trials and persecutions which our cause has to encounter from our own countrymen; it is hard to endure the insults and ingratitude of Americans; but God, helping us, we will defy them all, and we will look with pitying contempt upon all insults to freedom, whether from the foes or the apostates of liberty, whether for-eign or domestic. . . . I repeat, that a mighty resolution is going steadily on in this country and will result—and that in no distant day—in the utter overthrow of American Slavery. The day is not far distant, we confidently hope and believe, when the soil of this country will be unpolluted by a sin-gle stain of slavery. [28]

An additional irritant during this period was continuing disagree-ments within the black community. Purvis and his friend William Whip-per had backed away from their stand against attending meetings that were purely "complexional," for the American Moral Reform Society de-cided at its 1848 meeting that it was necessary to meet the issue of white exclusion on "complexional grounds." But they continued to work closely with white colleagues in the Pennsylvania and the American Anti-Slavery Society, especially with William Lloyd Garrison. Elected as a vice presi-dent of the AASS in 1846, Robert Purvis prided himself on never miss-ing an annual meeting. By the time of its dissolution in 1870, he had missed only one.[29]

Frederick Douglass, however, had broken some of his ties with Gar-rison when he founded his own paper, *The North Star.* The Garrisonians had attempted to dissuade him from establishing what they saw as a rival paper. Douglass felt he was asserting himself as a black man, and believed that black abolitionists should support him in this endeavor, as they had once supported the *Liberator.* In his paper, he upheld the political aboli-tionists and Liberty Party, feeling that the Garrisonian platform had be-come too narrow. The quarrel ebbed and flowed. In 1852, Charles Remond and Robert Purvis accused Frederick Douglass of accepting a bribe from Benjamin Coates of Philadelphia in order to publish Coates' letter extolling colonization in the *Frederick Douglass Paper.*[30] Douglass re-sponded by saying that he did not agree with Mr. Coates, but thought there was much in his letter to ponder. And though he received generous donations from Coates, he had never accepted a bribe.[31]

In 1853, stung perhaps by the criticism of some of the Garrisonians over his relationship with the white Englishwoman, Julia Griffiths, Douglass had attacked Charles Remond and Robert Purvis as "practical enemies of the colored people," and spoke of those who lived on "blood-stained riches," meaning the estate which Purvis's father had left him. Purvis wrote an impassioned letter to Garrison which was published in the *Liberator*, defending himself from this attack.

> As touching the matter of "blood-stained riches" to which this shameless ingrate and base slanderer alludes, I have but to say that my father (from whom I inherited my property) was never a slaveholder—that he made his money as a merchant, by honest mercantile pursuits—and was known while living as a friend and benefactor of the free and enslaved colored man (as there are living witnesses to testify). My own early detestation of slavery was owing doubtless to the seeds implanted in my bosom by my revered parent, by furnishing me with Dr. Torrey's *Portraiture of Slavery*, and the work entitled "Sanford and Merton." But why pursue this matter? A life's consistent hatred of slavery in every form, a willingness, to the best of my ability, to do and suffer with my oppressed brethren, to maintain a reputation "unspotted before the world," and thereby to live down the calumnies of the enemies of our race, is, in the fury and violence of this meanly ambitious man and foul-mouthed slanderer, of no account. To gratify his ire, and serve his bitter and malignant spirit, I am pronounced as being "practically an enemy of the colored people."[32]

Problems within the community of black abolitionists continued. James McCune Smith, a black New York doctor, was a backer of Douglass, and one of the organizers of the Radical Political Abolitionists, a group that attempted to enter national politics in 1855. Writing for *Frederick Douglass's Paper* under the pseudonym of "Communipaw," Smith questioned the motives of the white abolitionists, and claimed they discriminated against their black members. Specifically, he picked out Robert Purvis:

> Last spring when Robert Purvis rose to speak in the presence of his host, his manhood was insulted by Mr. Garrison who distinguished him as a colored man and his holiest feeling outraged by Mr. Furness, who said that he had demeaned himself by marrying a dark brown woman when he could have had a white one.[33]

Purvis had, in fact, protested at the May Anti-Slavery meeting in 1854 when the Reverend William Furness had made his unfortunate remark, saying that he was proud of his 25 percent Negro blood, and that he hoped no such remark would be made again.[34]

Smith also stated that Purvis's son Robert Jr, as well as Joseph C. Cassey, had been turned down for positions in the accounting house of Edward M. Davis because of their color. (There are no records to indicate whether this in fact happened.) Purvis did not reply directly to these allegations, but urged William Lloyd Garrison to do so, and thanked him most heartily afterwards for his "well-timed castigation of McCune Smith."[35]

Quarreling between abolitionists was temporarily put aside as the nation was gripped by the conflict in Kansas between pro- and antislavery settlers. In May 1856, a group called the "Border Ruffians" attacked many homes in Lawrence, Kansas, and burned down the offices of the *Herald of Freedom*, an antislavery newspaper. In retaliation, John Brown, an abolitionist, with six companions attacked and killed five pro-slavery settlers at Pottawatomie Creek. In Congress, Senator Charles Sumner delivered an impassioned address, "the Crime Against Kansas," during which he attacked several pro-slavery senators, including Andrew P. Butler of South Carolina. Several days later a nephew of Butler physically attacked Sumner while he was seated in the Senate; he beat him so severely with a cane that he was incapacitated for many months.

Against this background, Purvis was called to the platform during the annual meeting of the American Anti-Slavery Society in June 1856; he made a short extemporaneous speech full of fire. He declared himself to be a Disunion Abolitionist, and castigated the "abject servility of the North," in refusing to stand up to the slaveowning South."[36]

> I trust, Sir, I am not wanting in proper appreciation of the eminent services of the distinguished Senator from your state either in or out of Congress, who now lies convalescing from the wounds he has received from the hands of brutal and cowardly assassins; but, Sir, I feel that the deed was timely; the hand that inflicted the blows was fitting. Anything, anything, in God's name, that will tend to establish a backbone for the north, in asserting and maintaining its rights without regard to peril or to consequences![37]

On every side, it seemed to Purvis, there was betrayal. David Paul Brown had been a good friend of the slave, appearing at many trials in the defense of the fugitive. He had particularly distinguished himself as counsel for the defense at the Christiana trials. But now, at his instigation, Purvis felt, his son had accepted the role of U.S. Commissioner, vacated by the death of the hated Edward Ingraham, and he had presided over a hearing which had sent Michael Brown, an alleged fugitive, back into slavery. At a mass meeting of Philadelphia blacks held on February 3, 1857, Purvis denounced David Paul Brown, calling him a Judas Iscariot and a Benedict Arnold. He ended, however, by saying no such betrayal could stay the course of those committed to justice. The spirit of the black man and his determination to be free was now so developed that he would choose liberty even if it meant sacrificing his life.[38]

> . . . allowing no man, however clothed by human authority, be he a poltroon U.S. Marshal or a contemptible, puerile Commissioner, to decide that question for him. The right to be free is his against all the powers upon earth. The idea of equal rights cannot be wrested from the soul of any man; no power so omnipotent as can destroy this essence of Divinity, which is inseparable from his nature. The holy ardour of inspiration may be smothered, lofty desires for valorous deeds annihilated, the spirit of the man may lie bruised, bleeding, humbled at the feet of a remorseless despotism; but still the living, ethereal spark which God has placed in the heart of man is there. The time for its full development is at hand. Our manhood and claims to equal rights will yet, and speedily, be acknowledged by this oppressive and guilty nation. Take courage; trust in God and our own right arms.[39]

There were soon other matters to claim his anger. The Dred Scott decision handed down in March 1857 by Chief Supreme Court Justice Robert Taney, ruling that a black man could neither claim any of the rights of citizenship, nor had any rights which white men were bound to respect, angered and depressed Purvis. Speaking at a meeting held on April 10, 1857 in the Israel Church in Philadelphia, he offered a series of resolutions:

> Resolved, that this atrocious decision furnishes final confirmation of the already well-known fact that under the Constitution and Government of the United States, the colored people are nothing, and can be nothing but an alien, disenfranchised and degraded people.[40]

Persons of color, he argued, should not argue that the Constitution and essential structure of government did not support slavery. Instead, they and their allies should cease to support such a government and the only duty a colored man had to the government was to denounce and dispute it. Asked by someone in the audience if he had not been acknowledged and treated as an American citizen, he told of obtaining a passport in 1834 through the good offices of Roberts Vaux and President Andrew Jackson.[41] But this small individual concession did not change his mind.

By the time of the May meeting of the American Anti-Slavery Society in New York in 1857, Purvis's anger was at white heat. He had been reluctant, he said, to allow his name to be published, despite the desire of the committee, because his feelings were so strong:

> Sir, I envy those who, with cooler blood or more mental self-command, can rise before an audience like this, and deliberately choose their words and speak their thoughts in calm, measured phrase. This is a task, sir, to which I am not adequate. I must either say too much or too little. If I let my heart play freely and speak out what I think and feel, I am extravagant, as people call it. If I put a curb on my feelings and tried to imitate the cool and unimpassioned manner of others, I cannot speak at all. Sir, how can any man with blood in his veins, and a heart pulsating in his bosom, and especially how can any coloured man, think of the oppression of his country and of the wrongs of his race, and then express himself with calmness and without passion? (Applause)[42]

While some abolitionists, including Gerrit Smith, whom he admired, were claiming that the Constitution was actually an antislavery document, he believed it benefited those who made it, "slaveholders and their abbettors."

> And I am free to declare, without any fears of contradiction that the Government of the United States, in its formation and essential structure as well as in its practice, is one of the basest, meanest, and most atrocious despotisms that ever saw the face of the sun.[43]

In October, he joined with a group of Pennsylvania abolitionists, black and white, in signing a call for a national convention "to consider the practicability, probability, and expediency of a Separation between the Free and Slave States, and to take such other measures as the conditions of the times may require."[44] A Disunion Convention was held in Ohio, but, because of the financial panic of the period, few attended.

In January 1857, Purvis's only surviving brother, Joseph, age 45, died suddenly.[45] Joseph had at first made a success of his farm in Bensalem; he raised prize stock, and sold it at a profit. In 1853, he sold this farm also at a profit, and bought another farm in Bensalem called "Fair View." He began to buy and sell real estate in Bucks and Philadelphia Counties, as his brother Robert had done. Joseph, however, lacked the business acumen of Robert and was soon badly in debt; he took out mortgages and he borrowed money to keep afloat. When he died suddenly on January 17,

1857, he left eight children (one of them pronounced an "idiot") and a widow deeply in debt.[46]

Robert assisted his grief-stricken mother and his sister-in-law in arranging burial at St. Thomas Episcopal Church on Fifth Street, and did what he could to untangle the financial mess. Joseph left no will, and Sarah Forten Purvis chose not to serve as administrator, accepting the services of a court-appointed lawyer instead. Margaretta Forten, Sarah's older sister, took on the responsibility of guardianship of some of the children, and helped Sarah to hang on to the farm until 1875.[47]

Her sudden widowhood at age forty-two was a blow from which Sarah Forten Purvis evidently did not recover. An abolitionist and a poet of note in her early days, she had lost her bearings during the years when she had child after child while Joseph proved a poor land manager. Visiting her farm, Fair View, in 1858, her niece, Charlotte Forten, remarked on the state of the household:

> Went to Aunt Sarah's this morning. As usual a scene of confusion and disorder greeted me. What a contrast to the elegance and order of Byberry. Everything, everybody is very, very different. It grieves me to think about it.[48]

A worse blow than the death of his brother was in store for Robert Purvis in the tumultuous year of 1857. His oldest son, William, had completed his education and was now working in Philadelphia, helping to manage some of his father's business affairs. But his health was fragile, and he apparently suffered from tuberculosis. He was ill all spring and summer, resting at Harmony Hall while Harriet nursed him. Finally, on August 28, he died, just short of his twenty-fifth birthday.[49]

William was buried in the Byberry Friends burial ground, across the street from Harmony Hall. A large number of people came to the funeral. Lucretia and James Mott were invited but they were unable to attend; they sent their daughter and son-in-law, Maria and Edward M. Davis in their place. Lucretia Mott wrote to her sister, Martha Coffin Wright, about the event.[50]

> A large concourse of people—all color distinction seemed for the time laid aside. Eliza Paxson preached. Edward and Maria stayed to tea. James and self went up last 5th day to tea. They feel the loss much. Harriet and her daughter fretted. She spoke of Ellen's [Wright] letters, said she had not heard from her lately. I told her that now Ellen would write to her and would sympathize with her.[51]

CHAPTER 10

❧

"Are We Not Men?"

$\mathscr{P}$erhaps in part to fill the empty place in her heart, Harriet Purvis invited her niece, Charlotte Forten, to live with them at Harmony Hall during the school year of 1858–1859. Charlotte, a schoolteacher, was to tutor the younger children, Georgianna and Granville, and to keep Hattie company. Charlotte was the daughter or Robert Bridges Forten and his first wife, Mary Woods. Mary had died early, and Charlotte had been raised in the household of her grandparents, James and Charlotte Vandine Forten; she was privately tutored. In 1854, she went to Salem, Massachusetts to attend an integrated school and live in the household of the black abolitionist Charles Remond. After graduating from the Higginson Grammar School, she took a one-year course at the State Normal School at Salem, and then taught for almost two years in the Salem public schools. She resigned in March 1858 because of ill health; she spent eighteen months in Philadelphia, living with her grandmother and visiting her relatives.[1]

Charlotte kept a journal at intervals during her life, including her visit in 1858 to the household at Harmony Hall. She described the farm, and the well-ordered and elegant family life which her Aunt Harriet oversaw. She and her aunt often read aloud together from the classics, or went to Philadelphia to attend cultural events. In April, they had gone together to see the paintings of Rosa Bonheur; in November they attended a lecture by George Curtis entitled, "Fair Play for Women." Charlotte thought the lecture was "as much Anti-Slavery as Women's Rights."[2]

She also admired her uncle Robert, enjoyed horseback riding with him, and accompanied him to lectures at the local lyceum. "Mr. P. very eloquent and excelled himself. I think the amount of good he does in

131

awakening and arousing the people is incalculable," she wrote on January 29, 1859. She read a letter he received from William Lloyd Garrison and enjoyed hearing him tell about his trip to England in 1834.[3]

Hattie, her cousin, was only two years younger than she, and the two were often together. For entertainment, Charlotte helped the children perform in tableaux. In one, Hattie and Charlotte were bride and groom, and Granville and Charles, traveling minstrels. In another, Hattie was Rebecca, a role which Charlotte thought became her because of her "decidedly Jewish features." Together, Charlotte and Hattie attended meetings of the Philadelphia Female Anti-Slavery Society, and of the antislavery sewing circle that met at the home of Edward and Anna Mott Hopper. Lue Hopper, the oldest Hopper daughter, became a special friend. In the fall, Charlotte went with the Purvises to Byberry Meeting to hear Lucretia Mott speak; afterwards she helped her aunt entertain the Motts and "a large company" for dinner.[4]

Tacie Townsend, the young Quaker woman who had attended Central College and written a poem about Joseph's death, was a constant companion to Charlotte during this visit. Together the two young women joined a literary society organized at Harmony Hall. In December, Ellen Wright, who had attended Eagleswood School with Hattie, came for a visit. "I like her very much—an independent, intelligent girl," Charlotte wrote in her diary. Ellen stayed through the holidays and was still at Byberry on January 9 when Hattie, Ellen, and Charlotte went to Bristol to visit an antislavery family, the Pierces. While there they performed tableaux.[5]

During her visit to Byberry, Ellen flirted with Robert Purvis Jr. They went horseback riding together, talked about "everything, from books to beasts to consumption" while they walked their horses. When it began to snow, they fantasized about "some sort of romantic scene such as being snowed up." But the storm abated, and the ten- mile ride came to a "safe conclusion" though Ellen confessed to her mother that, exhausted, she slid off the saddle "like so much lead" into Robert's arms at the end of the ride.[6] She confessed to her journal that she thought Robert was fond of her and might ask her to marry him. What then would she do? Her sister would never approve because of his African blood.[7]

During the following Christmas season, Robert Purvis Jr. commenced paying attention to Ellen's first cousin once removed, Anna Davis, daughter of Anna Mott and Edward M. Davis. Ellen, perhaps stung, wrote to Anna to commiserate. "I think there is the utmost of wretchedness in store for Bob! He is susceptible and very sensitive. Of course no *white* person would want to fall in love with him—and of course he wouldn't marry any other than white as his father did."[8] Two weeks later she renewed the attack, writing to Anna about Robert's attentions, "It must be very disagreeable. It seems rather hard that you should be called upon to endure so much—unwelcome attentions from a handsome fellow of African tint! Think of having an *octagoon* baby—Horror!! I have been thro' the wars and have scars and experience."[9]

Ellen's jealousy and its cause soon came to naught. Like his older brother, William, Robert became ill with tuberculosis, ending any thoughts of marriage, interracial or otherwise.

Domestic tragedy and public turmoil seemed to alternate with distressing regularity in the lives of Robert and Harriet Purvis. In April 1859, the household at Harmony Hall learned that another fugitive had been arrested. Daniel Dangerfield had run away from his female owner in Athensville, Virginia, seven years before and had been living quietly in Harrisburg, Pennsylvania, under the assumed name of Daniel Webster with his wife and two small children. Daniel had been at the market buying fish for breakfast when he was suddenly seized by three marshals and taken by train to Philadelphia.[10]

When he first heard the news, Robert Purvis got in touch with members of the General Vigilance Committee. They decided then and there to hire two antislavery lawyers, Edward Hopper, son-in-law of Lucretia Mott, and George Earle, son of Thomas Earle, to represent Dangerfield in court. These two managed to persuade the judge to put off the hearing until the following Monday.[11]

News of the arrest of Dangerfield spread throughout Philadelphia. Philadelphians had been unsympathetic to other escaped slaves, but the story of Dangerfield and his young family stirred public support. Crowds gathered to protest Dangerfield's arrest. On Monday morning, when the hearing was supposed to be held in the office of the commissioner, there was a mob congregating outside. Inside the office were Dangerfield and his lawyers, the lawyers representing the slave owner, members of the Vigilance Committee, and some women from the Female Anti-Slavery Society, all grouped around Lucretia Mott. Outside the door, others pressed to get in.[12]

The commissioner was forced to move the hearings to the jury room in the federal court building. Fearing that Dangerfield might be kidnapped by a pro-slavery mob, the women insisted on accompanying him down the street, serving as personal bodyguards. They, along with Robert and other members of the Vigilance Committee, remained with him throughout the hearings, which took three days. Feelings continued to run high in Dangerfield's favor, and at the end of the trial the judge ruled that the slave owner had not proved that Dangerfield answered the description of the slave she had lost.[13]

Charlotte Forten described the elation the antislavery group felt:

> Wednesday, April 6. Good news! After waiting with intense and painful anxiety for the results of the three days' trial, we are at last gladdened by the news that the alleged fugitive, Daniel Dangerfield, has been released.— The Commissioner said that he released him because he was not satisfied of his identity. Others are inclined to believe that the pressure of public sentiment—which was, strange to say, almost universally on the right side— was too overwhelming for the Com. to resist, particularly as his own family—even his wife, it is said, declared that they would discard him if he sent the man into slavery. It is encouraging to know that there was so much right and just feeling about the matter. It gives one some hope even for Philadelphia. Last night the court sat for fourteen hours, the longest session that has ever been held in this city. Many ladies stayed during the entire night, among them the noble and venerable Lucretia Mott, untiring and devoted to the last. She is truly lovely—saintly in look as in spirit, for a beautiful soul shines through her beautiful face. She is indeed one of the "blest of the earth" one of those whose "very presence is a benediction."[14]

On April 8, a large victory celebration was held in the Sansom Street Hall. According to Charlotte Forten, a crowd of Southerners surrounded the building, "stamping, hallooing and groaning," so that it was almost impossible to hear. But the police came, order was restored, and Robert Purvis spoke. "His speech was fine, decidedly the most effective," Charlotte said. The following day Purvis brought Dangerfield and his family to Harmony Hall as the first leg of the long journey to Canada, where they could be secure. Purvis arranged for the trip ahead, and two weeks later received the good news that the little family had arrived in Ontario.[15]

The Dangerfield victory was one bright spot in an increasingly discouraging climate. Other escaped slaves were being returned to their masters. In February, Robert Purvis, Jr., just twenty-four, had written to a state representative, C. A. Walbern, for the Philadelphia Junior Anti-Slavery Society; he asked him to present before the state legislature a petition, which was being circulated. The petition asked for a law "prohibiting the surrender of any person claimed as a slave on the soil of Pennsylvania." The effort got nowhere.[16]

In October, the abolitionist John Brown led eighteen followers, including five blacks, in an attack on the federal arsenal at Harpers Ferry, Virginia, an action which he and his followers had envisioned as the first step in a great insurrection of slaves in the South. Many abolitionists had supported his cause, and a group of well-to-do reformers—including Samuel Howe, Gerrit Smith, Thomas Higginson, Theodore Parker, and George Stearns—had financed the purchase of arms. But no slaves came to support the embattled Brown and his followers; they were soon captured, tried, and sentenced to hang.

Blacks in Philadelphia observed the day of Brown's death, "Martyr Day," as they called it, by draping their homes and businesses with black, and holding public prayer meetings at the Shiloh and Union Baptist churches. Hundreds went to the National Hall to hear the Unitarian minister William Furness, and Robert Purvis, speak in praise of the fallen Brown. According to a report in the *National Anti-Slavery Standard*, Purvis spoke well.

> Robert Purvis made the closing speech. He was interrupted somewhat but his eloquent words were heard by the larger part of the audience, and heard with satisfaction. The interruptions were, of course, somewhat annoying, but a friend who was present assures us that the meeting was a great success, marking a new era in the progress of the cause.[17]

At about this time, the Purvises acquired a portrait of Brown which thereafter adorned their dining room.

All of Purvis's struggles for justice seemed to have come to naught, and he was bitter. When he received a letter from the *Weekly Anglo-African*, asking his views on the recently established African Civilization Society, he answered scornfully that he regarded the new group, organized by Henry Highland Garnet and Benjamin Coates, a Philadelphia merchant and member of the Pennsylvania Abolition Society, and supported by Alexander Crummell,[18] as merely a euphemism for the old enemy, colonization.

> I have no faith in the wisdom or philanthropy of any such enterprise, and believe that this device, covered by the euphemism of the African Civilization Society, merits no other consideration at our hands but that of condemnation. Its advocates should all leave the country without delay. Africa needs their labors; a wide, almost boundless field, is before them, and why tarry in fruitless efforts to induce colored emigration from this country!

He quoted scornfully from a letter by Alexander Crummell published in the *Public Ledger*, praising Africa, and describing a trip up the Cavalla River, in which the inconvenience of sleet, rain, and mud up to the ankles was compensated for by the mountain scenery. While partaking of the simple fare of his wild country kin, Crummell had learned that the people of the "Carbo country are visited once in three or four years by other people who wear trousers." "What more is needed?" Purvis asked scornfully. "The best judgment of the colored people today is to remain in this country, for reasons as good—nay, better, than that of any other class—remain. The past and present inspire a faith that no far-off future will bring with it a practical acknowledgment of our just claims to a perfect equality of rights in this our native land."[19]

His passion and his eloquence had made him a favorite speaker at the conventions of the American Anti-Slavery Society. Speaking at the 1860 Annual Meeting of the AAS in New York, Purvis said that the United States government was not his:

> I say *your* government—it is not mine. Thank God, I have no willing share in a government that deliberately, before the world, and without a blush, declares one part of its people, and that for no crime or pretext of crime, disenfranchised and outlawed. For such a government, I, as a man, can have no feeling but of *contempt, loathing, and unutterable abhorrence!*[20]

Look at the facts in the case, Purvis said. What is the attitude of the boasting, braggart republic toward the six hundred thousand free people of color who swell its population and its wealth? Look at the Dred Scott decision, which revealed the animus of the whole country toward the black man. That decision was aimed to destroy the colored man, as a man, to prevent him from having any existence in the land except as a "chattel personal to all intents, constructions and purposes, whatsoever." With this purpose in mind the Dred Scott decision rules that a colored man

> . . . shall not sue and recover his lawful property; he shall not bear arms and train in the militia; he shall not be a commander of a vessel, not even the meanest craft that creeps along the creeks and bays of your Southern coast; he shall not carry a mail-bag, or serve as a porter in a post-office; he shall not even put his face in a United States court-room for any purpose, except by the sufferance of the white man.[21]

Purvis told about entering the United States courtroom in Philadelphia recently to provide bail for a group of blacks who had attempted the rescue of a fugitive, Moses Horner, on his way South to slavery. "As I was about entering the door, I was stopped, and ordered back; I demanded the reason—"I have my orders," was the reply. What orders? "To keep out all colored people." It was, he believed, an insult to the race. The mobs that ruled American cities were largely foreign born, he declared. Although some could not speak English, they had the franchise which was denied to blacks. He was neither a Nativist nor Republican, he said, for the Republicans favored emigration and conspired to expel the black man from his country. Horace Greeley, one of the founders of the Republican Party, had recently expressed his personal dislike for Negroes. To whom could the black man turn for understanding? Quoting from William Shakespeare's play, *The Merchant of Venice*, he asked:[22]

> Are we not men? Have we not eyes? Have we not hands, organs, dimensions, senses, affections, passions? Fed with the same food, hurt with the same weapons, subject to the same diseases, winter and summer? healed by the same means, warmed and cooled by the same weather. If you prick us, do we not bleed? If you tickle us, do we not laugh? If you poison us, do not we die; and if you wrong us, shall we not seek revenge?[23]

At the annual meeting of the Pennsylvania Anti-Slavery Society in the fall of 1860, held at the Town Hall in Kennett Square, Purvis was irritated when a clergyman from Long Island, Hiram P. Crozier, stated: "he had never had the consciousness of prejudice against color . . . he had eaten with black men; he had *slept* with a black man; and this perhaps was as severe a test as a man's antislavery character could be put to."

Purvis responded vigorously:

> But sir, I utterly repudiate the idea that social intimacy with colored men is a test of the antislavery character. Sir, what has eating with a man, or sleeping with a man, to do with the question of human rights? This, sir, is a novel antislavery doctrine; and in the name of the cause, I utterly, and in my own name, scornfully repudiate it! Sir, we ask no favors of any man or any class of men, in this contest. A white man may eat and otherwise associate with colored men, without conferring thereby any favor. It is quite possible that the favor may be on the other side! Sir, this is a question, not of complexion but of principle. Social intercourse is regulated by irreversible social laws. Every man will find his level. Gentlemen will associate with gentlemen; vulgarity will find its natural place, and true refinement will be respected without regard to color and that, Sir, is what this glorious antislavery enterprise is teaching the American people.[24]

Crozier replied that he had not meant to imply he was conferring a favor by associating with colored men. But Purvis was not appeased, and later in the meeting, the two tangled again. Crozier, a member of the newly established Republican Party, defended the U.S. Constitution as antislavery, adding that its author, Thomas Jefferson, was "a good antislavery man." This was too much for Purvis who pointed out that Jefferson was a slaveowner and reputedly had sold his own daughter. "If true, this proves him a *scoundrel* as well as a traitor." Though, he said, he had nothing but friendly feelings for the Republican Party, he had to point out that some of its members, such as Horace Greeley, supported colonization or banishment of the colored race. As for George Washington, he, too, had been a slaveowner, and had once tried to recover a slave who had fled to New Hampshire, "showing a truer courage then he [Washington] ever did."[25]

The next morning, Friday, the chairman announced that Robert Purvis had a word of apology to make. But Purvis said it was more a matter of explanation:

> I came to this meeting to keep as much as possible in the background; but I have not been allowed to do so. I know my vehemence when my feelings are touched, and I mean to speak guardedly. But, sir, it's no use; I can't be anything but Robert Purvis and when I speak I must speak in my own vernacular. He had not meant to hurt the sensibilities of Mr. Crozier, but when the latter defended Thomas Jefferson as "a good antislavery man" he said that he forgot his "resolutions to be silent, or to be guarded, and I speak with a vehemence which I afterward regret."[26]

The Philadelphia papers ran stories the next day, criticizing Purvis. The *Philadelphia Bulletin* reported:

> Mr. Robert Purvis (colored) took the floor, and delivered one of his characteristic ultra harangues. This Government was the meanest and foulest despotism that ever existed. [Hisses.] Washington and Jefferson were slave-drivers and thieves, whose memory should be held in detestation. The Constitution was an accursed scroll, which he trampled under foot. [Renewed hisses and exclamations of great disgust.] The audience might hiss until the crack of doom, for all the speaker cared, the founders of this country were man-thieves and murderers; he despised them and those who upheld them.[27]

The *Philadelphia Press*, usually more friendly to the abolitionists, also reported on Purvis's speech:

Mr. Robert Purvis, whose violence has never been questioned, came out on the evening of the first day with one of his characteristic intemperate and violent speeches, which threatened for the time not only to interrupt the quietude of the affair but even to drive off the pioneers.[28]

Upset by the coverage, Robert Purvis wrote to Miller McKim asking him to respond. Miller prepared a short paragraph that appeared the next day in the *Philadelphia Dispatch* and succeeded, Purvis thought, in "'staying' the minds of all who may see it," and inviting fair-minded citizens to read the next issue of the *National Anti-Slavery Standard*. In this issue, Purvis denied that he had called Washington a slave-driver or a thief and said he was no "Bedlamite."[29]

The controversy did not, however, go away. Citizens of Kennett Square, where the meetings were held, were incensed at this attack upon the "sacred and venerated dead," and responded with a card in the *Press* for November 3, signed by a number of local men. Miller McKim decided to investigate, and interviewed a number of citizens of Kennett Square and signers of the card. He was told that several of the men who signed were not known to the oldest inhabitants of Kennett Square, and that several were boys away at school. Even the author of the card acknowledged he had not heard the speech, and could not vouch that Purvis had said the things attributed to him.[30]

Purvis noted that these men were all Republicans, and many shared the surname of Taylor. Bayard Taylor, a travel writer, had stated in one of his books his belief that the Egyptians could not be considered members of the "Negro race." Blacks were represented in the tombs as slaves or captives of war, never as rulers.[31] Purvis had remarked at the meetings that a celebrated traveler (whom he did not name) was using his popularity to depress further a race ground into the dust. In a letter to the editor of the *National Anti-Slavery Standard*, Purvis stated that he believed it was this remark, not his comments on Jefferson or Washington, that had produced the response.[32]

Taylor answered in the next issue of the paper:

I am charged with using my "popularity" "to depress still further a race already in the dust," and with "gratuitously speaking against the colored race," and this charge is made the excuse for public attacks of an unusually vulgar and personal character. I now distinctly state that I never even mentioned the negro race in any lecture or speech until within the last eight days; and that the only reference to that race in my published writings is that statement of the fact that they are represented in the ancient Egyptian tombs only as slaves—or captives taken in war, and that the Egyptians themselves did not belong to the negro race. . . .

Whatever my views regarding the negro race may be, they have nothing to do with the question of human rights. I appeal from the morbid sensitiveness of that 1/8th of him which was insulted to the sober commonsense of the 7/8ths which cannot possibly have been insulted."[33]

Purvis countered that Taylor's beliefs about Negroes in Egypt was at variance with those of Herodotus, Stanhope Smith, Alex and Edward Everett, and many other writers. Taylor's remark about human rights was ridiculous, he asserted, and about 1/8th versus 7/8ths insulting:

This is as if some *man* were to get up at a Woman's Rights Convention and say, "I believe after much travel and research that woman is the natural inferior of man, but that has nothing to do with the question before the Convention." Imagine Mrs. Mott, Miss Grew, Miss Anthony rising in reply.

It takes a woman to understand woman's wrongs, and it takes a man of African blood to understand the contempt which is cherished by a certain class of people against people of African blood.[34]

The outbreak of the Civil War in April 1861 might have lifted Robert Purvis's depressed spirits. But now there was fresh anxiety at home. His beloved son Robert Jr. was ill with tuberculosis, the dread disease that had carried off William just four years earlier. Robert had shown signs of following in his father's footsteps in every respect. He had been an active member of the Junior Anti-Slavery Society of Philadelphia. In 1854, when he was nineteen years of age, he had sponsored a meeting at which a speaker from New York, Giles Stebbins, had spoken on "the glaring wickedness of the American Colonization Society."[35] Later, Robert Jr. had entered business as a commission merchant in his own right. He had formed a partnership with Joshua Pierce, the son of Cyrus Pierce of Bristol, the white abolitionist who had sold Robert Purvis his farm. Working with Pierce, Robert Jr. had amassed a modest capital, including real estate worth $50,000. But by the early spring of 1859, he was ill with a sore throat and had begun to lose weight. Two years later he was confined to his bed.[36]

In addition to the anxiety over his son, Robert Purvis was upset by the refusal of the army to accept the proffered services of black troops. In May 1861, he wrote to the editor of the *National Anti-Slavery Standard* from the bedside of his son, sharing his belief that the inevitable end of the war would be the destruction of slavery. He and others were annoyed

by General Butler's offer to suppress slave rebellions, and especially by
General Patterson's declining the offer of colored volunteers:

> Loyalty and unswerving devotion to the interests of this country, in war
> and peace, have ever characterized the conduct of the colored Americans.
> In the Revolutionary War, the first blood shed in the cause of independ-
> ence was that of a black man. In the War of 1812, when Philadelphia was
> threatened, after the capture of Washington, none were more forward to
> enroll themselves as soldiers, and none labored with more patriotic devo-
> tion in throwing up earthworks of defense against the apprehended
> enemy, than the colored people of that city. My honored father-in-law, the
> late James Forten, used to narrate, with glowing feelings, stories of the
> courage and patriotism of the colored people in the Revolutionary strug-
> gle. He, as you know, was a soldier and prisoner of war in that contest.
> With others of his race, while yet a youth, he enlisted, and on board the
> *Royal Lewis*, Stephen Decatur commanding, did good service and a full
> hand's duty. He was for seven months a prisoner on the *Old Jersey* prison-
> ship. What is true of him, as to patriotism and courage, is true of thou-
> sands of others of his complexion; and I apprehend that a realizing sense
> of the services which colored people have rendered, and can again render,
> will yet be reached by the people of this country, and that the time will
> come, and is not far distant, when they will be glad to avail themselves of
> the assistance which they now so contemptuously and so foolishly reject.[37]

He regarded the war as a struggle between freedom and despotism
the world over. He was not sure of the good intentions of either the Republican party or of Lincoln at first, and in October, at the twenty-fifth
anniversary of the founding of the Pennsylvania Anti-Slavery Society, he
urged members to continue the struggle. Though some said that the work
of the abolitionists was being done for them by the government, that government continued to protest that it had no purpose to abolish slavery.
Why abandon an agitation which had so far had good results?[38]

The fact that the government refused to accept black soldiers, and
that when Colonel John Charles Fremont had freed the slaves in Mis-
souri in August 1861 he was relieved of his post, made Purvis dubious of
Lincoln's interest in ending slavery. On the other hand, the news that the
government had nullified the Dred Scot decision, and that Secretary of
State William Henry Seward had issued a passport to a black man, made
him hopeful.[39]

With other black leaders he urged that the black man be allowed to
fight for his country. He was cheered by the news of the heroism of two

black sailors in the summer of 1861. William Tillman, a navigator, had almost single-handedly recaptured a vessel from the Confederates and sailed it into New York Harbor. Shortly thereafter another black sailor, Jacob Garrick, was aboard another ship captured by the Confederates when a Union vessel, the USS *Albatross*, hailed her. The confederate captain claimed his vessel to be a legitimate cargo ship, but Garrick jumped overboard, swam to the *Albatross* and assisted in her recapture. The exploit of Robert Smalls, who captured a Confederate steamer in Charleston Harbor and sailed it into contact with the Union fleet guarding the harbor, rejoiced in his heart, as it did that of every black man. Robert Purvis could not help but think of the heroism of his father-in-law, James Forten, in the Revolutionary War.[40]

The capture by Union Troops of the Sea Islands off the coast of South Carolina was a source of delight to all Union supporters. Robert Purvis was pleased when his friend and comrade, Miller McKim, who left the Pennsylvania Anti-Slavery Society in January 1862 began work with the Port Royal Society, organizing relief and reconstruction on those islands. The following year Harriet's niece, Charlotte Forten, was among the black teachers who went south to work among the newly freed slaves. She was assigned to Beaufort and there played an active role in establishing a school.[41]

Sadly, his son Robert's illness progressed, and on March 19, 1862 he died; he was buried next to William in the little Quaker burial ground across the road. At his funeral too there was a large crowd and both Lucretia Mott and Miller McKim spoke of young Robert's gifts and his life. Elizabeth Paxson, a Quaker minister and abolitionist, and a Byberry neighbor, wrote the obituary:

> In the position to which he attained, he has left to his race a bright example of what a truly aspiring soul, a resolute and persevering spirit may accomplish, despite the difficulties and discouragements which beset its path. To him, these difficulties, far from causing him to despond, were but an incentive to more earnest and energetic action. He fought the life-battle bravely and well, and *compelled* the respect which high principles and a courageous self-assertion must ever compel—even from the most prejudiced.[42]

"I found Mrs. Purvis still very deeply afflicted at the recent loss of their beautiful and noble son," William Lloyd Garrison wrote to his wife after visiting the Purvises a few months later.[43]

In her journal Charlotte Forten mourned Robert:

> In March, Robert died. When I saw him lying so cold and still, and witnessed the agony of the loving hearts around him, I wish, dear A! that I

could have been taken instead of him. He had everything to live for, and I so little. It seems hard, yet we *know* it must be right.[44]

Robert Purvis could find some relief from his grief in renewed efforts to win equal rights for blacks in the Civil War and in continuing efforts to try to destroy "that Hydra-headed monster, colonization." When Samuel Clarke Pomeroy,[45] the government emigration agent, argued that the nation consider colonizing free blacks in Central America as a remedy for its racial ills, Robert Purvis responded indignantly. His letter to Pomeroy, published in the *Liberator* in August 1862, was regarded as a classic, and was widely reprinted.

Purvis reiterated the history of the attempts to woo blacks to the colonization scheme, beginning in 1817 with the famous gathering in Mother Bethel Church where his late father-in-law had presided, and where those present had passed a resolution stating their determination to remain in the United States.

> Those were the sentiments of the colored people of Philadelphia, and of the whole land in 1817, they have been their sentiments ever since, and they will be found to be their sentiments now . . . Sir, for more than twenty years the question of Colonization agitated and divided this country. The colored people stamped it with the seal of their reprobation, the whites acquiesced in the justice of their decision, and the vexed and vexing question was put to rest. Now it is revived. The apple of discord is again thrown into the community, and as though you had not already enough to divide and distract you, a new scheme is hit upon, and deliberately sent upon its errand of mischief.[46]

Purvis argued that from the government's own point of view the plan did not make sense. Exiling a portion of the working class would deplete the economy of the nation, which was already feeling the effects of the draft. It would also antagonize foreign governments, on whose goodwill the nation now depended.

> These nations have none of this vulgar prejudice against complexion. What, then will they think of the wisdom of a people who, to gratify a low-born prejudice, will deliberately plan to drive out hundreds of thousands of its most peaceable, industrious, and competent laborers.[47]

Purvis described a slaveholders convention held in Maryland several years before to discuss the problem of free blacks. Was it best to reenslave them, or banish them? The committee entrusted with this question had reported that to reenslave them would be inhuman and to banish them would be to rob the state of needed labor. Now the U.S. Government proposed to do what that Slaveholders Convention had decided against. Even President Lincoln had said that he could not discuss whether it was right or wrong.[48]

> Great God! Is injustice nothing? Is honor nothing? Is even pecuniary interest to be sacrificed to this insane and vulgar hate? But it is said that this is the "white man's country." Not so, sir. This is the red man's country by natural right and the black man's by virtue of his sufferings and toil. Your fathers by violence drove the red man out and forced the black man in. The children of the black man have enriched the soil by their tears, sweat and blood. Sir, we were born here, and here we chose to remain. . . . I elect to stay on the soil on which I was born, and on the plot of ground which I have fairly bought and honestly paid for. Don't advise me to leave, and don't add insult to injury by telling me it's for my own good; of that I am to be the judge. It is vain that you talk to me about "two races" and their "mutual antagonism." In the matter of rights there is but one race and that is the *human* race.[49]

Figure 1. Robert Purvis, 1833
(*Sophia Smith Collection, Smith College*)

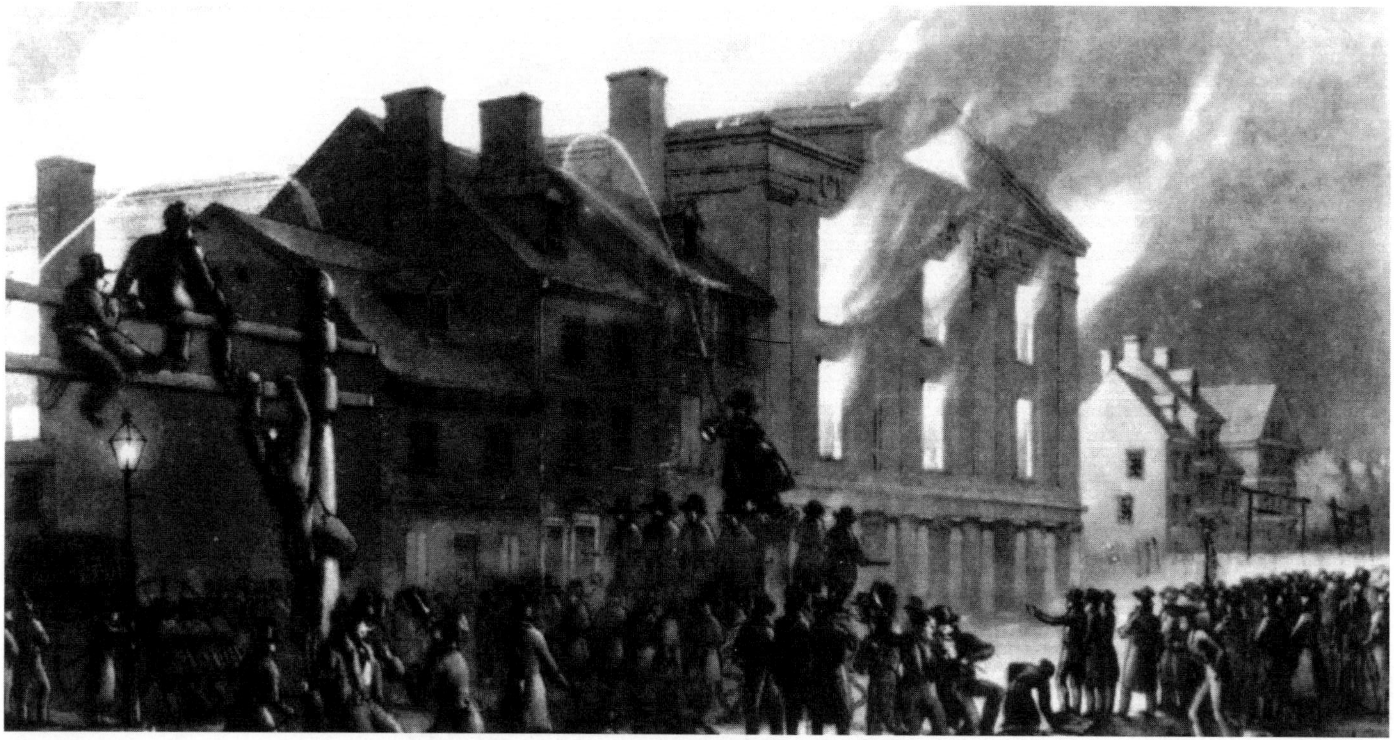

Figure 2. Burning of Pennsylvania Hall, 1838

Figure 3. *Cinque: The Chief of the Amistad Captives*, by John Sartain, ca. 1841
(*Library Company of Pennsylvania*)

Figure 4. Silver spoon from Purvis step-descendants
(*Marcus Huey and Barbara Graf*)

Figure 5. Forten table, ca. 1790–1800, from Purvis step-descendants
(*Marcus Huey and Barbara Graf*)

Figure 6. Elijah Lovejoy Commemorative Plate, Staffordshire,
ca. 1840, earthenware and whiteware
(*The Colonial Williamsburg Foundation. Gift of Mrs. John Robie*)

Figure 7. The Board of the Pennsylvania Antislavery Society, 1851.
(*Friends Historical Library, Swarthmore College*)

Figure 8. Byberry Friends School and Meeting, photo taken by Gilbert Cope, 1895

(Library, Byberry Meeting)

JAMES AND LUCRETIA MOTT

From a Daguerreotype by Langenheim about 1842.

Figure 9. James Mott and Lucretia Mott
(*Friends Historical Library, Swarthmore College*)

C. B. PURVIS.

Figure 10. Charles Burleigh Purvis
(*Library Company of Philadelphia*)

Figure 11. Harriet ("Hattie") Purvis
(*Sophia Smith Collection, Smith College*)

Figure 12. Robert Purvis in his later years
(*Sophia Smith Collection, Smith College*)

CHAPTER 11

"A Proud Day for the Colored Man"

$\mathcal{T}$he Emancipation Proclamation of January 1863 lifted Purvis's sagging spirits. Although he knew it was the result of a political compromise and only applied to freed slaves in the rebel states, it established the principle of equality. At a meeting of the Pennsylvania Anti-Slavery Society on January 10, he said he regarded the great fact of emancipation as a result of the long years of labor and self-sacrifice made by the abolitionists. He was ready to say, "God bless Abraham Lincoln." He agreed with an old friend and comrade who was now able to say, "I am proud in being an American citizen."

> I agreed with that friend, and with every other man, in that expression; for, forgetting the past, and looking forward to the future, I, too, am proud of the land of my birth—proud of this mighty young nation—this awakened young lion, with power so vast, varied, and exhaustless as to fill with consternation and terror the haughty despotisms of the Old World. Proud of a country whose soul is for freedom, and who, in the grandeur and sublimity of her position, will welcome under the aegis of her protection people of every nation and every clime.[1]

He was still rejoicing in the Emancipation Proclamation when he spoke to the American Anti-Slavery Society annual meeting in May. He had not prepared an address, he said, but spoke extemporaneously. This sometimes led to overstatement:

> It is the misfortune of natures born near the sun that their blood will not obey the helm of their judgment. My friends would urge me to moderate

145

my tone, but it was impossible; out of the bitterness of the heart the mouth would speak. I was a victim, stricken, degraded, injured, insulted in my person, in my family, in my friends, in my estate; I returned bitterness for bitterness and scorn for scorn.[2]

But he knew that on this occasion the committe had asked him to speak because he was a colored man, and therefore he was glad to accept the invitation.

Mr. Chairman, this is a proud day for the "colored" man. For the first time since this Society was organized, I stand before you a recognized citizen of the United States (applause). And let me add, for the first time since your government was a government is it an honor to be a citizen of the United States! Old things are passing away, all things are becoming new. Now a black man has rights, under this government, which every white man, here and elsewhere, is bound to respect (applause). The damnable doctrine of the detestable Taney no longer rules at Washington. The slaveholders and their miserable allies are biting the dust, and Copperhead Democracy has come to grief. The black man is a citizen, all honor to Secretary Bates,[3] who has so pronounced him. The black man can take out a passport and travel to the uttermost parts of the earth, protected by the broad aegis of the government; all honor to Secretary Seward, who was the first to recognize this right.[4] The black man is a citizen, soldier, standing on an equality in the rank and file with the white soldier; all honor to Secretary Stanton[5] and the rest of the Administration.[6]

He knew, he said, that the government was not all that it might be, and that some of the men he praised had not always been friendly to the colored people. His friends urged him to moderate his tone and suggested that it was too early to rejoice. But he was too full of joy to hold back, and left to others the job of censure. He had denounced the United States in the past under Presidents James Buchanan and Franklin Pierce, when it was, he said, a slaveholding oligarchy, full of slave-breeding traitors such as Jefferson Davis, Howell Cobb, John Floyd, Isaac Toucey, and Roger Taney, Chief Justice of the Supreme Court. He had hated it then with a wrath which words could not express. Now however, he could only rejoice in his belief that the good times were at last coming:[7]

I feel it, I see it in the air, I read it in the signs of the times; I see it in the acts of Congress in the abolition of slavery in the District of Columbia, in its exclusion from the Territories, in solemn treaties for the effectual suppression of the infernal foreign slave trade, in the acknowledgment of the black republics of Hayti [sic] and Liberia. I see it in the new spirit that is in the army; I see it in the black regiment of South Carolina (applause).[8] I see it in the 54th Regiment of Massachusetts[9] I see it in the order of Adjt. Gen. Thomas,[10] forming a Black Brigade at Memphis; I see it, above all, and more than all, in the *glorious and immortal proclamation of Abraham Lincoln on the first of January* 1863. (cheers).[11]

The year before, on July 17, 1862, Congress had enacted a bill authorizing the president "to employ as many persons of African descent as he may deem necessary and proper for the suppression of the rebellion and for this purpose he may organize and use them in such manner as he may judge best for the public welfare." But fear of arming the blacks remained widespread, and there was no recruitment of black troops until early in 1863, when the state of Massachusetts permitted the raising of the 54th Regiment, Massachusetts Volunteers. This was followed by permission to raise the 55th Regiment. Since the black population of Massachusetts was sparse, abolitionists turned to Pennsylvania for volunteers. Major George Stearns of Massachusetts created the Philadelphia Supervisory Committee for Recruiting Colored Regiments, and invited Robert Purvis to take part.[12]

When Richard P. Hallowell, a great-grandson of Lucretia Mott, and one of four brothers to serve in the Civil War wrote to Robert,[13] asking his help in recruiting for the Massachusetts regiments, Purvis was at first reluctant to agree, feeling that it was unfair for black troops to be commanded by white officers. He wrote to a friend, possibly Wendell Phillips, for advice:

> Yet notwithstanding the advance made by the government in forming regiments of colored men—it argues a sad misapprehension of character, aspirations and self-respect of colored men, to suppose that they would submit to the *degrading* limit which the government imposed in regard to the officering of said regiments.[14] From that position and error, the government must recede or else I opine that failure to secure the right kind of men will be the result.[15]

Nevertheless, Robert Purvis finally agreed to help recruit for the Massachusetts regiments. In June 1863, he wrote to Elizabeth Gay, wife of his friend, journalist Sydney Gay, asking Sydney to convey to Sarah Shaw, the mother of Robert Shaw, who commanded the 54th Regiment, his regrets that ill health had prevented him from going to Boston to see the departure of the troops.[16]

The 54th was stationed on St. Helena Island at Beaufort, South Carolina, where Charlotte Forten was engaged in teaching school. Charlotte met young Colonel Robert Shaw and Major Edward Hallowell on July 2 when they came to tea with the whole Port Royal Relief Association team. Afterwards, the officers stayed to attend the black "shout" or praise group meeting. Only sixteen days later, on July 18, Robert Shaw and many of his men were killed in an assault on Fort Wagner, on Morris Island which guarded Charleston Harbor. The news reached Charlotte Forten on July 20. She recorded in her journal:

> For nearly two weeks we have waited, oh how anxiously, for news of our regiment which went, we know to Morris Island to take part in the attack on Charleston. Tonight comes news, oh, so sad, so heart sickening. It is too terrible, too terrible to write. We can only hope it may not all be true. That our noble, beautiful, young Colonel is killed, and the reg. cut to pieces! I cannot, cannot believe it. And yet I know it must be so.[17]

News of the heroism of black volunteers also came from Louisiana, where the First Louisiana Native Guards fought bravely at Port Hudson, on the Mississippi, and ten days later at Milliken's Bend, where fierce hand to hand fighting occurred between black and Confederate troops. The arrival of a Union warship turned the tide, and the southern troops retreated. A federal captain wrote to General Ulysses Grant: "The capacity of the Negro to defend his liberty, and his susceptibility to appreciate the power of motives . . . have been put to such a test under our observation as to be of no further doubt." Another general wrote: "It is impossible for men to show greater bravery than the Negro troops in that fight."[18]

Philadelphia abolitionists were eager to raise black troops, and began meeting in March to discuss ways and means. In June 1863, a large number of prominent citizens, all white, were named to a committee for that purpose. The federal government had still taken no action to enlist black soldiers. A bill introduced into Congress by Senator Charles Sumner of Massachusetts in February, which called for raising three hundred thousand black troops, had been ignored. But in June 1863, Lieutenant Charles C. Ruff of the U.S. mustering office in Philadelphia announced that he had received orders to "authorize the formation of one regiment of ten companies, colored troops, each company to be eighty strong, to be mustered into the United States service and provided for, in all respects, the same as white troops."[19]

Within a week of this order, Camp William Penn was established on the property of Jay Cooke, the financier of the Civil War. The fact that the North Penn Railroad had recently been constructed to give easy access to Philadelphia, and that most of the surrounding farms were owned by Quakers—including James and Lucretia Mott—made this an ideal location. Later, as the needs of the camp expanded, Edward M. Davis, the Mott's son-in-law, leased his property, Oak Farm, to the Camp. Davis also helped to organize the Union League, to support the black troops, and this group quickly raised $34,000 to outfit and equip the new regiments. Lieutenant Colonel Louis Wagner, of the 88th Regiment, Pennsylvania Infantry, a German-born volunteer, who had been badly wounded in the Battle of Bull Run, was put in charge of the camp. By July 4, 1863, the first black troops were being trained.[20]

Robert Purvis was delighted by the establishment of Camp William Penn, and the fact that blacks were being inducted into the Union Army. He redoubled his work in recruitment, and in September presented a flag to Colonel Louis Wagner, for the Sixth U.S. Infantry.

> You will prove yourselves worthy of the gift; you will see that the flag of your country suffers no dishonor at your hands. I am fully satisfied that the loyalty, prowess, and devotion of the colored soldiers will take care of the interests committed to them by the country. What are the facts? Let Milliken's Bend[21] answer. Said Adjutant Gen. Thomas, "the negro soldiers repulsed the enemy; to the brave black men are we indebted for the possession of that important post." Let Fort Wagner answer! Led by the noble and heroic Colonel Robert G. Shaw, no men fought more bravely, no soldiers bore in hospitals their wounds more patiently. Let Port Hudson[22] answer! Let no one who reads the official report of Major-General Banks, bearing testimony to the valor of colored soldiers, dare to scruple and say the black man will not fight, unless he belongs to that tribe of the meanest of God's creeping things, the copperhead.
>
> Soldiers, in this momentous struggle between freedom and slavery, in other words, between a true democracy and a tyrannical despotism, I thank God that the Government, from a sense of duty, and therefore in the exercise of its highest wisdom, recognized your manhood, and evidences it by calling on you to share the sacrifices necessary to establish the doctrine of equal rights.[23]

Robert Forten, Robert Purvis's brother-in-law, had moved to England after his father's death and the dismantling of the business, but returned to enlist in March 1864, just short of his fiftieth birthday. He was made a Sergeant Major and assigned to Colonel S. M. Bowman, the chief mustering and recruiting officer of the 43rd Regiment, United States Colored Troops, stationed in Baltimore. "In the many speeches he made to those of his race in Baltimore, so full of logic and true eloquence, he in a great measure contributed to the great success which attended Colonel Bowman's efforts during the past two months," a newspaper columnist reported. "That officer in reporting to the Philadelphia Supervisory Committee, commended him as a scholar and a gentleman."[24]

Unfortunately, Robert Forten soon fell ill of what the reporter said was erysipelas, an infection leading to a deep inflammation of the skin (another report said typhoid fever) and shortly died, on April 25. According to the reporter, he was buried with full military honors, the first time they had been accorded to a colored man. Many prominent citizens spoke at the funeral including Lucretia Mott, Miller McKim, and Thomas Webster. He was buried at St. Thomas Episcopal Church, where three volleys were fired over his grave.[25]

Another family member, Joseph Purvis Jr., the son of Joseph Purvis and Sarah Forten Purvis, also had enlisted and was mustered in on March 16, 1864 to Company B, 43rd Regiment. But he soon fell ill with rheumatism, as a result, he thought, of having to sleep outdoors in a flimsy tent during the rainy season. Colonel Wagner eventually took pity on him, and excused him from drilling and standing guard. Instead, he was placed in charge of the horses. Later, when the regiment was ordered into action, and was marching from Annapolis to Alexandria, Joseph collapsed and was transported to the army hospital, the forerunner of Freedmen's Hospital in Washington, where his cousin Charles Purvis was serving as a nurse. Joseph was pronounced unfit and discharged on July 15, 1864. In March 1865, he reenlisted, and was discharged in October. He eventually became an alcoholic, blaming his addiction on his war service.[26]

Conditions for the blacks at Camp William Penn were unequal, with white officers living in the barracks, while the troops were stationed in leaky tents. The black community was also outraged to learn that while white soldiers were paid $13 a month and provided with clothing, the black soldiers got only $10 a month from which they had to provide their own clothing. In addition to these indignities, black families found they could not visit their soldier boys at Camp William Penn without riding on the segregated trolley lines that operated between the train station and the camp. The blacks had endured this segregation on other lines, being asked to ride outside when the cars were full of whites, or even to leave. Now, emboldened by the Emancipation Proclamation and the organization of black troops, leaders of the black community organized a massive boycott campaign, with support from such groups as the Philadelphia Female Anti-Slavery Society, Pennsylvania Anti-Slavery Society and the Pennsylvania Abolition Society.

Many blacks rode on the cars but refused to obey the order to move back. White allies such as Lucretia Mott refused to take their seats while the blacks were denied theirs.[27]

Harriet Purvis was among those active in the campaign. On September 13, 1866, she reported to the Female Anti-Slavery Society about a talk she had heard the night before:

> The speaker, Judge Pitkin, of Louisiana, said that the nation had more to fear from the conservatism of the North than anything else; even the Radicals were not ready to go as far as the Union men of the South, who knew from actual experience that negro suffrage and negro equality could alone save the Union. He was loudly applauded. Mrs. Purvis said she felt in coming out how useless was all this applause when she could not be allowed, weary as she was, to take a seat in the cars. She expressed her feelings to the group around the door and was heard with respect. She thought there was very little discussion on the part of Philadelphians that the colored people should ride in the cars. Even the committee who had the matter in charge had done nothing for fear of injury to the Republican Party.[28]

William Still headed up a committee of prominent blacks who supported the campaign. At an indignation meeting held at Concert Hall on January 13, 1865, Purvis spoke passionately. "We ask no favors, but in the name of the living God, give us justice!" Later, seeing some black soldiers evicted from a streetcar, he wrote an angry letter to the *Press*. He continued to support Still, who headed a committee that waited upon the heads of all the railway companies, urging the end of discrimination, and sought the support of prominent citizens, black and white, in signing petitions calling on public officials to demand the end of the discrimination.[29]

In addition to Still and the groups he had rallied, some younger black leaders, including Octavius Catto, a teacher at the Institute for Colored Youth; William Forten, Harriet's youngest brother; Joseph Bustill; and Alfred Cassey, were active in the campaign. In 1864, they met in Philadelphia to form Pennsylvania State Equal Rights League, and began the job of organizing branches. By February 1865, when the group held its first statewide convention in Harrisburg, Pennsylvania; it had organizations in sixteen of the larger cities. Later, Robert's nephew, William B. Purvis, became active (Robert Purvis was not present at the organizing convention but later played a supportive role in the organization). This group lobbied not only for black teachers to teach in all black schools, but also for an end to discrimination on the streetcars.[30]

Octavius Catto is generally credited with leading the fight for leg-
islative action against discrimination on the streetcars. Catto had come to
prominence in 1863 when he led a contingent of male students from the
Institute for Colored Youth to Harrisburg to enlist in the state militia, in
answer to a call for recruits. When a major in the army refused to allow
the blacks to be inducted, a number of prominent white Philadelphians,
including members of the newly formed Union League, protested this act
of discrimination. Eventually black recruits were accepted, and Catto
became a major in the Pennsylvania National Guard.[31]

In 1866, returning to his civilian concerns, Catto took up the struggle for an end of discrimination on the streetcars. As head of a three man
committee appointed by the Equal Rights League, he went to Harrisburg
to lobby for a statewide ban on such discrimination. At Harrisburg, he
was able to gain the support of Thaddeus Stevens, William Kelley, and
Morrow W. Lowry. The struggle was also supported by Colonel John W.
Forney, owner of the *Philadelphia Press*. The passage of the Fourteenth
Amendment, introduced in June 1866, seemed likely. This amendment
would give the blacks the right to vote in 1870. Legislators realized they
would need the black vote. In March 1867, the Pennsylvania Assembly
passed and the governor of Pennsylvania finally signed an act forbidding
the railways to force blacks to sit in the back of the streetcars.[32]

The year before, William Still and a friend, William Whipper, had
persuaded eight other prominent blacks to go in with them to purchase
the former home of the Institute for Colored Youth, at Seventh and Lombard, as a place where blacks could hold meetings. (The Institute had
moved to Ninth and Bainbridge.) They remodeled it, providing rooms for
shops in the lower floors, and a meeting room above. When it was finished, they renamed it Liberty Hall. To celebrate the end of the battle for
the trolley cars, blacks held a massive victory celebration at Liberty Hall,
chaired by Robert Purvis.[33]

The celebration was marred by criticism of William Still by the
younger and more radical black men; they claimed he took credit for the
victory, used elitist arguments, and depended on white allies primarily.
Feelings ran high, and some blacks threatened to boycott Still's newly
developed coal yard. In defense of his friend and colleague, Purvis called
a second meeting on April 8 at Liberty Hall to give Still a chance to
respond to the criticisms, and state his position.[34]

Following the tumultuous meeting at Liberty Hall, Robert Purvis
was invited by Still to join the Social, Civil and Statistical Association, an

organization which William Still and a number of other blacks had developed in 1861 to collect information on the status of black Philadelphians as well as to arrange a series of lectures and other cultural events. This group had played a prominent role in the streetcar campaign. Purvis declined, however, on the basis of conscience, once more making the point that he was opposed to all separate organizations "when the necessity of the case does not demand it."

> Our aim and end should be homogeneity with the American people—we being in fact Americans—with all the elements of character so peculiar to the natives of this country. Now what is to be gained . . . in collecting facts in regard to the material prosperity or worth of the colored people? Is it to astonish the people (whites) of this State? May they not console themselves, and say that after all, our oppression of these people serves as a good stimulant. See how they thrive. . . . The great fundamental law of our Republican Government is *Equal rights for all men by virtue of their common humanity.*[35]

As the streetcar battle began, the Civil War still raged. In March 1863, Congress passed a Conscription Act, making all men age 20-45 liable for military service. There was a catch, however. If you could pay $300 or procure a substitute for three years, you could be exempt. This provision inflamed the anger of the working classes, who saw the sons of their employers avoid the draft, while they were sent to fight. The antagonism which existed in Northern cities at the time between black and white working-class men (the latter largely new Irish immigrants), was exacerbated by the new law. In New York City rioting broke out on July 13 and continued for several days. Blacks were strung to lampposts, the homes of prominent abolitionists—including the Purvis's friends James and Abby Gibbons—were attacked and burned, businesses employing blacks were ransacked. For Robert Purvis, and his fellow black abolitionists, it was a clear sign that nothing had changed. Despite the Emancipation Proclamation, the country was still pro-slavery.[36]

William Lloyd Garrison felt differently. He believed the Republicans intended to grant suffrage, and that the need for the antislavery crusade was essentially over. From the outbreak of the Civil War, he had felt that the abolitionists should mute their criticisms of Lincoln and the Republican Party, and attempt to enlist more and more of their fellow citizens in a broad campaign to support the war effort, in order to ensure that emancipation of the slaves became its goal. Spurred by Maria Chapman, Garrison supported an Emancipation League, which was organized in Boston in 1861 and which not only called for the emancipation of all the slaves without compensation in the rebel states, but also with the payment of a "fair pecuniary award" to slaveholders who were loyal to the government.[37]

For many of the founding members of the American Anti-Slavery Society, this was heresy. Robert Purvis said: "He wouldn't give a dollar to so-called loyal slaveholders whose devotion remained contingent on the government's protection of their rascality." Others, however, followed Maria Chapman and Garrison; they were delighted to be less isolated, more in the mainstream of public opinion. In 1863, Elizabeth Cady Stanton and Susan B. Anthony organized the Women's National Loyal League, to circulate a giant petition asking for a constitutional amendment banning slavery; another effort to enter the mainstream, which the purists rejected. The women aimed at one million signatures, but came up with only four hundred thousand, still an impressive number.[38]

In December 1863, when the American Anti-Slavery Society gathered in Philadelphia to celebrate three decades of struggle, Garrison announced that if Congress abolished slavery, he would abolish the American Anti-Slavery Society. Perhaps this could be the Society's last session.[39] Robert Purvis spoke on the second day of the sessions, but his speech was not included in the published proceedings of the convention. According to the reporter from the *National Anti-Slavery Standard*, "with deep feeling, yet great magnanimity, he referred to the past wrongs under which he in company with his race had labored, while in contrast he drew from the hereafter, a picture of consolation and hope."[40] He must have made other comments as well, for Frederick Douglass referred to them:

> My respected friend, Mr. Purvis, called attention to the existence of prejudice against color in this country. This gives me great cause for apprehension, if not for alarm. I am afraid of this powerful element against color. While it exists, I want the voice of the American Anti-Slavery Society to be continually protesting, continually exposing it.[41]

Among the speakers at the Third Decade celebration was Colonel Louis Wagner, the commander of Camp William Penn. Asked by Lucretia Mott about stealing at the camp compared to camps for white soldiers, Wagner insisted that he had found blacks "in this respect far superior to white soldiers in a similar position":

> I have never yet seen a camp of white soldiers where depredations were not committed; but at Camp William Penn there have been no depredations.

It is not owing to a more rigid discipline there; we have no other rules than those that govern white camps. But the men seem to feel the dignity and responsibility of their position.[42]

Ironically, the only person who got into difficulties for "depredations" at Camp William Penn was William Still. Early in 1864, Edward M. Davis had arranged for Still to be offered the position of sutler or civilian provisioner for the camp. The former sutler had been lazy and dishonest, and had allowed some bad practices to develop. Davis believed William Still could correct all these. William Still was honored by the offer, but torn. He had recently left the office of the Pennsylvania Anti-Slavery Society to establish a small business selling stoves. On the side, he was serving on a committee established by the Pennsylvania Abolition Society and the Freedmen Aid Commission to find homes and jobs for black refugees from the South pouring into Philadelphia. But he felt it was his duty to accept the post of sutler, whatever its effect upon his fortunes; he did so.[43]

The first months at Camp William Penn were difficult. Some of the young soldiers were given counterfeit money when they went to town, and insisted on using it to pay for their purchases at the camp store. When William Still refused to accept it, they spread rumors that he was cheating them. The former sutler had ordered some clothing for the soldiers from a friend, paying a large price for inferior goods. His enemies blamed William for this rip-off. In April, he was arrested and briefly imprisoned on charges of having cheated the government. Miller McKim, who was visiting the Motts, heard about the charges and hurried to camp headquarters to clear the charges made against Still. He was soon freed and resumed his duties, which he continued until the end of the war.[44]

Despite Northern victories, news filtering back from the South was not good. In recaptured rebel areas, there was little done to provide former slaves with either land or the vote, and without these protections it was clear the whites would soon achieve dominance again. When the administration announced a reconstruction plan in which loyal states would be readmitted to the Union without giving suffrage to the blacks, the radical abolitionists protested, and declared it was necessary for the antislavery crusade to continue at least until the freedmen obtained the shield of suffrage.

Lincoln's Second Inaugural Address, delivered on March 4, 1865, seemed to suggest a deepening commitment to the abolition of slavery, and a determination to bind up the wounds of war, "with malice toward none, with charity toward all." Slightly over a month later, on April 9, 1865, General Robert E. Lee surrendered his forces at Appomattox Court House, Virginia, and the war appeared to be over. But what triumph the abolitionists felt was short-lived. On April 14, Abraham Lincoln was assassinated at Ford's Theater in Washington by John Wilkes Booth, a disgruntled southern actor. However much the abolitionists had criticized Lincoln's hesitant policies on antislavery, they felt his loss keenly. Whatever hopes they entertained that his successor, Andrew Johnson, would carry forward a reconstruction program favorable to the newly freed blacks was soon dissipated when Johnson admitted loyal governments in Arkansas, Louisiana, Tennessee, and Virginia without black suffrage, and granted amnesty to Confederates.

The abolitionists were in a dark mood when they gathered in May in New York City at Dr. Cheever's Church of the Puritans. William Lloyd Garrison had come to the meeting from a triumphal visit to Charleston, South Carolina, on April 14, to celebrate the recapture of the city by Northern forces. He believed he was now with the mainstream of public sentiment; he saw no further reason for the existence of the American Anti-Slavery Society. A group of radicals, under the leadership of Wendell Phillips, felt otherwise. Debate, heated at times, flowed back and forth. Robert Purvis was torn between his longtime commitment to Garrison, and his strong feelings that the Society must continue until black suffrage was firmly established. His speech was short, and he sounded heartbroken:

> Mr. Chairman, the words that I desire to utter have already been spoken by the speakers this morning; and the reasons which have been given why this Society should not be dissolved are my reasons. I do not desire and shall not attempt to reiterate what has been said. The trusting confidence of the colored people in this Society—and which, sir, has never been betrayed—will not permit a dissolution at this particular juncture. I have now simply to say, that I trust in God that my very heart may cease to beat when its pulsations fail to bring with them stirrings of gratitude, and a lasting ever-enduring sense of my obligations to you (turning to Mr. Garrison) and to ask of you, to beg of you, to entreat of you, to remain at your post until slavery goes down so effectually that about it we can have no question or doubt.[45]

But Garrison did not relent, and made a motion that the American Anti-Slavery Society dissolve. He was defeated by a vote of 118–48, and the remaining members voted Wendell Phillips as their president.[46]

In keeping with his passionate nature, Robert Purvis took the break with Garrison seriously. The man who had been his hero now seemed like a traitor to the cause. At the fall meeting of the Pennsylvania Anti-Slavery Society, he joined with Wendell Phillips and others in rejecting a resolution floated by Garrison for the dissolution of the Society. A few months later, when Garrison came to deliver some lectures in Philadelphia, Purvis refused to attend. Garrison heard that Purvis had said that when the *Liberator* came to hand, "he threw it from him as far as possible with feelings of disgust."[47]

For the next several years, Purvis continued to back Phillips and attack Garrison, and to a lesser extent, Miller McKim, who had also withdrawn from the Anti-Slavery Society. The depths of Purvis's feelings of betrayal surfaced when a court ruled that the legacy left to the abolitionists by Francis Jackson, a Boston merchant and president of the Massachusetts Anti-Slavery Society, should go to Garrison and his colleagues who had left the American Anti-Slavery Society with him, rather than those who had stayed on under the leadership of Wendell Phillips. Purvis wrote a letter to the *National Anti-Slavery Standard*, revealing his anger:

> MY DEAR FRIEND: My blood with unwonted celerity moved to fever heat as I read the letter of the Boston correspondent to the *Standard* of last week, touching the matter of the bequest of the late Francis Jackson.[48]
>
> The inquiry is naturally suggested to the mind, who are the persons to whom the trust was reposed? It is stated that they were "associates of Mr. Jackson in reformatory labors," and that the subject was referred to a "Master in Chancery," the aforesaid trustees were to be conferred with, and "then he was to report his opinion as to the disposal of the bequest." Now, that report being adverse to the manifest purpose of the testator, who devised that the fund ($10,000) be used "for the preparation and circulation of books, newspapers, the delivery of speeches, lectures, and such other means as in their judgment would put an end to negro slavery in this country.[49]

Who was responsible for the accomplishment of these goals today? Purvis asked. Was it not the men and women who were not under the delusion that "the nation is converted," and "the work is done;" and who meant to be faithful to the end of the struggle for Negro freedom? those who mean to be faithful to the end?[50]

He was equally concerned that the American Anti-Slavery Society be represented at the World Anti-Slavery Conference to be held in June 1867 in Paris.

The American Anti-Slavery Society is the only legitimately authorized exponent of the colored race, in this country, and can speak for them as no other association can. To guard, therefore, against wrong impressions being made, as to the condition of the freedmen, and that the necessity for the continued existence of our antislavery organizations (Emancipation Proclamation, Civil Rights bills, etc. to the contrary not withstanding) is as imperatively the duty and obligation which civilization and humanity require at our hands, to secure freedom to the colored race today, as at the beginning of our antislavery labors. For practically, the black man throughout the South, and nearly so at the North, fulfils, as the victim race, the satanic sentiment, that he has no rights which the white man is bound to respect. Absolute justice, in the complete habiliment of all that constitutes a freeman, is our pledged duty to the slave, and *short of it our work is not accomplished*. Therefore, we hold that the fitting representative to the Nation's Conference is to be delegated from the American Anti-Slavery Society.[51]

Purvis's sense of betrayal came to a head at a meeting of Progressive Friends at Longwood in June 1868 where he attacked Garrison angrily. Garrison wrote to his wife Helen that Robert took exception to some remarks by Miller McKim about comparative importance of the ballot and the educational movement under the auspices of the Freedmen's Commission. "He vociferated, ranted, and showed himself to be in a volcanic state of mind, reflecting severally upon what Mr. McKim had said, and upon those who had withdrawn from the Anti-Slavery Society—fulsomely eulogizing Lucretia Mott, Mary Grew, Edward M. Davis, and Wendell Phillips." Garrison in his speech had supported McKim and said he thought any one who attacked him had come to the meeting in a spirit of controversy.[52]

This remark roused Purvis to the utmost pitch of wrath. He again took the platform, and poured upon my head all the vials of his vituperation, with eyes flashing fire and voice raised to its highest pitch—accusing me of being to the antislavery cause what Benedict Arnold was to the Revolutionary struggle and Judas Iscariot was to Jesus, and also ill-mannered and insulting, && I took no notice of his scandalous imputations, but he was pronounced by Mr. Johnson as chairman to be flagrantly out of order in the use of such language; from which decision he took an appeal to the house, and was pronounced disorderly by an overwhelming vote. He sneeringly remarked that being a colored man, he could expect no better treatment! and sat down in a towering rage. He spoke several times, evincing the same bitter spirit.[53]

Having lost William Lloyd Garrison as a hero, Robert Purvis turned his ardent affection to Wendell Phillips. In 1864, he wrote Phillips to praise Phillip's recent speech at Cooper Union, in New York, and to express his appreciation for his stand: "We thank God, that a *leader is preserved* us; who amid the entangling besetments of the day, keeps in view the great landmarks of our cause."[54]

A few years later, writing to Mrs. Sargent, who had taken Maria Chapman's place in the Boston Anti-Slavery Society, Purvis praised the abolitionists who had continued faithfully, especially Wendell Phillips:

> Of Wendell Phillips (Heaven's blessings upon him), I accept most heartily every word of reference you make. No man, at this moment, wields a greater power in the nation! Every word that falls from his lips or his pen is eagerly caught up by the press of the country, and thus widely circulating, the most beneficent results *must* follow. We shall not despair of our cause or our country whilst life and light are dispensed by our cherished, honored, and distinguished leader.[55]

Purvis's belief that the struggle was not yet won surfaced again and again in his letters and speeches in this period. Writing to the New England Anti-Slavery Convention, which had invited him to speak in June 1868, he sounded the same theme:

> Could I be with you, and called to say a word to the men and women of the New England Anti-Slavery Convention, it would be to repeat the words of our peerless LUCRETIA MOTT, in her letter to the late Anniversary Meeting of the American Anti-Slavery Society *that our duties still press upon us, and urge perseverance,* until we have obtained the goal of our labors, to which we are pledged in "removing public prejudice" and securing "equality" of rights and privileges to all classes of American citizens. That this is not yet accomplished needs no argument. Let me repeat, *our duties still press upon us.*[56]

CHAPTER 12

"Equality of Rights for All"

$\mathcal{D}$uring the Civil War, the children of Robert and Harriet Purvis had come of age. Charles, the oldest remaining son, enrolled in the preparatory course at Oberlin College in 1860, at age eighteen; he graduated in 1863, and in 1865 graduated from Wooster Medical College (later, Western Reserve Medical School). In the summer of 1864, he worked as a military nurse at a large contraband relief center in Washington, in the barracks of Camp Barker near Thirteenth and R Street, a forerunner of the Freedmen's Hospital. He contracted typhoid fever, but he was able to return to Cleveland to complete his studies. In 1865 he graduated, and he enlisted in the Union Army as an acting assistant surgeon, with the rank of first lieutenant; he was assigned to Washington, D.C. to work among the freedmen. He began attending meetings of the American Anti-Slavery Society; he was a principal speaker in 1869 and 1870.[1]

Henry, the next son, also attended Oberlin College from 1863 to 1866, then went south to work in the reconstruction effort. Granville attended Oberlin from 1865 to 1867, and then went to the newly opened Howard University; he studied pharmacy for two years. Hattie was enrolled for one year at Theodore and Angelina Grimké Weld's school in Eagleswood. Nothing is known of Georgianna's education beyond the fact that she attended the Byberry Friends School and that Charlotte Forten was her tutor. Despite their belief in women's rights, the Purvises evidently thought that college education was not as necessary for daughters as for their sons.[2]

Although they commuted to Philadelphia even more frequently to engage in wartime duties, Robert and Harriet remained at Byberry. Robert

161

recruited and supported black soldiers, and Harriet engaged herself in the campaign against the streetcar segregation of the Philadelphia Female Anti-Slavery Society. Together they attended the meetings of the American Anti-Slavery Society held in New York.

Through the years, women abolitionists had worked side by side with men in the antislavery societies. Following the election in 1840 of a woman (Abby Kelley) to a committee of the American Anti-Slavery Society, women began rising to leadership positions in the organization. In addition, spurred by the struggle within the antislavery movement over women's rights, Lucretia Mott had joined with Elizabeth Cady Stanton in organizing a women's rights convention in Seneca Falls in 1848; and she had continued to give spiritual leadership to the women's rights movement.

There is no record of Robert and Harriet Purvis attending any of the subsequent woman's rights conventions prior to the Civil War. But the fact that they both supported women's rights is obvious. At the time of the split in the American Anti-Slavery Society, Robert had voted for the election of Abby Kelley to a committee; at the various colored conventions, he had articulated his praise, and he honored the work of the antislavery women.[3]

Now that slavery was officially abolished, the women abolitionists had felt the time had come to work for suffrage for both blacks and women. Following the anniversary meeting of the American Anti-Slavery Society in 1866, the comrades gathered in May to organize the American Equal Rights Association, which was dedicated to obtaining the vote for both blacks and women. At the initial gathering, Lucretia Mott was elected president and Elizabeth Cady Stanton, vice president. In the call to the convention, the organizers outlined their argument:

> Let the gathering, then, at this anniversary, be in numbers and character, worthy, in some degree of the demands of the hour. The black man, even the black soldier, is yet but half emancipated, nor will he be, until full suffrage and citizenship *are secured to him in the Federal Constitution.* Still more deplorable is the condition of the black woman; and legally that of the white woman is no better! Shall the sun of the nineteenth century go down on wrongs like these, in this nation, consecrated since its infancy to justice and freedom? Rather let our meeting be pledge as well as prophecy to the world of mankind, that the redemption of at least one great nation is at hand.[4]

The following year, when Lucretia Mott was absent from the beginning of the meeting because of ill health, Purvis rose to speak on her behalf, saying that he believed that no one had accomplished more in the work of antislavery, and that it was her influence that had caused the Society to aspire to "a more comprehensive work for freedom."

> Our simple yet imperative demand, founded upon a just conception of the true idea of our republican government, is equality of rights for all, without regard to color, sex, or race; and inseparable from the citizen, the possession of that power, that protection, that primal element of republican freedom—the ballot.[5]

The Radical Republicans in Congress were pressing for a Constitutional Amendment, penalizing any state that denied any male resident over twenty-one the right to vote. The franchise was needed to protect the blacks from the efforts of many Southerners to terrorize them back into submission. It was also needed to keep the Republicans in power, since the Democrats otherwise controlled the vote in the South. In early 1868, when the abolitionist women learned that the word "male" was being inserted in the proposed language of the amendment, they were alarmed. Susan B. Anthony and Elizabeth Cady Stanton launched a newspaper, *The Revolution*, devoted to suffrage for women, and began collecting names for a giant petition asking that the word "male" be removed from the proposed amendment. Black women needed the protection of the franchise as much as black men, they argued, and if women were passed over in this amendment, it would be many years before they would be given the vote.

By the third meeting of the Equal Rights Association in May 1868, sides were drawn between those who supported suffrage for blacks alone, and those who desired to wait for a bill which gave suffrage to both blacks and women. The fact that Anthony and Stanton were receiving support for *The Revolution* from George Francis Train, an eccentric Copperhead, a Northern supporter of the South, who opposed the vote for blacks while supporting it for pure, educated women, alienated many. Frederick Douglass argued that for blacks it was a question of life and death:

> When women, because they are women, are hunted down through the cities of New York and New Orleans, when they are dragged from their houses and hung from the lampposts, when their children are torn from their arms, and their brains dashed out upon the pavement; when they are objects of insult and outrage at every turn; when they are in danger of having their homes burnt down over their heads, when their children are not allowed to enter schools; then they will have an urgency to obtain the ballot equal to our own.[6]

The black poet, Frances Ellen Watkins Harper, declared that when it was a question of race, she let the lesser question of sex go. But, she said: "The white women all go for sex, letting race occupy a minor position. If the nation could handle one question, she would not have the black women put a single straw in the way, if only the men of the race could obtain what they wanted."[7]

Robert Purvis was torn. No one felt more bitterly the sting of prejudice than he. But he remained convinced that all rights were indivisible. In the end, he alone of the blacks present supported the women's side.[8]

The split with Garrison had deepened Purvis's appreciation of James and Lucretia Mott, whose colleagues he had been for thirty years. Following the New York meetings in 1866, Purvis joined with Lucretia Mott in attending the meetings of the Pennsylvania Equal Rights Association, arguing for the inclusion of women's rights. On December 22, 1869, he was present at a meeting at Liberty Hall to found the Pennsylvania Woman Suffrage Association, where Mary Grew was elected president, and Robert's wife Harriet made a member of the executive committee.[9]

In February 1868, James and Lucretia Mott had gone to New York to visit their youngest daughter, Patty Mott Lord. At the Lords, James fell ill with pneumonia, which proved fatal. Purvis temporarily assumed the role of president of the Pennsylvania Anti-Slavery Society in James Mott's place, and attended his funeral, which was held at the home of Edward and Anna Mott Hopper on Clinton Street, Philadelphia. He delivered a eulogy, and then accompanied James Mott's casket to the Fair Hill Burial Ground. His tribute to James Mott was reprinted in the *National Anti-Slavery Standard*:

> We who have, during so many years, shared his labors in the antislavery field, who have been aided by his wisdom and blessed by his friendship, who in the dark and stormy days of our enterprise stood side by side with him, can testify to his deep, earnest, unwavering devotion to the cause of human freedom and equal rights for all men. Unmoved by obloquy, undaunted by peril, unwearied by years of labor, he kept the even tenor of his way, firm, gentle and just, refusing all compromise with wrong, claiming all human rights for the colored man, illustrating in his daily life, the religion taught in the Sermon on the Mount. . . . In our meetings for counsel we shall miss the lessons of his ripe experience and the inspiration of his presence, his patriarchal greeting and benediction; the abolitionists of the country will mourn the loss of a faithful coadjutor, the community in which he lived has lost a fellow-citizen of rare worth, and the colored people of this country, in the North and in the South, a friend indeed.[10]

In January 1869, Susan B. Anthony called a woman's suffrage convention, the first to be held since the war, and the first in Washington, D.C. Here again the former comrades argued against the Fifteenth Amendment. Most of the men present, including Edward M. Davis, Frederick Douglass, and Robert Purvis's own son, Dr. Charles Burleigh Purvis, responded that the black man needed the shield of suffrage to protect him from terror in the South. Robert Purvis disputed with Charles, favoring the women's position. According to Susan B. Anthony's later recollection, Purvis said: "If need be, I would prefer to bide my time for twenty years before I shall deposit a ballot, if at that time I may be allowed to take my wife and daughter with me to the ballot box."[11]

Martha Coffin Wright, accompanying her sister Lucretia Mott to the convention, wrote her husband David about it:

> Mr. Purvis's son Charles, a member of the Colored Convention, a physician in Washington, made an earnest protest against Mrs. Stanton's idea—After Downing and several others with Edward had spoken—Mr. [Robert] Purvis came forward and said that deeply as he felt the wrongs of his race, and anxious as he felt for that long delayed measure of justice, he could not help feeling the justice of your demand, and seeing the danger of so much added ignorance and bigotry to weigh down our cause therefore he must stand with us. You can imagine the vehement applause. He alluded to his son's arguments and his strong sympathy for them, but on the other hand, stood his daughter, palpitating in every nerve for the recognition of her rights.[12]

According to Martha Wright, Charles responded, saying that, of course, his sister's interests were as dear to him as his own and could anyone doubt that, as soon as his own rights were secured, theirs would be his first care.[13]

A reporter for the *Denver News*, covering the convention, reported on Robert Purvis's speech, saying that an elegant looking gentleman of sixty or over had risen from his seat and begun to speak, until Susan B. Anthony beckoned him to the platform. By the gaslight in the hall, he appeared to be white, the reporter said, but he was told he was Dr. Charles Purvis's father. He was also told that Robert Purvis was a man of wealth and culture, able "to surround his family with all the gratification of the intellectual, esthetic, and moral desires, and carefully developed his children at home and at the best schools into which they could gain admission."[14]

He spoke but a few words. They were all of a character of the generous impulse upon which he rose. In his gratitude for what those noble women had done for the colored race *with which he is identified*, he was willing to wait for the ballot for himself, his sons, and his race, until women were permitted to enjoy it.[15]

Troubles among the antislavery comrades continued. Following another tumultuous meeting of the American Equal Rights Association in 1869, Susan B. Anthony and Elizabeth Cady Stanton organized the National Woman Suffrage Association in May 1869; the Association was devoted to obtaining the vote for women. Other abolitionists/feminists, concerned about worsening conditions for blacks in the South, developed the American Woman Suffrage Association, under the leadership of Lucy Stone, in November 1869.

In 1870, Robert Purvis was unable to attend a convention of the newly organized National Woman Suffrage Association, held January 19 in Lincoln Hall in Washington, but addressed a letter to the group, supporting them; the letter ended with a justification for his own position:

> Censured as I may be for apparent inconsistency, as a member and officer of the American Anti-Slavery Society, in approving a movement whose leaders are opposed to the passage of the XV Amendment, I must be true to my own soul, to my sense of the absolute demands of justice, and hence, I say that, much as I desire (and Heaven knows how deeply through life I have antagonized therefor) the possession of all my rights as an American citizen, were I woman, black or white, I would resist, by every feeling of self-respect and personal dignity, any and every encroachment of power, every act of tyranny (for such they will be) based on the impious and infamous assumption of superiority of sex.[16]

On February 15, 1870, the new organization celebrated Susan B. Anthony's fiftieth birthday with a gala dinner in Riggs House. Robert Purvis presided, sitting on Susan B. Anthony's left, next to Isabella Beecher Hooker, while Elizabeth Cady Stanton and Senator Henry B. Blair, of New Hampshire, a supporter of woman's rights, sat on Susan's right.[17]

Robert Purvis's regard for women was based in part on his intimate connection with two impressive women, his mother, Harriet Judah Miller, and his wife, Harriet Davy Forten Purvis. Having raised her three sons to manhood, Harriet Judah had seen two, William and Joseph, die. She took an interest in Robert's many antislavery activities, including hiding fugitive slaves in her house on Seventh Street. She was interested in both Robert and Joseph's children, and entertained them frequently.

In the late fall of 1869, Harriet Miller, aged eighty-five, determined to visit her half-sister, Mary Bird, who lived in Charleston; she had not seen her sister in many years. Traveling by train, she made the trip successfully, but on her way home she evidently had a stroke. According to the newspaper account, she was "stricken with paralysis, which rendered her unconscious and helpless." Harriet Miller was taken to her home on Seventh Street in Philadelphia; she died a few days later.

Under the headline: "Internment of a Remarkable Woman," *Forney's Weekly Press* stated that she had been born a slave.

> While living in South Carolina, she became the property of Mr. Purves [sic!] to whom she was most faithful. Purves was a single man, and at one time, a conspiracy was formed among a band of desperadoes to take his life. His faithful slave got an inkling of the conspiracy and she advised her master of the plot, and by so doing saved his life. He shortly afterwards gave her her freedom and made her his wife.[18]

Another paper had a slightly different account.

> She was manumitted in her nineteenth year. While she was yet unmarried, she discovered a plot to take the life of William Purves, an Englishman, who was residing in Charleston as a merchant. Her information saved his life and he subsequently married her.[19]

Harriet had managed well the money left to her by William Purvis; she left an estate of $100,000 to Robert Purvis and his children. According to a later codicil, she left $500 to a niece, Sarah Judah Vickers, who had been living with her in the house on Seventh Street, which she had occupied for many years. If Sarah predeceased Harriet, the money was to go to her sister Mary Bird, "for her sole and separate use, free from the control of her husband."[20]

Harriet had maintained her membership in St. Thomas Episcopal Church. After a funeral service at her home on Seventh Street, she was buried in the cemetery of that church; William Aston presided according to her wishes. When the St. Thomas burial ground was closed in 1887, Robert Purvis moved the remains of his mother, as well as his brothers Joseph and William, to the Fair Hill Burial Ground where he had purchased a family lot.[21]

At the time of the death of his mother, Robert Purvis was preoccupied with concern for the worsening conditions of blacks in the Deep South. Reconstruction had been a bitter disappointment to all radical abolitionists, black and white. Robert Purvis had a personal stake in the matter, through his son Henry. Henry had gone to Columbia, South Carolina, in 1867 to serve as vice president of the Union League with the mandate of rallying blacks to exercise their suffrage. In 1868, he was elected as a delegate from Lexington County to the House of Representatives.[22] He wrote home of the efforts of the Southerners to regain control of the government.

The rebels are "moving Heaven and Earth" to carry the election next fall, and it will require all the energies of the Republicans to secure the success of Grant and Colfax. You can have no idea of the bitter and malignant feelings existing among these rebels against us. We are daily in expectation of an outbreak. It is reported that arms are being sent into the state by the Democracy of the North. In regard to the recent "affray," it was caused by some rebels attempting to force their way into a *house* occupied by a number of "colored" members of the Legislature, who in self-defense shot into them, killing one of the ruffians. Violent threats are made to blow us up, to drive us out of the State, etc. We are obliged to go armed, and keep close to our rooms at night.[23]

Robert published this letter and added his own bitter comment:

I suppose there is enough in the daily reports of murder, rapine, and blood, from the Southern section of our *"Converted"* country, to convince the obtuse, deluded and malignant enemies of our cause, that the jubilee for freedom has not yet come; and that the abolition of chattel slavery, about which there was so much idle prattling and affected exultation, is to a great extent practically void, and unsubstantial, and that warfare, earnest, persistent, aggressive warfare, is the need, and alike the pledged duty of every *consistent* and *faithful friend* and *advocate* of the Black Man's Cause.[24]

In addition to his anger about the treatment of his son Henry by Southern whites, Robert Purvis was outraged that his son Charles was being discriminated against because of his race. In 1869, Charles was appointed assistant surgeon of the Freedmen's Hospital, and at the same time, made a member of the medical faculty of Howard University, becoming the second black ever to teach medicine in an American university. As such, he was one of eight black doctors practicing medicine in Washington, D.C. Three of them, including Charles, applied for membership in the Medical Society of the District, affiliated with the American Medical Association; they were refused, clearly on the basis of race. Senator Charles Sumner introduced a bill in the U.S. Senate to repeal the charter of the Medical Society, but his legislation was not acted upon. Charles Purvis and his colleagues then organized an interracial National

Medical Society of the District of Columbia. This organization declared that the United States was the only country, and medicine the "only profession in which such distinction is made. Science knows no race, color or condition, and we protest against the Medical Society in the District of Columbia for maintaining such a distinction."[25]

Robert Purvis was incensed at the slight to his brilliant son, and to all black physicians. He wrote a letter to the editor of the *National Anti-Slavery Standard* enclosing an article from the *Washington Chronicle*, describing the action of the Medical Society; he once more attacked the Garrisonians who believed that the struggle was finished:

> Let me, however, in way of premise, say:—that this Devil of Caste, a very omnipresence, as daily events show, alike indicates the wisdom of faithful adherence to pledge and to duty of our honored and trusted friends, who are not impatient or tired in well-doing. "Anti-slavery work finished! The nation converted! The existence of the American Anti-Slavery Society an absurdity!" Such language may suit those who are not victims of this living death. What is life to us, when encircled and hampered by this accursed prejudice, we but agonize the torments of hell, or with deadened sensibilities exist in unserviceable barrenness. ROBERT PURVIS.[26]

Robert Purvis himself had hoped to play a role in reconstruction, but he never received the sort of appointment he had hoped for. In 1867, he had been approached by George B. Halsted, a member of Andrew Johnson's administration, about accepting the post of Commissioner of the Freedmen's Bureau then held by General Oliver Otis Howard. According to Halsted, Johnson planned to remove the General. Purvis was told that the president wanted a "colored man" in the post. In fact, Johnson had already approached Frederick Douglass, who had declined, and then made the offer to John Mercer Langston of Ohio; he had also refused.[27] Purvis apparently did not know of these previous efforts to recruit black candidates for the office. Nor at the time did he know much about General Howard. When he received the offer he decided to consult Wendell Phillips:

> I write for your judgment, and it is desired, by our friends here to whom I have submitted the matter, desiring, of course, first and last, as the only view to be taken, the effect upon the "good cause."—With me, in this matter—yr. Judgment "hangs the law and the prophets"—please let me have it at your earliest convenience.[28]

Wendell Phillips apparently counseled Purvis against accepting the bogus offer, as Purvis's next letter to Phillips makes clear:

> I beg yr acceptance of my heartfelt thanks—yr words command themselves to my judgment, and to that of every member of my family—with you, we now see, that the whole purpose of his execrable Excellency, to put a "colored" man in Gen. Howard's place is a mere "trick." I have learned that Halsted, who wrote me on the subject, stands in relations of private sec'y to the President—I hope his Excellency (!) Will be foiled in any attempt to shield himself from the indignation of the people which will be sure to follow his removal of Gen. Howard.[29]

There the matter ended. Purvis was evidently considered for other posts, but not until 1874 was he offered a government position. Meanwhile he came to admire General Howard, praising him in 1869 for the establishment of Howard University, where his son Charles taught medicine:

> You know that Gen. Howard, "fighting on *our* line," sees the necessity of securing to the "colored" race equal civil and political rights, hence, upon the broad and catholic basis of a common humanity, in the just exercise of large discretionary powers granted him by Congress, as well as laborious efforts in other directions, has erected the magnificent University (which bears his honored name) unequalled in architectural beauty by any institution of learning in this country, and to be unsurpassed in all of its departments for thorough and complete instruction. All honor, to the noble General for the work he has accomplished, and our heart in grateful feelings shall follow him in his continued efforts to make practical and permanent these ideas of justice, equality and freedom, for which the "American Anti-Slavery Society," in fulfillment of its pledges, so faithfully labors to accomplish.[30]

Along with other abolitionists, Robert Purvis was watching anxiously as the Fifteenth Amendment was ratified state by state. This took longer than expected. In December 1869, he signed a letter addressed to "Fellow Abolitionists" along with Lucretia Mott, Benjamin Bacon, William Still, and others, stating that it was necessary to continue the work of the American Anti-Slavery Society, and the publication of its paper, *The National Anti-Slavery Standard*, until ratification was secure:

> The personal freedom of the colored men in the South cannot be complete and secure without the right of suffrage. The ratification of the Fifteenth Amendment will so secure to them and to colored men in the

North this right, that they can never be deprived of it, except by the consent of three-fourths of the States of the Union. To promote this ratification is the end to which the American Anti-Slavery Society and its coadjutors are now working. . . . Now we appeal to you for a generous donation toward the support of the *Standard* until the work to which we are pledged shall be finished.[31]

When Pennsylvania voted for ratification in the spring of 1869, Robert Purvis was gratified, but angry that members of the Democratic Party had voted against the amendment in both branches of the Pennsylvania House. It brought back memories of the Reform Convention of 1838, which had stripped blacks of the right to vote. He was glad, he said, that Pennsylvania was among those states that had adopted the Fifteenth Amendment to the Constitution,

> . . . regretting however, the incompleteness of the Amendment in its provisions, in not ignoring sex as well as color. Thirty years ago the political disenfranchisement of the "colored' citizens of the State was effected, by the infernal Democracy in their mis-named "Reform Convention," and how consistently and persistently they have continued their persecution of their victims! From the profoundest depths of my indignant soul, I pledge eternal hostility to this accursed party, who makes to-day its record of infamy complete, in the unanimous vote in both branches of the legislature against passage of the Amendment.[32]

The ratification of the Fifteenth Amendment on March 30, 1870 was cause for rejoicing. At last the American Anti-Slavery Society had accomplished its goal, and could disband. Robert Purvis had been asked to speak at the final meeting, but he was prevented from attending by a heavy cold, a condition to which he was frequently subject. He had been present at every meeting but one since December 1833; he was deeply disappointed. He wrote instead, enclosing a short speech he had planned to make.

> How marvellous the change from that time to the present! It bewilders, it puzzles me, and fruition of the mighty change steals upon my senses, leaving me in a half-conscious existence of indescribable happiness![33]
> Free! absolutely, unconditionally free! Not that in body we were fettered, but invisible and corroding chains ever bore heavily their cankerous weight upon our soul. This, though long labored for, yet, as it seems, sudden emancipation, excites strange emotions. Is it to be wondered at? "A long communion tends to make us what we are." But still I joy in the happiness which this freedom gives.[34]

In the enclosed text of his speech, Purvis quoted Daniel Webster as having contemptuously referred to the Abolitionists as being engaged in a "rub-a-dub agitation." But that agitation had brought the members of the American Anti-Slavery Society to the realization of their goal and had all but changed the government into adhering to its original principles.[35]

> I say almost, for our government will not have perfected itself, as truly Republican, until administered in accordance with the received maxim or principle "by the consent of the governed," thereby repudiating all exercise of power and rule, founded not only upon conditions of race and color, but also that of sex . Then, Sir, and not until then, will we have a government "of the *whole* people and by the *whole* people."[36]

Purvis referred to the beginnings of the antislavery agitation, and to Benjamin Lundy, who was, he felt, its founder and pioneer. But he spoke also of all the noble men and women who had worked for so long, and so hard, for the present victory.

> And now, in parting words, allow me, Mr. President, to say, and not alone for myself—but as I feel assured, I represent the views of the large and intelligent class of the colored race, who with feelings of gratitude recognize the fact—that to your enlightened wisdom and sagacity, in the last five years, of imminent peril to our cause, (you gave the same unselfish devotion, in unceasing labor, as well as pecuniary aid, which marks preeminently for more than thirty years your connection with it), are they mainly indebted, under God, for the great benefaction which to-day invests them with all the rights and privileges of AMERICAN CITIZENS.[37]

In Philadelphia, blacks and their supporters celebrated the franchise on Tuesday, April 26, 1870. The Union League Club presented Octavius Catto, the teacher at the Institute for Colored Youth and a founder of the Pennsylvania State Equal Rights League, with a commemorative silk banner, and behind him a huge procession marched through the city streets and out to Horticultural Hall, across the river. There were marching bands, and regiments, and neighborhood groups in the lineup. At Horticultural Hall, the stage was filled with members of the Union League and other prominent citizens, among them Lucretia Mott, Robert Purvis, Passmore Williamson, Judge Paxton, and Colonel John W. Forney. After election of the officers of the day, Robert Purvis spoke, introducing the president, David B. Bowser, who in turn introduced Purvis as the first speaker of the evening.[38]

I am here, for the first time, by the highest constituted authority of the land to address you as "fellow citizens" regardless of your color, whether it be the cream of the Anglo-Saxons or shadowed bronzes of a burning sun. We are here to ratify the declaration that has become a truth, that "all men are created free and equal." I congratulate you on this new birth from death unto life. Slavery dead? No power on earth, none in hell, can alter that fiat. Let us be alive to our duties and responsibilities. I will not suggest what you should do. I know you will never forget the bridge that has carried you over to freedom, and as a fitting corollary, you will never forget your enemies—those who prate of this as a white man's Government. Where is the probate that devotes it to the white race! Our Democratic friends insist that this is a white man's country. This is their standing argument. This is the idea promulgated by their paper. The age is progressive: the age comes freighted with the joyful news of fetters falling—the joyful mind of freedom. I must stop, my voice has broken down. I say one word: I like the idea of our friend, Charles Sumner, who believes in cherishing a sacred animosity to all slaveholders.[39]

Among the resolutions passed by the euphoric gathering was one giving tribute to the "martyrs and apostles of liberty." The names mentioned included: John Brown, Abraham Lincoln, Ulysses S. Grant, Charles Sumner, William Lloyd Garrison, and Horace Greeley. Robert Purvis offered an amendment, which was adopted, that the name of Lucretia Mott be added to the list.[40]

Eight days later, Robert Purvis presided over the final meeting of the Pennsylvania Anti-Slavery Society, in which Lucretia Mott had been his colleague for more than thirty years. An epoch was ending.

CHAPTER 13

The Freedmen's Savings Bank

The Fifteenth Amendment was ratified, but blacks were quickly finding that it seemed to do little to overcome the effects of discrimination. Robert Purvis turned his remarkable energies to finding new ways to struggle for equality for blacks in the nation at large, and in his hometown, the City of Brotherly Love. He began to take a lively interest in city politics, in order to do what he could to protect black interests.

That protection was badly needed. There were rumors of racial violence on election day in 1870. The U.S. Marshal of the Eastern District of Pennsylvania sent in a company of Marines to maintain order, an action which the Democratic mayor of Philadelphia, Daniel M. Fox, protested vigorously, and the governor questioned. Nevertheless, there was little violence. The next year at election time, local police rather than federal troops were called in to restore order. This time there were bloody riots and three fatalities. On the morning of Tuesday, October 10, violence erupted at several of the river wards, resulting in the murders of two black men, Isaac Chase and Jacob Gordon. The mayor called out the state militia, and Octavius Catto, a major, went home to get his uniform. In front of his house at 814 South Street, he was accosted by a young man with a bandage around his head. When he turned to respond, the man shot him twice. Catto was mortally wounded and died instantly.[1]

Purvis was both grieved and angered by this murder. The year before, Catto's admission to the Franklin Institute as its first black member had resulted in public protests, bringing back memories of Purvis's son Robert's ejection from that institution.[2]

On October 13, 1871, a mass meeting was held at National Hall to express the community's indignation at the death of Catto, and the failure of the authorities to find the assassin. The majority of persons present were prominent white citizens; they passed a series of resolutions deploring the violence and the inefficiency of the police. They praised Catto. Robert Purvis was the first speaker: his talk, as paraphrased by the reporter from the *Public Ledger*, was conciliatory.

> He said he was present to give expression to that confidence and trust which inspired the action of colored citizens. The action of today gives assurance of protection to every American citizen. In the death of Mr. Catto, liberty has been strengthened. The blood of a black man was the first shed in the Revolution; the blood of a black man was the first shed in Baltimore during the Rebellion, and now let us hope that the blood of our friend will be the end of resistance to the right. For colored men he now demanded equal rights, in their fullest sense, so that citizenship may not be a mockery.[3]

As had been so often the case, Robert Purvis's confidence was misplaced. The assassin of Catto was identified as a man known as Frank Kelly, who had fled to Chicago after the murder. In 1877 he was discovered and arrested. William Forten, Harriet's youngest brother, was part of a delegation from the Republican Party which went to Chicago to identify him. Kelly was returned to Philadelphia, and brought to trial, but exonerated. It was a shattering blow to many blacks, who had really believed that things were going to be different. At the protest meeting, black minister J. Walker Jackson had asked: "Could it have been because of his erudition and his eloquence that his life was taken?" The audience responded: "That's it," and "That's right."[4]

Catto's funeral was attended by five thousand people, black and white alike. There was a funeral procession that included one infantry brigade, three regiments, eight military detachments, and 125 carriages. It took three hours to move down Broad Street, which was packed with spectators, to the Mount Lebanon Cemetery. Like other blacks, Purvis was gratified by this display of solidarity but infuriated that Mayor Daniel Fox, a Democrat, chose not to attend.[5]

In common with most of his contemporaries, Robert Purvis had put his reliance at first on the Republican Party. At a meeting at Liberty Hall in October 1871, he said, as paraphrased by the reporter, "that his instincts were averse to politics and that this was the first time he had appeared in Philadelphia to make a political speech. He knew something of parties and their leaders, but would not attempt to advise or direct his hearers how to vote. He took pride in knowing that the colored man, with that mighty instrument of power—the ballot—would cast it but one way and that was for the party that gave him the right to vote."[6]

He spoke of the troubles of the blacks in the South, and their martyrdom in supporting the Republican Party under the present circumstances. The president should use his mighty power to save them from outrage, and protect their precious right to vote.

> The enemies of the colored people in the South are of three classes of men who are at war with the colored race. They compose part of a respectable minority who insist that this is a white man's country, who have in our own city put forth a manifesto signed by twenty-five of their leaders, claiming such to be their views, and he regretted to see ex-Mayor Vaux's name at the head of it. He was galled by these continued attacks upon the colored man, and regretted that men claiming to be respectable and intelligent would permit the use of their names to be attached to such pernicious documents.[7]

He spoke of the attempt of Philadelphia mayor Fox and others to woo black voters by naming a school "James Fortin." If the spirit of Forten had been present, he said, he would have denounced Fox and others as enemies of his race. A third political party, the Citizen's Democratic Reform Party, was also trying to influence black voters, without providing them with the support and respect they deserved.[8]

In 1872, Robert Purvis was a delegate to the Republican National Convention held in Philadelphia on June 5; he was one of fifty black men present. "No more useful or influential man will sit among the delegates," John W. Forney, editor of the *Press*, commented. Purvis, however, was not so totally wedded to the Republicans that he did not feel free to criticize them, and even shift his vote whenever he felt the Republicans were not doing their duty by black voters.[9]

Thus, on March 10, 1874, he and his friend and colleague William Still held a meeting in Concert Hall in which they advised black voters to choose candidates not by party, but by the question of whom they thought would do the most for them. Purvis spoke, but the newspapers did not record his remarks. William Still gave the principal speech, entitled "On Laboring and Voting."[10] Some voters were enthusiastic. S. A. Newby wrote to William Still to praise their courage. "You and Purvis are the pioneers," he said. "You and Mr. Purvis have but taken the initiary steps in this direction which is destined ultimately to convulse this great nation. As Purvis has justly remarked, 'there are no rights or liberties for colored men to be put in jeopardy by the late municipal elections.'"[11]

Others were less enthusiastic. M. A. S. Carr wrote to complain that Robert Purvis was trying to pass for white. "I knew his mother, a tight-headed negro lady and a dear good woman. I am not surprised at him. They would marry their great-grandmother if white."[11] And William Still received an anonymous threat to burn down his coal yard addressed to "Mr. Nigger" though apparently written by an angry black man. Ultimately, the police had to protect him.[12]

In addition to persecution throughout the North, the blacks found they still had to deal with efforts to persuade them to leave the United States and colonize elsewhere. Robert Purvis had been fighting this concept for more than forty years. In 1871, he wrote to Gerrit Smith to congratulate him on the letter he had written on Grant's proposal to annex the Dominican Republic as a home for blacks, saying that Smith's opinion coincided with that of Charles Sumner. "I saw Mr. S. a few days ago in Washington, and he referred, with much feeling, to a letter he had from you and which he partly read to me—" Purvis wrote. He concluded the letter by enclosing a photograph of "our dear Lucretia Mott" and asked for an autographed photograph of Smith in return. (The exchange of photographs was a custom of the times.)[13]

Despite the efforts of allies like Smith, it was beginning to be apparent that in the postwar era blacks had made few gains. As one by one the promises of emancipation went unfulfilled, black voters began to look for ways to remind the country of the sacrifices their men had made during the Civil War. In May 1873, Robert Purvis spoke at a gathering of black leaders to discuss the upcoming Centennial of the Declaration of Independence, scheduled to be held in Philadelphia in 1876, saying he thought the celebration of one hundred years of American history would be a chance for the blacks to tell the truth about their contribution to the nation:

> We have been hypocrites and liars with respect to our real history long enough. We must tell the truth, which will reveal as an incontestable fact that the blood of a Negro was first shed for liberty in the Revolution, and that blacks had taken an active part in the War of 1812 and in our late Civil War for freedom.[14]

His interests in human rights remained broad. Shortly after speaking at the meeting to prepare for the Centennial he attended a meeting of the Universal Peace Union, a group to which Lucretia Mott and many of the former abolitionists belonged, to protest the government's policy of removing Native Americans from their homelands to reservations. A group of Modoc Indians, who had resisted this forced move by arms and had shot and killed a soldier, were to be hanged. The members of the Peace Union were outraged and prepared a protest in the Modocs' behalf. Purvis objected to the word "criminals" being used in relation to the Modocs. He said the Indians were not criminals, but heroes.[15]

But while active in Philadelphia, Robert's interests were shifting somewhat to Washington, D.C. His brilliant son, Charles, was making a name for himself in that city not only as a surgeon at the Freedmen's Hospital and a professor of obstetrics and diseases of women and children at Howard University, but also as a member of the small elite black community, composed of persons of light skin and education such as himself. He boarded in the home of Dennis Smallwood, a black civil servant, (along with his cousin, Sarah Purvis, daughter of Joseph Purvis, who was teaching school in Washington at the time), and participated in the rich cultural life of the District.[16]

Sometime in 1869, Charles met Ann Hathaway, daughter of Warren Hathaway and Hannah Peavey Hathaway, of Eastport, Maine who had been sent by the New England Freedmen's Aid Association to Richmond to teach the freedmen. Ann had moved to Washington in 1869 to take charge of the Home established by the National Association for the Relief of Destitute Colored Women and Children, during the Civil War. Then in January 1871, she was hired to teach at the Normal and Industrial Institute of Hampton, Virginia. She was white, and at thirty-eight, eleven years older than Charles. The two were married on April 13, 1871 and shortly thereafter moved to a house at 1118 Thirteenth Street, North West. Here, their daughter Alice was born in 1872, and a son, Robert, in 1874. Another of Robert's cousins, Charlotte Forten, boarded with them in 1872. Charlotte taught at the Sumner High School in Washington and later became a clerk in the U.S. Treasury Department.[17]

Despite this busy household, Ann Purvis continued to be active with a number of charitable organizations, as well as with the Unitarian Church. She was a volunteer at the Colored Home, finding placements for the orphaned children, as well as serving on the board.[18]

There are no family papers to help us understand how Robert and Harriet Purvis reacted to Charles' marriage to a white woman. There were subsequent interracial marriages in the family, but this was the first. Robert, who could have passed for white and had instead staked his life on identifying with the blacks, may have felt a twinge of regret, and so may the darker-skinned and proud Harriet. But their philosophy of accepting humans as individuals, of believing that there was "but one race, the human race," would indicate that they accepted the marriage fully, and later developments would bear this out.

Whether or not the Purvis family accepted the marriage, the black community in Washington did not. Later, when Charles and Anne sent their daughter to the white public school, Charles, a member of the District School Board, was criticized for "advancing his own interests by claiming to be Negro at the same time disdaining any association with the black people."[19]

At the time of the 1873 financial crisis, the board of trustees of Howard University announced to the medical faculty that they could no longer pay salaries. Only three members of the faculty stayed on under these conditions. One was Charles Purvis, who wrote General Howard: "While I regret the University will not be able to pay me for my services, I feel the importance of every effort being made to carry forward the institution and make it a success." Purvis remained an unpaid faculty member until 1906, when he resigned. (The following year the University began to pay salaries again.) Shortly after the suspension of salaries in 1873, Charles was elected secretary of the medical faculty, and worked hard to keep the medical school open. He has been credited with saving medical education at Howard.[20]

Despite not receiving a salary from Howard, Charles did well financially. He had learned from his father the importance of investing his money wisely, in real estate and other ventures. In 1878, when Frederick Douglass wanted to move to a larger home, Charles was able to make him the loan that made the move possible.[21]

Granville Purvis, the youngest son, having completed his studies at Howard University, had moved to Detroit, where he, too, became part of the black elite. He started as a clerk for a Dr. Samuel Watson; in 1873 opened his own pharmacy. He was also a man of affairs, serving as a director of Detroit River Savings Bank. Much later, in 1885, he entered into a partnership with a man called Peter J. Spieleses to run the Wolverine Nickel Works, plating and polishing metals. Granville remained committed to the radical causes his family espoused. In 1871, he wrote to the *National Anti-Slavery Standard,* to renew his subscription, saying that the *Standard,* "is the only thoroughly radical newspaper in the country."[22]

Henry Purvis had continued to live in South Carolina. He served two terms in the South Carolina legislature, voting with the conservatives unless the question was clearly one of race.[23] In 1870, he was elected Adjutant General and in April 1872, he married Ella Zenobia Barre, the daughter of a Frenchman, John Augustus Barre and his mixed-race housekeeper, Virginia Ann Ferrette. Robert and Harriet journeyed to South Carolina for the wedding. John W. Forney wrote of Robert's homecoming, after more than fifty years:

A few weeks since he returned to his native city, and was eagerly welcomed by his own people, and by many of the old citizens, who favorably remembered his father and mother, and had watched his career with friendly eyes. The changes wrought in this more than half a century were more than revolutionary. The stone rejected by the builders had become the head of the column.

Mr. Purvis stood among his kindred like another Rip Van Winkle, with the difference that he was not forgotten; and as he walked the streets of Columbia and received the ovation of his friends in Charleston, he saw and felt that, although slavery was dead and the old slave-lords deposed, the sun shone, the grass grew, the flowers bloomed, the birds caroled, and the waters ran, as when the magnates lived on the labors of others as good as themselves, and often died confessing that their bad work must come to a bitter end.[24]

Nine months after their marriage, Henry and Ella welcomed their first son, whom they called Robert, after his grandfather. The following year another son, Augustus, was born, and probably the year after, Charles. Ella had several miscarriages, then a daughter, Marie, was born in 1877, and much later another daughter, Louise, in 1895. A nephew of Ella's, Clarence Farrell, also lived with the Charleston Purvises.[25]

Henry continued to serve as state Adjutant General until the end of black rule in 1877. The election of Rutherford B. Hayes to the office of U.S. President, after a long drawn out dispute, was based on a compromise which included the withdrawal of federal troops from the South and thus the end of Reconstruction. Henry himself may have contributed to this result in South Carolina. In 1875, he was selected as one of five members of the Board of Canvassers to certify the results of a hotly disputed election for Governor between David Chamberlain, the Republican candidate, and Wade Hampton, the Democrat. Accusations of fraud were made both by and against this board, in an election that dragged on for months, resulting in both men claiming victory, and two separate sets of legislators claiming to represent the state. Finally the Hayes administration intervened in favor of the Democrats. They declared Wade Hampton to be governor, the Democratic legislators to control the South Carolina House of Representatives in Columbia, and the Democratic electors who had voted for Hayes to be victorious. Both Henry Purvis and Robert Smalls were later accused of accepting favors in return for using their power on the Board of Canvassers in ways favorable to the Democrats.[26]

On the other hand, as Adjutant General, Henry had warned Governor Chamberlain that state arms were in the hands of white rifle companies, some of them the Red Shirts, who prevented blacks in rural areas from voting, and thus were able to swing the election to the Democrats and Hampton.[27]

Moving to Charleston, Henry found it hard to find employment to support his rapidly growing family; starting in 1880, he accepted a series of federal jobs including Inspector of Customs for the Port of Charleston—a position which entailed the granting of much patronage—bailiff in the Federal Court in Charleston, and clerk in the office of the United States Marshal. Since federal patronage was now in the hands of the so-called Half Breeds, Congressmen favoring the South, he was regarded by some as a traitor.[28]

In 1880, the *Philadelphia Times* ran a racist article, datelined Columbia, South Carolina, and entitled: "How the Negro Lost Self Government," blaming the blacks themselves for their overthrow after the withdrawal of federal troops, and singling out Francis Cardozo, Robert Smalls, William Whipper, and Henry Purvis:

> . . . the shrewd and unscrupulous Purvis, who dishonored an honored name in Philadelphia . . . Purvis was a prominent leader in the House as chairman of a most important committee, and he did as much as any one to hasten the overthrow of negro rule. He now resides in Charleston and is a beneficiary of the national government.[29]

Robert evidently felt that Henry had compromised; relations between father and son became cool, then frosty. The two were never reconciled.

Robert himself had never given up his hope of serving the government during the Reconstruction period. In 1874, he had finally been chosen for a government job, as one of three commissioners of the Freedmen's Saving Bank, charged with the difficult task of winding down its affairs after its failure.[30]

This institution had been initiated at the same time as the Freedmen's Bureau and had operated thirty-four branch banks in every state of the South and in New York, Pennsylvania and the District of Columbia. The object was to give the freedmen a safe place to deposit their savings, as well as to make small loans to worthy projects. It was, however, not well managed and made large investments in risky enterprises, including the Union Pacific Railroad and Jay Cooke and Company. With the financial collapse of Cooke in the 1873 Depression, the bank verged on disaster. In April 1874, Charles Purvis, a member of the board of managers, urged that Frederick Douglass be appointed to manage the bank. Douglass accepted, eager to save the bank. He even invested some money of his own in an attempt to ward off failure. He soon concluded, however, that it was financially unstable, and recommended that it be closed in June.[31]

The board concurred and appointed three commissioners, John Creswell, a Radical Republican, who had served in Congress during the Civil War and was Postmaster General in 1869–1874, with a reputation of appointing blacks to office; R. H. T Leipold, a Treasury accountant, and Robert Purvis. Though there had been a recommendation against nepotism, Robert obviously owed his appointment, at least in part, to his son. He understood his assignment as representing blacks on the commission, and acted accordingly. Critics claimed he did little of the work of the bank, other than signing checks, and keeping a watchful eye on black interests.[32]

The commissioners were to receive a salary of $3,000 a year and were required by the Secretary of State to make a joint bond of $100,000. They had their offices in the bank's Washington headquarters, a tall, elegant structure at 1507 Pennsylvania Avenue, flanking Lafayette Square, and diagonal to the White House. It had been built at the cost of a quarter of a million dollars, and featured filigreed walnut cages where the bank tellers worked.[33]

The duty of the commissioners was to close up the branch banks, consolidating remaining funds in Washington, manage the properties that the bank owned and eventually selling them, collecting debts owed to the bank, settling claims, and paying dividends to the depositors when funds became available.[34]

It was heartbreaking work. Many small town Southern blacks had put their tiny savings in the bank, as recommended to them by Reconstruction workers, and now faced the pitiful downfall of their dreams of owning land. Many felt distrustful of the new commissioners, hearing rumors that it was the Democrats who had closed the bank. Some feared that Leipold was a thief. As a result, many small depositors refused to turn in their passbooks, or sold them for a fraction of their value to unscrupulous traders. They therefore missed receiving funds when a 20 percent dividend was declared on November 1, 1875; 10 percent on March 20, 1878, and 20 percent on September 1, 1880. Though the dividends were announced in the black press, many other depositors failed to come forward, and they were never found.[35]

Among the persons who invested their small savings in the Freedmen's Bank may have been some relatives of Robert Purvis. In Charleston, South Carolina, Margaret, the widow of a William Purvis, and her sons Thaddeus Purvis and Thomas Baker, had become depositors in the

Charleston Bank on October 30, 1871. William Purvis was earlier listed in the Charleston Free Negro Capitation tax books, 1863 as a stevedore, with a net worth of $1,950. There was also a Harriet Purvis, a seamstress, worth $10 in the enumeration the following year, as well as several blacks named Judah. These relationships remain obscure.[36]

The commissioners' work was made more difficult by constant wrangling among the commissioners. Leipold, appointed by the U.S. Treasury, was regarded as a thoroughly unpleasant man, even by his supporters. He had no use for blacks, and treated Robert Purvis with constant disrespect, refusing to turn away from his work in order to speak to him, and smoking heavily in the office despite Purvis's pleas for him to abstain. He was also rude to the blacks with whom he was required to deal.[37] As the only accountant among the three, he was forced to do the bulk of the work, a situation about which he complained bitterly. At one point Creswell commented on Leipold:

> Mr. Leipold is a very competent accountant. I believe he has faithfully and rigidly looked after the interests of the depositors, but he is the most disagreeable person with whom I have ever associated. His temper and manners are exceedingly disagreeable and at times, almost insupportable.[38]

After Leipold complained to the U.S. Treasury that he was being forced to do all the work, Purvis spoke in his usual hyperbole:

> In making such a sneaking assault [Leipold] was guilty of an act of perfidy so treacherous that there is no parallel in the scope of my experience of bad men and bad acts. I paid Leipold $500 purely as a benefaction on account of his sniveling whining about his poverty. There was, however a faithfulness in the discharge of his duties.[39]

Creswell and Purvis experienced some friction in their relations at first, but soon made common cause against Leipold. The Secretary of the Treasury worked almost exclusively with Leipold, thus deepening tensions. When it was necessary to hire lawyers, Purvis wanted to employ blacks, but Leipold refused. The accountant also constantly threw suspicion on the trustees, including Charles Purvis, implying he had benefited from his dealings with the bank.[40]

In 1876, a Congressional Committee was appointed to investigate the affairs of the bank and the work of the commissioners. Chaired by a southerner, Beverly Brown Douglass of Virginia, who had served in the Confederate Army, the Douglass Committee was scathing in its condemnation of the former bank trustees, blaming the blacks and the Radical Republicans. A similar committee set up in the Senate under B. K. Bruce of Mississippi, a black, was equally critical. Reporting to the Senate in 1880, the Committee recommended that the Commissioners be discharged, and the work handled by the Comptroller of the Treasury.[41]

Despite all the negative criticism and the constant wrangling, the commissioners proved to have fulfilled their function fairly well. In the end, they had paid what depositors they could reach 40 percent in dividends, had left the accounts in fairly good order, and had disposed of most of the property belonging to the bank.[42]

Robert Purvis believed throughout the ordeal that the bank would eventually pay its debts in full. When Frederick Douglass wrote to him in 1878 wishing to withdraw his $2,000 note before expiration of its term, Purvis begged him to reconsider.

> I have learned through Mr. Leipold that you wish the anticipated payment upon yr note, to the am't of two thousand dollars.
>
> The balance due is not payable until Sept 1st'/79—the security is quite good, in *every* respect, and I believe, that the money, for me "Is doing the most good," *where it is*—I beg therefore to decline yr offer, preferring to wait until the expiration of the time for payment—I would now, if agreeable to yrself, substitute the obligation of a new note, extending the time, to a fair estimate of our life's time here, ten years. What say you?[43]

Douglass refused the extension. Other creditors did likewise, and before Purvis could realize his hopes, Congress acted on the recommendation of the Bruce Report, prepared by a committee of the 46th Congress, that the work of the commissioners was terminated in 1881.[44]

For Robert Purvis, it was a blow, one more proof that the nation cared little for the rights of the black man. He had struggled throughout his tenure at the Freedmen's Bank to represent the interests of the small black investors; he had continued to believe until the very end that it was going to be possible to salvage their dreams.

Despite their disagreement over the future of the bank, the relationship between Robert Purvis and Frederick Douglass had warmed slightly over the years. In 1876, the two were chosen to accompany the body of Vice President Henry Wilson from Washington, D.C. to his home state of Massachusetts, together with a third black man, a fact which Frederick Douglass chose to mention in his autobiography. However, it was not until 1886 that a full reconciliation occurred. Robert Purvis authorized his son Charles to deliver to Douglass the message:

"You may say to Mr. Douglass, I will meet him cordially and rub out from memory all of the unpleasantness of the past."[45]

In order to give his full attention to the work of winding up the affairs of the Freedmen's Bank, Robert Purvis commuted back and forth to Washington, making his home there with Charles and Anna at 1118 Thirteenth Street, NW. With their sons grown and gone, and only Hattie and Georgianna at home, Harriet and he had little use for Harmony Hall with its empty bedrooms, and the long commute into Philadelphia. In June 1873, they purchased a residence at 1601 Mt. Vernon Street in Philadelphia from a John and Bertha McDowell. A few months later they moved there, returning to the city after an absence of over thirty-one years. Perhaps finding it hard to break all ties, they retained the farm, renting it to members of the Pierce family, until April 1881, when Robert sold the house and remaining acres to Thomas and Tacy Hall.[46]

Robert Purvis was sixty-four at the time of his appointment to the Freedmen's Bank. He was approaching the status of an elder statesman, honored in both Philadelphia and Washington. It should have been a rich time in his life. Unfortunately, it was shadowed by the illness of his beloved Harriet. She developed a sore throat and a cough, and it soon became apparent that she was suffering from the consumption which had carried away two of her sons.

To make matters worse, as Harriet became alarmingly ill, things began to go very wrong with members of her Forten family. In January 1875, her older unmarried sister, Margaretta, died of pneumonia. Margaretta had always been present to live in the household of her aged mother Charlotte, to manage the affairs of the Forten family, and to take a lively interest in her sister's children. Then in April her sister Sarah, who had been fighting to hold on to her farm in Bucks County, gave up the struggle, declared bankruptcy, and moved into the city to take the place of Margaretta in the household of Charlotte Forten.[47]

On June 11, 1875, Harriet died, bringing to an end a companionship of forty-four years. Robert did not want to bury her at the cemetery at St. Thomas Episcopal Church, which was threatened with relocation, nor at Byberry, now that they had moved away from that community. He decided to buy a lot at the Fair Hill Burial Ground at Ninth and Cambria, owned by the Green Street Meeting of the Religious Society of Friends, where his longtime comrade James Mott was buried. Here Harriet Davy Forten Purvis was laid to rest on June 14, 1875.[48]

Harriet and Robert's marriage had been a happy one, according to all observers. Robert had respected his wife's many talents, and had made it possible for her to exercise them, employing what help she needed to run her household and still have time for public affairs. It had come close to being a marriage of equals, rare in the nineteenth century. Harriet clearly loved and admired her handsome and well-spoken husband. They should have been able to look forward to many happy retirement years together. To lose her when she was just sixty-five was cruel. For several years, Purvis grieved. "Old age is not desirable," he frequently told his son Charles.[49] The fact that Georgianna was also ill with tuberculosis did not help. In July 1877, Georgianna died and was buried on July 14 in the grave with her mother at the Fair Hill Burial Ground. She was just twenty-seven.[50]

Both Harriet and Georgianna had been deeply loved by their Byberry neighbors. One of these, Tacie Townsend, a poet who had been close to both Harriet and Hattie, had been a friend of Charlotte; she had written a poem about Joseph. Following Harriet's death, Tacie often visited Hattie and Georgianna at the house on Mt. Vernon Street, nursing Georgianna as she grew ill. In the course of these visits, she had grown to know Robert better. He was seventeen years her senior, a huge gap when they were younger, but less formidable at his sixty-five to her forty-eight.

On March 5, 1878, Robert Purvis and Tacie Townsend were married in a Quaker ceremony in Bristol, Bucks County. Whether any members of his family objected to his marrying a white woman is not known. Charles had married Ann, and Henry's wife Ella was very light-skinned. Robert, moreover, would have felt that "complexional differences" should not be considered important in this relation of his life, as in any other. He was proud of Tacie's accomplishments as an author, and supported her in her work. Later, when Frederick Douglass shocked the black community in 1882 by marrying a white woman, Purvis defended him, saying it was nobody's business but his.[51]

In 1878, Tacie's first book, *Abi Meredith*, a collection of stories and poems, was published by the Friends Book Association. This book was evidently in press before her marriage, for it bears her maiden name, Tacie Townsend. The preface, however, is signed T. T. Purvis. A second book followed three years later, *Hagar, the Singing Maiden*, published in Philadelphia by Walton and Company, and bearing her married name, T. T. Purvis. In this second volume, Tacie included the poem she had written at the time of the death of Joseph Purvis, "The Martyr Student," as well as a series of poems on the Underground Railroad. There were sketches of her early life as a student at the Byberry Friends School, and several poems on women's rights.[52]

For marrying a man "not in membership with Friends," Tacie was visited by a committee of women Friends from the newly formed Bristol Monthly Meeting. They reported that "her marriage had been accomplished without any violation of our testimonies, but she had no desire to continue [as] a member of the Society of Friends." She was subsequently removed from membership.[53]

Six months after Robert Purvis's marriage to Tacie Townsend, his niece by marriage, Charlotte Forten, married, on December 19, 1878, Francis James Grimké, pastor of the First Presbyterian Church in Washington, D.C. Grimké was the natural son of Henry Grimké, the Charleston lawyer who had represented the Purvis family in suing for unpaid debts owed their father, and a slave woman, Nancy Weston.

The Grimké sisters, Sarah and Angelina, who had belonged to the Philadelphia Female Anti-Slavery Society and had known Harriet Purvis, had discovered the existence of three illegimate biracial nephews, Archibald, Francis and John, at the end of the war. The sisters acknowledged them, and supported their enrollment in Lincoln University in Pennsylvania. John showed no aptitude for higher education, but Archibald and Francis thrived and went on to distinguished careers. Francis Grimké and Robert Purvis's son Charles became fast friends, and corresponded for many years.[54]

During his years at the Freedmen's Bank, Robert Purvis continued with his many commitments to equal rights in Philadelphia. In 1875, he was in Philadelphia for the 100th anniversary of the founding of the Pennsylvania Abolition Society, to participate in a program coordinated by his old friend William Still, who had finally been elected to membership in 1867. The celebration was held in Bethel Church and Robert Purvis reminded the audience that this was the very spot in which his honored father-in-law, James Forten, had presided over the first meeting to protest colonization.[55]

Again in 1876, he was in Philadelphia for the opening of the Centennial Exposition. This proved a bitter disappointment. The fact that the organizers of the fair ignored the blacks, after all their preparation, was a cause for grief. A guard at first refused to seat Frederick Douglass, who had a ticket to the opening ceremonies. The commissioners did not make room for an exhibition honoring the blacks who had fought for their country. The black community had collected money from all over the country to erect a permanent statue of a black hero, Richard Allen, at the fair. The black sculptor, Edmonia Lewis, was commissioned to make the edifice on which the likeness of Allen was to sit, in her studio in Rome. Hopes were high for its installation. Instead, the officials grudgingly gave the committee a small plot of land behind the other buildings, and told them that the statue must be removed at the end of the fair. The installation was postponed from week to week due to a series of problems. Finally, en route to the fair, the edifice was destroyed in a train wreck, and only a small dispirited group gathered to see the bust alone installed in a pouring rain just a few days before the exhibition closed. Purvis and his colleagues were disheartened.[56]

During these years, he did not neglect his interest in women's rights. While in Washington, Robert Purvis had attended the meetings of the National Woman's Suffrage Association whenever he was able. In 1877, he could not attend, but wrote a letter to Elizabeth Cady Stanton to be read at the convention, congratulating her on the progress of the cause:

> Wherever I have been, and with whomsoever I have talked, making equal rights invariably the subject, I find no opposing feelings to the simple and just demands of our cause. The chief difficulty in the way is the indifference of the people: they need an awakening. Some Stephen S. Foster or Anna Dickinson should come forward, and with their thunder and lightning, arouse the people from their deadly apathy. I am glad to know that you are to have with you our valued friend, E. M. Davis of Philadelphia. We are indebted to him more than all for whatever of life is found in the movement in Pennsylvania. He has spared neither time, money, nor personal efforts.[57]

Working with the Citizen's Suffrage Association of Philadelphia, Robert Purvis called on Lucy Webb Hayes, the wife of Rutherford Hayes, nineteenth president of the United States, to present an address adopted by that society, calling for the suffrage for women.

> I have just returned from a very satisfactory and delightful interview with Mrs. Hayes. She received me most cordially. I read to her the eloquent address from the Citizen's Association. She listened with marked attention, was grateful for the high favor conferred upon her, and sent her best wishes for the success of the cause. I made reference to the fact that the address bore the honored name of Lucretia Mott, which she received with a ready acknowledgment of her great worth and usefulness and her distinguished place as a reformer and philanthropist.[58]

CHAPTER 14

"We are To the Manner Born"

$\mathcal{A}$t the national convention of the Republican Party, held on June 2, 1880, there was wrangling between two groups, the "Stalwarts," who wanted to elect General Ulysses S. Grant, and the "Half Breeds," who nominated James A. Garfield. A compromise was reached after Chester A. Arthur, a Stalwart, was made the vice presidential nominee. In the November election Garfield won an extremely tight election, but left a much-divided Republican Party, which quarreled over cabinet appointments. In July 1881, a disappointed office seeker, Charles J. Guiteau, shot and killed the newly elected President Garfield at the Washington Railroad Station. Dr. Charles Burleigh Purvis was the first doctor to arrive on the scene to attend the dying president, a fact which made the black community in general, and his father Robert Purvis in particular, very proud. In recognition of his care of Garfield, he was appointed surgeon-in-chief of the Freedmen's Hospital by President Chester A. Arthur.[1]

At the time of the assassination of President Garfield, Robert Purvis was no longer in Washington, his role as commissioner of the Freedmen's Savings Bank having ended in April 1881. Shortly thereafter, he had moved back to Philadelphia permanently, to live with Tacie and Hattie in the house on Mt. Vernon Street. Settled at last, Purvis began to play a role as elder statesman in the black community and in city politics.

Philadelphia had grown beyond recognition from the colonial city of 135,000 persons he had known in 1820 to a city of 847,000 in 1880. The influx of southern blacks had raised the black population to approximately 31,700 in 1880. At the same time, the arrival of Irish working-class families had slowed. Most of the black newcomers were former slaves, starting out as unskilled laborers; they competed for jobs with other newly arrived immigrants. Racial tensions continued.[2]

In appearance, the city had also changed beyond recognition, stretching far west beyond the Schuylkill River, and spreading to the north and south. The new Industrial Age produced factories along the two rivers that distinguished Philadelphia. The Pennsylvania Railroad was erecting a giant station in the center of the city, across the square from the elaborate new city hall building which was rising in the old center square. A statue of the founder, William Penn, sat waiting to be mounted on its tower. Elsewhere, architect Frank Furness was designing a series of graceful buildings: the Pennsylvania Academy of the Fine Arts (1876), the Library Company (1879); the Unitarian Church at Twentieth and Chestnut Street, the library at the University of Pennsylvania.[3]

Along with the growth of industry had come corruption in government. Mayor William Stokley, who had begun as a reformer, was widely thought to be receiving bribes and kickbacks, and the police were said to be under the control of the Gas Ring. Any efforts of the incipient labor unions to strike was put down brutally by the police and sometimes the Marines.[4]

If he felt a little like Rip Van Winkle, Robert Purvis at seventy-one was far from retiring. Having struggled long and hard for the vote, he was determined that blacks should get the most advantage for casting their ballots, and should back those politicians who seemed to offer the best hope of providing jobs and advancement. This did not always mean backing the Republican Party.

Never totally dedicated to the Republicans, Robert Purvis had been further disenchanted by the actions of President Rutherford B. Hayes in 1877, when he withdrew federal troops from the South. He had also been angered when the City of Philadelphia had done nothing to see that space was devoted to black history in the 1876 Centennial Exhibition. The fact that the murderer of Octavius Catto had been exonerated in two separate trials infuriated him. And most exasperating of all, the Republicans in power in Philadelphia provided no jobs of any importance to the blacks.[5]

While his brother-in-law, William Forten, remained faithful to the Republicans, Purvis had voted for a reform candidate in 1877 against the Republican incumbent Mayor William Stokley. When Stokley won again and continued to ignore black demands, Purvis became determined to make a difference in the next election. In 1880, he accepted appointment to the Committee of 100, a group of leading independent Philadelphia citizens with a bent toward reform, and backed the election of Samuel King, a reform Democrat, as mayor. King won, and shortly appointed four carefully picked black men to the police force. When asked about this action, he said he had attended a Quaker school and thought it was the right thing to do. Robert Purvis and William Still organized a victory celebration at Liberty Hall where two thousand people gathered to mark this advance for Philadelphia blacks.[6]

In his speech on this occasion, Purvis reviewed the history of the abolition of slavery, and the passage of the Fifteenth Amendment, that gave blacks the right to vote.

> We were given the right to vote, but were still denied our right to participate in the government, excepting to deposit our ballots. In this condition we stagnated until we unexpectedly found in the chair of the chief magistrate of this city an honest man. His action in appointing colored policemen was due to no outside pressure. It was not expected of him but originated in his own sense of justice. Only congratulations have greeted him in the act. Not a whisper of dissent has even come from the police force.[7]

Purvis corrected himself. One policeman, a Mr. Jordan, had resigned, refusing to serve "by the side of men whose faces were shadowed by the livery of the burning sun." His scornful remarks about this man were vintage Purvis:

> He awoke to find himself in the detestable pre-eminence of the biggest fool in Philadelphia. He is proud of his white skin. I can tell him that he comes of a lineage that he would be sorry to learn about. This graceless and impudent scoundrel dares to set himself in the way of the progress of a race that never harmed him. Here I brand and gibbet him in the scorn of popular opinion as a man who dared to raise his atheistical voice against the everlasting God.[8]

Later Purvis said of King that "the only man in Philadelphia who ever carried out those principles of equality, which the Republican Party professed, was Samuel King, a Democrat."[9]

By the time of the next election, King had appointed fifty-five blacks to the police force. Nevertheless the Seventh Ward, where most of the black vote was congregated, was now under the control of the Republican machine, and voted overwhelmingly for King's opponent, William Smith. One of Smith's first acts in office was to fire Lewis Carroll, one of King's original four black appointments. Thereafter most city jobs went to blacks who were party loyalists. They were placed in lowly positions, and their progress was painfully slow.[10]

Robert Purvis continued to campaign on the issue of more employ-ment for blacks in meaningful jobs, backing whatever candidate he thought most likely to aid the blacks. In 1882, he met with the reform Re-publicans, and in 1884 he sat on the dais at a rally for Benjamin Butler of the Greenback Labor Party. When the head of the Philadelphia De-partment of Public Works, German-born General Wagner, treated a black job applicant unfairly in 1889, Purvis called him an "alien," by which he meant a person who was not a native American. He castigated Wagner at the end of a "brilliant and temperate speech" he had prepared for an occasion to celebrate the twenty-fifth anniversary of freedom, an event sponsored by the Pennsylvania Abolition Society and arranged by William Still.[11]

Describing how an educated black man had come to him for advice, having been turned down by two prominent public officials, Purvis said he had inquired after the applicant's qualifications, and had assured him he would have no difficulty.

> On the contrary, he was treated like a dog and ordered out of the presence of this alien. The applicant was an American born citizen. The two offi-cials to whom he applied for employment were aliens.[12]

Purvis did not say who the other "alien" was, but the name of the man he meant was whispered around the audience. "This was freely com-mented on after the adjournment of the meeting, which took place amid considerable confusion," the *Press* reporter commented.[13]

In 1883, the U.S. Supreme Court had ruled in five separate deci-sions that the Civil Rights Act of 1875, which had been introduced by Charles Sumner, and vigorously supported by the Pennsylvania Equal Rights League, did not apply to social, but only to political rights. The Court had argued that the Fourteenth Amendment prohibited invasion by the states of civil rights, but did not protect the invasion of civil rights by individuals. Thus, national redress for discriminatory practices was de-nied, and the concept of "separate but equal" introduced.

This ruling, plus continuing news of the lynchings and persecution of blacks in the Deep South, caused Purvis to despair of change. In 1886, word of lynchings in Carrolton, Mississippi reached Philadelphia blacks. The Afro-American League called a protest meeting at the Musical Hall Fund on May 17, 1886, chaired by Robert Purvis, which published several "resolutions of indignation." He pleaded that he was physically unable to perform the duties of chair, but he was shouted down. When he stepped onto the podium, he was greeted with wild applause; it was a few moments before he could calm the crowd, and begin to speak in a "rich, round, full voice."[14]

> My blood boils when I see the gingerly, mealy-mouthed manner in which the press of my country has handled the subject. I am almost compelled to believe we are looked upon as aliens. We are to the manner born; we are native Americans.[15]
>
> I read an article recently relative to the Colonization Society, headed, "Africa for the Africans." There is not a single African in the United States. Simultaneously with the landing of the Pilgrim fathers in 1620 came a slave ship from Africa into the Virginia colonies. Congress stopped the miserable trade in 1808. The Reverend Bryon Sutherland, of Washington, recently delivered an address on colonization in a church in this city. He said colored men are waiting and watching to be wafted to Liberia. This clerical wolf, who has stolen the livery of heaven to serve the devil in, tells a lie. I wonder at the man's audacity and impudence. This is the land of our birth. Here we will live and here we will die.[16]

Purvis next attacked Welsh Dulles, the treasurer of the Colonization Society, who was repeating the assertion that black men and women were eager to go to Africa. Why did these "superannuated fossils" go about the country raising funds for "Africa for the Africans?" It was a tremendous fraud and a hatred of the black race. "The Colonization Society has no desire to do good for the African descendants."[17]

> The first clause in its [The Colonization Society] charter says: "To Liberia or anywhere else." Yes, we may go to hell—but we are not going. The fathers of the white race drove out the red man and forced the black man in. Our claim to remain here comes from the blood and sweat which has enriched the soil. Let any set of men get up an association to send back the Irish, the German, or the Italian. Don't you think there would be indignation meetings from all classes of foreigners?[18]

Purvis ended with a plea for black men to vote for Samuel King, and sat down to great applause.

What was desperately needed in Philadelphia was better jobs for blacks. Black women were primarily employed as domestics, though a few became wig makers and caterers. An apparent chance for them to enter the garment industry in numbers came in 1890 when a large number of garment workers, primarily Jewish women from Eastern Europe, struck for better working conditions. The Reverend B. F. Christian, new pastor of Shiloh Baptist Church, thought this might be an opportunity. He persuaded Robert Purvis, along with the lawyer T. J. Minton, to call upon the Blum brothers, spokesmen for the manufacturers, to ask for jobs for black women. After several weeks, Gabriel Blum announced that the industry would now be open to black women.[19]

There was jubilation in the black community, but it was short-lived. It soon became apparent that the garment manufacturers meant only to give the black women piecework to do at home, rather than jobs in the factories. When the strike was settled, even the piecework dwindled. Discrimination against black workers in the garment industry continued to be the order of the day for many, many years.[20]

In terms of public employment, what was needed in Philadelphia was legislation mandating that the candidates for city office with the highest test scores get the jobs. Under current regulations, the supervisor could hire whom he wanted, as long as the person had passed a test. Thus, whites with Ds were regularly appointed, while blacks with As were passed over. Black Councilman Constantin Hubert, representing the Fifth Ward, tried to introduce legislation into the City Council which would put a black candidate on the same footing as his white counterpart. When the Council refused to pass such legislation, claiming it did not have jurisdiction to pass laws covering Philadelphia County, Hubert and his friends decided to try Harrisburg. In November 1890, Robert Purvis was present at a meeting with city councilmen to discuss a bill to be sent to the state legislature. He spoke with his usual eloquence:

> It seems to me that to every unperverted mind these things which Mr. Hubert has mentioned are common sense. As colored people we labor under the terrible proscription of caste, and that is destructive of the rights of citizens. We claim that we should have the rights of every other citizen. It seems to me that the mere fact of the difficulties under which we labor, and that we are proscribed from all the advantages and benefits of citizenship, are too plain to make it necessary to draw special attention to them. The time has come when we should assert our rights.[21]

The following March, Purvis accompanied Hubert and others in presenting an Equal Rights Bill to the Senate at Harrisburg. The bill had reached a second hearing in April when he chaired "an immense gathering" at the Musical Fund Hall to hear a report on the bill's progress. Hubert reported that one of the senators had asked: "Have you not messengers, policemen, and doorkeepers?"[22] Purvis answered indignantly,

He did not ask us, "Have you a lieutenant of police? Have you a member of the Park Commission? Have you a member of the Board of Public Charities? If a few are raised to a place of higher citizenship, it will advance the rest of the race.[23]

Despite all the enthusiasm, and all the effort, the senate found a way to bury the Equal Rights Bill, and it never came up for a vote.[24]

Robert Purvis had been active in the fight against prejudice for almost sixty years. He continued valiantly, but he felt increasingly isolated among younger men and women. Many of his old comrades were gone. While still living in Washington, he had reconciled with his old hero and later nemesis, William Lloyd Garrison. Garrison apparently made the first overture. Writing to Purvis in November 1878, he told of his plan to submit a picture of George Thompson to *Harpers Weekly*. He went on to deplore President Rutherford B. Hayes's "conciliatory" policy to the South, and ended with an old rallying cry: "Yours to giving the enemy no quarter." Purvis responded warmly:

> I have several letters from Mr. T., the first on shipboard from Liverpool, on the eve of his embarking for this country in 1834—and another of especial interest from New York, soon after my arrival from England. This latter, is a letter of wonderful power and eloquence, it refers mainly to yrself & the "Liberator."
>
> Spending an evening at our dear Lucretia Mott's, I took with me this letter and one from yrself to me, written in 1832! The reading of them contributed largely to delight our venerable friend, and a number of visitors, who were present—our enthusiastic friend Davis, considered them so valuable, as to deem them unsafe in my custody, unless placed in a fire proof vault![25]

Purvis wrote again a month later, thanking Garrison for his note and asking Garrison to write a letter "protesting the recent political outrage to which the 'colored' people of the South have been subjected." The correspondence continued. In March 1879, Purvis's tone was warm:[26]

> I bow reverently and gratefully to you, my dear friend Garrison, for your grand reply to Senator Blaine on the Chinese question; none other than the "Great Liberator" could have demolished so effectually the sophistry of the Senator. God bless you. In view of the continued *making* of the "bloody shirt," at the South, and the merciless persecution of the Chinese, does it not seem now imperative that our scattered Anti-Slavery forces, should be gathered up, and under your leadership, meet in anniversary week in New York?

With many thanks for the papers you have sent me, and the prayer that your health may be preserved, and your days greatly lengthened, I am most truly yours.[27]

Purvis's prayer was not answered. Two months later, on May 24, 1879, William Lloyd Garrison died. The man who had been variously his hero, his betrayer, and finally his hero again, was gone, leaving an empty place in his heart.

Worse was to follow. In November 1880, Lucretia Mott died at the age of eighty-seven. Robert Purvis had come to reverence Lucretia Mott, for she shared his belief that there was "but one race"; she had taught by example that gender also made no difference. A memorial meeting was held in the Bethel African Methodist Episcopal Church in late November, under the auspices of the Literary and Historical Society of the Church. A number of notables spoke, including William Still, Dr. B. T. Tanner, Dr. Hannah Long-shore, Dr. Jacob Paxson, and Frances Ellen Watkins Harper. Robert Purvis's remarks were "eulogistic" according to the *Ledger and Transcript.* Fanny Jackson, principal of the Institute of Colored Youth, concluded her remarks by saying: "We are not here to say goodbye to Lucretia Mott but to welcome her to a place of undying remembrance. She is no longer the possession of Pennsylvania but belongs to the whole country."[28]

In 1883, a handful of survivors celebrated the fiftieth anniversary of the founding of the American Anti-Slavery Society. Of the original sixty founders only four survived, including Robert Purvis and John Greenleaf Whittier. A celebration was planned for Horticultural Hall on December 4, 1883, and a group including Edward M. Davis, Daniel Neall, and William Still, met for several weeks at the Purvis house at 1601 Mt. Vernon to prepare for the event. They tried to persuade the New York Historical Society to lend them the original Declaration of Sentiments, however, they were told this was against the society's bylaws. At the celebration itself, letters were read from the sons of William Lloyd Garrison, from Wendell Phillips, Samuel May, and Parker Pillsbury among others.[29]

Purvis served as master of ceremonies and spoke about the pioneers, men and women who were loyal to the principles of the Declaration of Independence, and the teaching of Christianity in the fatherhood of God and the brotherhood of man.

They came and pledged themselves to purge this guilty nation from the curse and deadly sin of human slavery. To this end they declared, come what might to their persons, their interests, their reputations, or their lives; whether they lived to witness the triumph of their cause, or perish untimely as martyrs, they would be steadfast in their object. Their trust for victory was solely in God. Their weapons were not carnal but spiritual, mighty through God to the pulling down of the strongholds of sin. Conscious of the invincibility and resistless power of truth they said, "We may be personally defeated, but our principles, never." And they went forth in the name of indignant justice, outraged humanity, and insulted religion, and demanded an immediate and unconditional emancipation as the right of the slave and the duty of the master. How they labored, how they worked, in season and out of season, in storm as well as whatever sunshine they may have had, it is not at this time for me to speak. It is enough to know, and we exultingly point to the fact, that five millions of American slaves were enabled, to spring out *instanter,* from the vileness and degradation of being chattels, to the higher and nobler condition of freemen and American citizens.[30]

Edward M. Davis was unable to attend the event, and sent a letter of apology which he had hoped Purvis would read to the group. Purvis failed to do so, and the day following the celebration, Davis wrote an angry letter saying, "I am greatly mortified to find that you did not think it of sufficient importance to read [my letter] to the meeting." He went on to say that one of the sorrows of his life was that he was not present at the founding of the American Anti-Slavery Society. He had, however, joined less than a year later, "and have done what I could to uphold its principles and measures." He had missed no more than three of the Anti-Slavery meetings held in Philadelphia. He said he hoped his letter would be included in the proceedings, and ended on a somewhat conciliatory note:

> I know all this was not intentional, had it been, I probably should not have taken any notice of it. It may be very weak of me to feel as I do, but I was involved socially, religiously, politically for so many years because of my open-hearted advocacy of freedom and I do not mean to be seemingly ignored.[31]

He was further mollified when Daniel Neall Jr. apologized and promised to include him in the printed program of the proceedings.[32]

Women had not been included in the 1833 meeting, though Lucretia Mott had spoken anyway. In 1883, two women, Mary Grew and Susan B. Anthony, were present at the celebration. Mary Grew spoke and emphasized the opposition they had encountered in the "martyr days," especially in the churches. Now the specific work of the American Anti-Slavery Society was done.

Its lessons remain for instruction to the generations to come. God grant that these lessons may be heeded; that man may learn the great truth, that injustice cannot prosper; that he who fastens a chain upon his brother fetters himself thereby; that though the footsteps of Nemesis may be slow, they are sure, because the Lord God Omnipotent reigneth.[33]

Robert Purvis worked closely with Mary Grew and the Pennsylvania Woman Suffrage Association in these years; Mary was president. This association was affiliated with the American Woman's Suffrage Association headed by Lucy Stone, a rival to the more radical National Women's Suffrage Association headed by Susan B. Anthony. Purvis generally favored the National Association, and appeared at many of their annual meetings. However, he and Mary Grew were good friends, and cooperated on many occasions. In 1886, he spoke at the annual meeting of the Pennsylvania group, held on October 27 at the Association Hall, Fifteenth and Chestnut Streets.[34]

His wife, Tacie Townsend Purvis, was supportive of the women's rights movement, and included several poems and stories about the struggle for women's rights in her book, *The Singing Maiden*. His daughter, Hattie, was also becoming active in the women's rights movement, working with the Pennsylvania Woman Suffrage Association and the National Woman Suffrage Association. In 1884, Hattie became an officer in the Pennsylvania Woman Suffrage Association; in 1888, she was placed on a committee to enroll visitors at a meeting of the International Council of Women in Washington, D.C.[35] Many pioneers of the movement were honored, including Robert Purvis, who was asked to sit on the platform. He was introduced by Susan B. Anthony, who recalled his courageous stand for women in 1869 against his own son.[36]

In his brief speech on this occasion, he began by saying that it had been the most natural thing in the world to side with the women in 1869.

I value the honor of being ranked as a pioneer in this cause, although I cannot claim, as my friend Douglass can, to have been a member of the first Woman's Rights Convention at Seneca Falls; but I owe it to myself to say that anterior, some few years at least, to the matter to which Mrs. Blackwell has referred, in the test vote touching the appointment of Abby Kelley, subsequently Abby Kelley Foster, I stand rightly upon the record in that vote which I gave that time. I had before committed myself to the belief that whatever was morally right for a man, was equally so for a woman.[37]

This struggle for women's rights, Purvis said, was analogous to the battle waged against the slave power. Many of the women present, including Susan B. Anthony, Elizabeth Cady Stanton, Lucy Stone, and Mary Grew had been involved in that struggle.

> You know how we boasted then and we boast now, but with a little more consistency, that our land is the freest land upon the face of the globe. We exultingly pointed to the truth, as in our Declaration of Independence, that all persons were born free and equal, and were endowed with an inalienable right to life, liberty, and the pursuit of happiness, and yet at that very time we held one-sixth portion of the people of this country as chattels, slaves, to be bought and sold, and to be branded and whipped, and killed all the day long. With sublime independence we boasted that this was the land of the free and the home of the brave. We were, in truth, a country
>
> > *"Where the fustian banner proudly waves*
> > *In splendid mockery o'er a land of slaves."*
>
> Turn from that inconsistency to another. We yet hold and declare as a parallel and a paradox, that the right of voting and representation are reciprocal; and that all governments derive their just powers from the consent of the governed; and, in the face of this, in the presence of women, who constitute one-half of this population, we ignore the application of what we consider to be truths.[38]

It was not his purpose, he said, to dwell on the past, but rather simply to congratulate the women on the marvelous success that had followed their labors—"a success that portends, in the near future, your emancipation."

> I possess no gift of prophecy: I cannot penetrate the vistas of the future, but I believe I can name the day of "good time coming." I see it, I feel it. Our good President told us that the signs of the times indicated this. It is so. It comes to us in its animating and inspiring force. It enables us to see throughout the world, that despotism is becoming, to use a mild word, unfashionable; that scepters are being respected only as they rule in righteousness, to effect purposes of mercy and benevolence. That the thrones of all despots, great or small, wherever found, whether as rulers over kingdoms or lesser ones in our domestic homes, rest upon shallow, sandy, uncertain foundations; that the genius of liberty and freedom is moving on—moving on—demanding in tones not to be misunderstood, demanding in the name of justice and outraged humanity, a practical recognition of the doctrine of equality of rights for all, without regard to sex, color, race, or condition.[39]

In connection with his work with the women's suffrage organizations, Purvis was active in the cause of Prohibition. He continued to take a lively interest in Home Rule for Ireland, and attended the meetings of the Universal Peace Union, which worked for rights for Native Americans, labor unions, and to oppose lynching. The black poet, Frances Ellen Watkins Harper, was also a member of this largely white organization.[40]

He continued to be interested in the history of the Underground Railroad, in which he had played a pioneer role. In 1872, William Still published a book, *The Underground Railroad,* based on notes he had kept while working in the office of the Pennsylvania Anti-Slavery Society. In the book, which Still promoted vigorously as the official record of the Underground Railroad, the author wrote a short and complimentary biography of Robert Purvis, but failed to credit him with the establishment of the Vigilant Committee and the operation of the Underground Railroad from 1837 to 1851. Purvis made no comment on this omission, and continued to support Still in his many endeavors, civic and financial. At one time he loaned him money for the operation of his coal yard.[41]

Among the white allies with whom Robert Purvis had worked was Dr. Robert Smedley of Chester County. Smedley was at work on a book on the Underground Railroad, however, he became ill and died before he could complete the manuscript. In 1883, therefore, Robert Purvis agreed to join Marianna Gibbons of Lancaster, a granddaughter of Lucretia Mott's cousin Mary Earle, in editing the book. In it he included a chapter on the case of the Dorsey brothers, which had first impelled him to organize the Vigilant Committee, the methods the Committee used to spirit blacks out of the Deep South, and a sketch of himself, giving the story of his parentage.[42]

In December 1895, Wilbur Siebert, the first historian of the Underground Railroad, came to Philadelphia to gather material for his study. He interviewed William Still, who suggested that the Underground Railroad had started with the General Vigilance Committee in 1852. On Christmas Day Siebert called on Robert Purvis at his home on Mt. Vernon Street. Purvis told him that he had destroyed all the records of the Vigilant Committee at the time of the Fugitive Slave Law, but that he still remembered the operations of the committee; he estimated that they had helped an average of one slave a day to escape. There were few records of the operation of this earlier Underground Railroad—and, with the exception of the notations in the minutes of the Philadelphia Female Anti-Slavery Society—there was no documentary evidence to back this assertion. Siebert was nevertheless impressed with Robert Purvis's alertness at age eighty-five, and included the interview in his subsequent study. If Purvis's estimate were correct, he had aided more slaves than the General Vigilance Committee under William Still.[43]

Robert Purvis had turned eighty on August 4, 1890. There were many letters of congratulation, among them one from John Greenleaf Whittier:

> I have just learned by a note from Mary Grew that thy 80th birthday occurs on the 4th next. My thoughts turn to the convention of 1833 when we first met in the Anti-Slavery Convention. Of the 63 members of that memorable meeting only thee and I remain. Thank God that we have seen the end of slavery. I have only a moment to write thee and can only assure thee of my affectionate interest and sincere good wishes. God bless thee.[44]

(Whittier died two years later, making Robert the only surviving founder of the American Anti-Slavery Society.)

On the occasion of his birthday, the *Philadelphia Press* sent a reporter to interview Purvis at his home on Mt. Vernon street. The result was a long feature story covering the highlights of Purvis's life, including his pranks at Amherst Academy, his trip to England in 1834, his successful efforts to save the Dorsey brothers in 1837, and the mobs that endangered his life in 1842. Asked about the future, he reiterated his belief in the rights of blacks to full American citizenship.

> Let this be said: if there is one thing fixed in the mind of the colored race it is that they believe they belong here because they have been born here for decades and almost centuries; here they'll stay and here they'll die, and here they'll hope for better things. . . . I never met a slave in the hundreds I helped to gain their liberty who thought that he was born a slave. They all believed in their natural right of freedom.[45]

Robert Purvis now had seven grandchildren: his son Charles had two, and Henry had five. (An eighth, Granville's only child, a daughter, Marion, was born in Detroit in 1903 after his death.) Like any proud grandfather, he delighted in the accomplishments of these offspring. By 1880, the oldest grandchild, Alice, daughter of Charles, was enrolled at Howard University, and Robert, son of Henry, was at the Avery Normal Institute before attending Atlanta University in Georgia.

Unfortunately, relations with Henry's family remained severely strained. In 1887, when Robert wrote his will, he named all his children as executors but Henry, and added a codicil awarding Henry's share of the estate to his wife Ella. Even this was not enough. In 1894, he added a second codicil stating that no money should go to Henry's family as long as Henry was alive.[46]

His daughter Hattie continued to share the house on Mt. Vernon Street with Tacie and Robert, but was often away, visiting friends and attending women's rights conventions. In New York, she sometimes stayed with Elizabeth and Sydney Gay, old friends of her father from the anti-slavery crusade. Robert Purvis wrote Elizabeth Gay in September 1896, thanking her for her good care of Hattie.[47]

> First and uppermost, allow me the expression of my grateful acknowledgments for yr generous care of my daughter, while with you.
> She feels, as I do—that only due to such nursing was she enabled to return home; in a condition so comfortable. I met her at the Depot, looking very much better than I expected, the cough is still harassing, but we are encouraged, in the hope she will soon be in her usual health.[48]

In addition to his own children, Robert Purvis kept a watchful eye on the offspring of his brother, Joseph. Two of the eight had died, Alfred in 1865, and James in 1870. Sarah had married a lawyer, William Boseman, and had moved to Kansas, taking her youngest brother, Alexander, with them. Emily had married a Philadelphia schoolteacher, John Quincy Allen. Annie, unmarried, had made a home with her grandmother, Charlotte Forten, and her mother, until the latter's death in 1884. She then moved into lodgings. Joseph had become an alcoholic following his war service and worked at various jobs in Bucks County when he was not drinking. Robert Purvis occasionally had to bail him out of jail. William worked at various low paying jobs while he experimented with inventions. He developed the Sterling Paper Bag Company, which went bankrupt in 1885. Robert Purvis stepped in to rescue him, accepting "all the debts real and personal of the said Sterling Paper Bag Company, and all its rights, credits, expectations, patents, and patent rights of whatsoever nature lying due and owing in the State of Pennsylvania."[49]

(William did not give up. In 1901, he formed the Union Electric Company, which was quite successful. But he continued to try to relaunch his paper bag business. In 1910, he tried to interest his wealthy uncle, Dr. Charles Burleigh Purvis to invest, but to no avail.[50])

Despite his family concerns, old age did not diminish Robert Purvis's interest in the improvement of race relations. He was supportive when a group of younger Philadelphia blacks organized the Afro-American

League, a forerunner to the National Association for the Advancement of Colored People. And he followed eagerly the efforts of this and other groups to secure equality under the law. The case of *Plessy v. Ferguson*, questioning the right of state laws to segregate blacks in railroad cars, was working its way through the court system, and led Purvis and others to hope for vindication on a national level. In 1896, the Supreme Court ruled to uphold a Louisiana law requiring segregated railroad facilities; the law stated that as long as equality of accommodation existed, segregation did not constitute discrimination, and blacks were not deprived of equal protection of the laws under the Fourteenth Amendment. The Pennsylvania Courts, which had been upholding the earlier laws against discrimination, began to weaken their interpretations. The gains that the Philadelphia blacks had made during the days of the streetcar boycotts were destroyed.

For Robert Purvis, it was a repudiation of the very principle on which he had staked his life, that men and women were fundamentally equal; that there was "but one race." Eighty-six at the time of the decision, he must have felt the court decision to be a bitter blow.

It was time to correspond with old friends—what few were left. For a time, he and Rowland Johnson had exchanged letters, reviewing memories of the early, exciting days of antislavery agitation. Robert Purvis remembered how he saved William Lloyd Garrison from the sheriff when the latter was en route to England in 1833, and from the angry mob in 1838, following the burning of Pennsylvania Hall. But Johnson died in 1886, leaving Purvis without further opportunity to rehash old memories.

As he approached the end of his life, Robert Purvis's thoughts turned to religion, which had not played a large part in his early life. Sometime after 1896, he became acquainted with a Unitarian clergyman, Frederick A. Hinckley. Born in Vermont in 1845, Hinckley was ordained a minister in 1878, and served parishes in Northampton, Massachusetts and Providence, Rhode Island, before coming to the Spring Garden Unitarian Church in 1896. He was interested in vocational education, and preached a very liberal theology with which the three Purvises, Robert, Tacie, and Hattie, all felt comfortable, though Hattie also explored the Ethical Culture movement. For several years, until he left Philadelphia, Hinckley functioned as a minister to the Purvis family.[51]

In March 1898, when Robert was eighty-seven, Edward Magill, a Quaker, ex-president of Swarthmore College, called on him twice at his home on Mt. Vernon Street to interview him about the Underground Railroad, about which Magill was gathering stories.

He is now past eighty-five years of age, and quite feeble, his memory of recent events (not those of his earlier life) showing the effect of age. He received me most cordially, with all the grace and dignified courtesy for
which he was so notably distinguished in early life, and at the close of each
interview of more than an hour, he dismissed me with the same dignified
and gracious manner, begging me to call at any time when he could render
me the least service upon any subject.[52]

Magill asked him about the case of the Dorsey brothers, which had
caused Robert Purvis to organize the Vigilant Committee; Purvis told the
story much as he had outlined it earlier for Robert Smedley. He added,
however, several postscripts:

> Twenty-five years after, during the war that ended slavery, the doorbell of
> Robert Purvis in Philadelphia was rung, and a young colored man, of re-
> fined appearance and bearing, was ushered into his parlor. When Mr.
> Purvis came in, he rose and said, "Is this Robert Purvis?" When told that
> it was, he said: 'My name is Robert Purvis Dorsey. You saved my father
> twenty-five years ago, and he has always told me that I must find your
> house first whenever I came to Philadelphia."[53]

> When Mr. Purvis first told me this story about three weeks ago, he was
> deeply affected, and seemed to dwell upon some parts of it, repeating them
> over and over before he would let me go. He also added that a few years
> after the war he visited Basil Dorsey and his family, and found Mr. Dorsey
> a well-to-do citizen, with an interesting wife and a number of children, all
> of whom had received or were receiving a good education. "The whole
> case of Basil Dorsey," said Mr. Purvis, "I have always considered the most
> interesting case of my long and eventful life."[54]

Edward Magill afterwards learned from Elizabeth Powell Bond,
dean of Swarthmore College, that she had spoken at Basil Dorsey's funeral in 1872; she had found among her papers a printed bill of sale for
Dorsey, arranged by friends in Boston who feared he might be retaken.

> As I afterwards told Robert Purvis about this interview with Mrs. Bond,
> the good old man was deeply moved and said: "Such coincidences, as they
> are sometimes called, are not accidental, and I firmly believe that you are
> divinely directed in the work which you have undertaken."[55]

CHAPTER 15

"His Magnificent Record"

$\mathscr{R}$obert Purvis had remained in relatively good health into his eighties. Though suffering occasionally from lumbago, rheumatic pains in the lower back, he was still erect and handsome. A newspaper reporter for the *Philadelphia Inquirer* had stated in 1890 that he had just celebrated his seventieth birthday, when in fact it had been his eightieth.

Although he had several times been threatened by the tuberculosis which had carried off his sons William and Robert, his daughter Georgianna, and his beloved wife Harriet, he had never succumbed. But in late March 1898, he suffered a stroke, and remained paralyzed for three weeks. He seemed to be improving, but on the afternoon of April 14 at 2:00 P.M. he experienced an apparent second stroke; he became unconscious. He lingered on until 6:00 P.M. in the evening of April 15, when he died at his home, with Tacie and Harriet by his bedside.

"The death of Robert Purvis removes the last member of the early Abolitionist Party in this city," the *Philadelphia Press* recorded in a headline obituary on April 16. "He lived to witness the success of the great causes to which he devoted his youth and manhood, to join in the jubilee song of the American slave, and the thanksgiving of the abolitionist, and to testify that his life had been one whose reward was in itself."[1]

The *Philadelphia Bulletin* also noted his long struggle against slavery:

In the death of the venerable Robert Purvis there has passed away a notable figure among the men who in former years struggled for the rights of the negro race. With some of the blood of this race, Mr. Purvis, in his personal appearance, had few of its characteristics. He might easily have passed, as he ordinarily did to strangers, as a white man, but he had the courage to avow his origin and to stand up manfully against the oppression and the ostracism which it once invited. . . .

. . . It was Mr. Purvis's good fortune to survive the era of prejudice and hate, and on the very day when he passed away the first of the soldiers whom the government of the Union directed to go into the South on the way to Cuba, and without a sign of Southern dissent, were two fine regiments of black men. How different from the days when even so accomplished a gentleman as Robert Purvis was not allowed to sit at a white man's table because there was the blood of another race in his veins.[2]

The New York Times said he was "known to the present and past generations alike for his great work in behalf of the emancipation of slaves" and called him the "President of the Underground Railroad." "Throughout the long period of peril his house was a well-known station where his horses and carriages and his personal attendance were ever at the service of the travelers upon that road."[3]

Among the publications that carried obituaries was *The Woman's Journal*, which reiterated much that had been said about him as a gentleman and a champion of the oppressed, and spoke well of his eloquence:[4]

He was filled with a deep earnestness, that glowed with white heat when he denounced the gigantic iniquity of human bondage; and his pent-up indignation and harrowing sense of wrong, rising to wrath and swelling with bitter resentment, often found vent in burning words of eloquence. On such occasions his ringing voice, always deep, rich and clear, gave an added power to his glowing sentences, as they fell with convincing force upon the ear.[5]

A funeral service for Robert Purvis was held at the Spring Garden Unitarian Church, on Monday, April 18, with the Reverend Frederick A. Hinckley officiating. In his sermon, Hinckley described his commanding appearance:

That tall, stately figure, that rare manly beauty, that courtesy of a gentleman of the old school, which were his, who can forget them? Together they made him a marked man in any company. Together they were the fitting shrine in which the knight errant of truth and justice and liberty might dwell. And how intensely the nature used this body, and beamed out his sympathy, and flashed out its indignation through the windows of the external eye; how intensely the nature within used the body as a protest or summons rolled from his external lips![6]

Hinckley described how the breadth of Purvis's concerns for equality and justice led him to support many causes, especially the rights of women:

> He believed in the cooperation of manly and womanly hearts; he believed in the home as created by the union of two equals in love and freedom. He believed the best results attainable in every department of life not when men work alone, not when women work alone, but when they work together.[7]

The minister spoke of Purvis's interest in Irish Home Rule, and of better working conditions for laborers. He described his support for prison reform, and his work with the Committee of 100 toward "the purification of the politics of our municipality."[8]

Discussing Robert Purvis's religious beliefs, Hinckley spoke of his belief in the fatherhood of God and the brotherhood of man:

> There were two articles in his creed. The first was: Truth is the summit of being; let us think and speak the truth. The second was: "to do good is my religion. I believe in the equality of men, and I believe that the religious duties consist in doing justice, loving mercy, and endeavoring to make our fellow creatures happy." Professions, form, ceremonies could not be taken for the substantial reality by such a man as he.[9]

Hinckley described the meeting of science and religion, and the "enthronement of reason" in contemporary religious thought, and the growing interest in world religions and their common elements, all touchstones of current Unitarian thought, and his belief that Robert Purvis shared these views.

> How naturally and inevitably this man found himself among the advance guard in religious thought and progress as thus shown and understood. I need not say, "Authority for truth," had no power over him. He looked to "Truth for authority."[10]

Following the service, Robert Purvis's body was conveyed to the Fair Hill Burial Ground, where he was interred next to his beloved first wife, Harriet Davy Forten Purvis.[11]

Letters of condolence poured into the house on Mt. Vernon Street. One was from an old comrade, Samuel May Jr., a Unitarian minister, who had served as general agent of the Massachusetts Anti-Slavery Society. May was as old as Robert Purvis, and was himself in ill health; he died the following year. Hattie acknowledged his thoughtfulness:

Thank you very much for the kind and comforting letter, and I appreciate the effort it cost you to write. While we rejoice that father has been released from the infirmities that oppressed him, still to me it is a *sad* loss. The house is very lonely without his dear presence, his increasing feebleness only made him all the dearer, we had so much in our lives that was congenial, from my childhood we had been close companions. The last days of his life were peacefully happy, he suffered no pain, quietly went to sleep. You and Mr. Pillsbury are, I believe, the only ones left of his old Anti-Slavery friends. When I go to Boston again it will be a pleasure to call and see you.[12]

Other letters and other obituaries arrived. The *Friends Intelligencer,* which normally covered only Quaker deaths, devoted several paragraphs to his death, mentioning also his wife, Tacie.[13]

The American Negro Historical Society held a large memorial meeting at Bethel Methodist Episcopal Church on Monday, April 18, 1898, where they passed a memorial minute:

Whereas, the late Robert Purvis, who not only sympathized for his people in their "enforced condition" but [also] with an earnestness and zeal, inspired by a cause, as great as any that has demanded the attention of the civilized world, and as noble as any that has enlisted the services of men to dare and die for its success, labored with hand, heart and means to check the triumphant march of slavery, to protect and defend the escaping slave, to blot from the statute books of the nation the recognition of that accursed institution, and to liberate the oppressed millions: and

Whereas, the same spirit dominated his character in his connection with and attitude in the first Anti-Slavery Convention, and later, in his defense of the cause of Ireland, in his efforts for justice to the Indian, in his pronounced views on the rights of women, and in his general advocacy of the reformation of the body politic along the higher lines of civil liberty: Therefore, be it resolved: that this body in memorial meeting assembled, hereby expresses its grateful recognition of the extended, sincere and untiring labors of the late Robert Purvis, humanely given for the oppressed, and for his generous contribution unselfishly made to the list of pioneers of the race. . . .

Resolved: that the life of Robert Purvis with its Magnificent record, will ever be reverently cherished and that to an indebted and sorrowing people consolation is given by the knowledge that he lived to see the greatest desire of his heart consummated, before he passed into the presence of "Him who is" no respecter of persons.[14]

Isaiah Wears, unable to attend the memorial meeting, sent a letter praising Purvis's influence on his own life:

> I knew Robert Purvis for more than fifty years. He was an intense, enthusiastic, and uncompromising abolitionist—one who gave his time, labor and freely of his means to the cause.[15]

Wears described how Robert Purvis had served as spokesman for the Pennsylvania blacks who assembled in Harrisburg in 1846, presenting their petition to the governor of the state of Pennsylvania, and how he had acquitted himself with singular ability.

> We remember how for years he fought for the recognition of the United States citizenship of the black man by efforts to secure for himself a national passport to Europe. We also remember how in 1863 when desperate exigencies in which the nation found itself compelled it to acknowledge our citizenship before it could dare to draft us into the military service in the United States, officially proclaimed that citizenship.[16]
>
> Then it was that Robert Purvis walked more proudly through this land, in the light of this official vindication of his claims which had theretofore been made the subject of contemptuous sneer and even personal ridicule. But time had vindicated the rectitude of his demands.[17]

He described talking recently with Purvis about the convention of 1846, and discovering that he and Purvis were the only surviving members of the delegation.

> One of the noblest and wisest traits in his public utterances was that in them you never found him descending to the low and marshy grounds of mere race advocacy or mere race lines, knowing that such a course would justify the enemy in acting on the same lines, for his deportment toward us which has always been and is now the danger point. He left such near-sighted work to the latter-day leaders whose faith is attached to mere temporizing *race* philosophies. . . . He embraced within the grasp of his ardent and intelligent interest but one race and that was the human race, regardless of either sex or color.[18]

Robert Purvis's devotion to the rights of women was long remembered by the pioneers of the woman's suffrage movement. A year later Elizabeth Cady Stanton paid tribute to him and to Parker Pillsbury as two who had taken the unpopular position of advocating both women's and black suffrage. "They are conspicuous as the moral heroes of the nineteenth century," she asserted.[19]

Purvis's own modesty, and his refusal to take credit for the establishment of the Vigilant Committee and the thousands of escaping slaves it aided, caused his name to gradually fade from the ranks of the nineteenth-century black heroes of the struggle for freedom, equal rights, and suffrage. Recently, this oversight has been somewhat remedied as interest in the Underground Railroad has increased, both among historians and the black community. But Robert Purvis must be remembered not only for his heroic work for escaping slaves and his eloquent demand for equal rights regardless of sex or race, but also for his advocacy, in season and out, of the indivisibility of all human rights. His vision of a common humanity still beckons the human race on to greater heights.

The following abbreviations are used for frequently cited sources:

Lib for *Liberator*

NASS for National Anti-Slavery Standard

Mott Papers for Lucretia Coffin Mott Papers, Friends Historical Library, Swarthmore College

PAS for Pennsylvania Abolition Society

Introduction

1. Julie Winch, *Philadelphia's Black Elite: Activism, Accommodation, and the Struggle for Autonomy, 1787–1848* (Philadelphia: Temple University Press, 1988).

2. *New York Times*, April 16, 1898.

3. Joseph Borome, "The Vigilant Committee of Philadelphia," *Pennsylvania Magazine of History and Biography*, 92 (July 1968): 320–351; In a letter from Robert Purvis to Sydney Gay, August 15, 1858. (New York: Columbia University Library). See Harriet A. Jacobs, *Incidents in the Life of a Slave Girl, written by herself*, ed. L. Maria Child, now with "A true tale of slavery" by John S. Jacobs. [Both] edited and with an introduction by Jean Fagan Yellin (Cambridge: Harvard University Press, 2000).

4. International Council of Women, *Report of the International Council of Women: Assembled by the National Woman Suffrage Association* (Washington, DC: n.p., 1888), p. 343; Elizabeth Cady Stanton, Susan B. Anthony, Matilda Joslyn Gage, *History of Woman Suffrage*, 6 vols (New York: Fowler, 1881–1922) 2: 265.

5. W. E .B. Du Bois, *The Souls of Black Folk* (New York: Blue Heron Press, 1953), p. 85. Abraham Shadd (1801–1882) was born in Wilmington, Delaware,

but moved in 1833 to West Chester, Pennsylvania, where he was active in the Pennsylvania Anti-Slavery Society. In 1852, he and his family moved to Ontario, Canada. Du Bois of New Haven was W. E. B. Du Bois' father. James G. Barbadoes of Boston was a clothing merchant.

6. Mary Ann Shadd Cary (1823–1893) was a well-known black woman journalist; Henry Highland Garnet (1815–1882) was active in the American Missionary Society; Alexander Crummell (1819–1898) was frustrated in his attempts to become a minister until he attended Cambridge University in England; Martin Delany (1812–1885) attended Harvard Medical School for one year but was not allowed to continue because of his race; Edward Blyden (1832–1912) was an eloquent spokesman for emigration.

7. See William S. McFeely, *Frederick Douglass* (New York: W. W. Norton and Co. Inc., 1991); Benjamin Quarles, *Black Abolitionists* (New York: Oxford University Press, 1969), p. 134; In a letter from Sarah Pugh to Mary Estlin, November 29, 1853, Estlin Papers, in Benjamin Quarles, *Black Abolitionists*, p. 134.

8. See P. J. Staudenraus, *The African Colonization Movement, 1816–1865* (New York: Columbia University Press, 1961).

9. Roger Lane, *William Dorsey's Philadelphia and Ours: On the Past and Future of the Black City in America* (New York: Oxford University Press, 1991), p. 262.

10. NASS (hereafter NASS), September 10, 1840; *Lib* (hereafter *Lib*) September 16, 1853. Frederick Douglass, *Life and Times of Frederick Douglass* (New York: n.p. 1892), p. 418.

11. Letter from Robert Purvis to William Lloyd Garrison, November 11, 1878. Anti-Slavery Papers, Boston Public Library. "Our friend Davis," refers to Edward M. Davis.

12. NASS, May 16, 1863; April 16, 1870. *Public Ledger*, April 27, 1870.

13. Robert Purvis, *Speeches and Letters of Robert Purvis, Published by the Request of the Afro-American League* (Philadelphia, Pa.: University of Pennsylvania Rare Books, n.d., n.p.)

Chapter 1. Of Southern Birth

1. Charleston City Directory, Charleston County Library (South Carolina Room) 1819. John Purvis, ed., *The Purvis Family, 1694–1988* (Tillicoulty, Great Britain: W. M . Betts Limited, 1988), p. 216.

2. *Philadelphia Press*, August 3, 1890. Robert Purvis to R. C. Smedley, in *History of the Underground Railroad in Chester and the Neighboring Counties* (Lancaster, PA: n. p., 1883), pp. 353–354. Letter from Mary. S. Carr to William Still,

May 11, 1874, in Alberta Norwood, "Negro Welfare in Philadelphia, Especially as Illustrated by the Life of William Still." Master's thesis, University of Pennsylvania, 1931, p. 172.

3. Marina Wilknamanayake, *A World in Shadow: The Free Black in Antebellum South Carolina* (Columbia SC: University of South Carolina Press, 1973), pp.20–21.For comparable laws in Virginia, see Winthrop D. Jordan, *White Over Black: American Attitudes Toward the Negro 1550–1812* (Chapel Hill, NC: University of North Carolina Press, 1968), p. 94.

4. *Philadelphia Press*, August 3, 1890; Smedley, *A History of the Underground Railroad*, p. 353.

5. The Bureau of the Census for Charleston Neck, 1840 and 1860 lists a Mary Phaman (born 1804) living with a John Judah (born 1815), a Sarah Weston, later Vickers (born 1808), with a boarder, Jonas Bird.·It is not clear whether Phaman was Mary's father's name, or her name from a previous marriage. By the Bureau of the Census of 1870, Mary was married to Jonas Bird. In a codicil to her will dated May 11, 1868, Harriet Judah Miller leaves a bequest to "my sister, Mary Bird." (Will 639 dated January 16, 1846, codicil May 11, 1868, probate December 17, 1869, Philadelphia County Archives.) Enumeration of "Dido" sales from the SC Department of Archives and History, Columbia, SC. Alphabetical Index. Will of Elizabeth Deas from Will Book D. 1800–1807, p. 292. I am indebted to Marianne Cawley of the South Carolina Room, Charleston County Public Library, for information on Dido, and to Reginald Pitts for research on Mary Bird's origins.

6. "Earliest Extant Minute Book of the Spanish and Portuguese Congregation Shearith Israel in New York 1728–1760," *Publications of the American Jewish Historical Society*, 21: 5 (1913). James William Hagy, *This Happy Land: The Jews of Colonial and Antebellum Charleston* (Tuscaloosa: The University of Alabama Press, 1993), p. 14.

7. Hagy, *This Happy Land*, pp. 6, 29, 112–116.

8. Ibid, pp. 55, 91, 126.

9. In a codicil to her will dated May 11, 1868, Harriet leaves to Sarah Vickers, "the daughter of my brother who has long resided in my family, $500. Should she die in my lifetime I give same to my sister, Mary Bird of Charleston, SC." Harriet Miller, will dated January 16, 1846, codicil dated May 11, 1868. Probate, December 17, 1869. Will Book 66, pp. 109, 639, Philadelphia County Archives. This will was signed by Harriet with her mark, indicating she was illiterate; she could not read the will. The question of the name of Harriet's brother is also puzzling. An article in the *Anti-Slavery Bugle*, November 3, 1860, states that the name of Harriet's father and brother was Daniel: it claimed that the brother Daniel died young. But there was also a Daniel Judah (colored) listed as the father of Sarah Ann Judah in

1818. See Elise Pinckey, ed., *Register of St. Philips' Church, 1810–1822* (Charleston, SC: National Colonial Dames of America, 1973), p. 53. Sarah Judah Vickers was the niece who lived with John Judah in Charleston and later with Harriet. The *Anti-Slavery Bugle* also states that William Purvis brought Dido to Philadelphia in 1819, to live with Harriet and her children, a highly improbable claim.

10. Myron Berman, *Richmond Jewry, 1769–1976* (Charlottesville: University of Virginia, 1979), p. 43; Herbert T. Ezekiel and Gaston Lichtenstein, *The History of the Jews of Richmond from 1769 to 1917* (Richmond, VA: H. T. Ezekiel, 1917), p. 135; George A. Kohut, "Oldest Tombstone Inscriptions of Philadelphia and Richmond," *Proceeding of the American Jewish Historical Society,* 6 (1898): 111; 1820 Federal Census of the City of Richmond, Henrico County, VA., p. 181. Also in that enumeration, Isaac H. Judah is listed as having six slaves, Manuel Judah, two slaves, and Moses H. Judah, one slave. Information supplied by Reginald Pitts.

11. Salo W. Baron and Joseph L. Blau, eds., *The Jews of the United States, 1790–1840: A Documentary History* (New York: Columbia University, 1963), pp. 206–209, 298.

12. William Miller, Harriet Miller, Robert and Joseph Purvis *v.* John and Robert Purvis, Charleston County Court of Equity Decree #74, 1836, South Carolina State Department of History and Archives, Columbia, SC. *New York Times,* April 16, 1898; *The Purvis Family,* p. 216; *Morning Press,* December 14, 1869; *Sunday Dispatch,* December 1869; *Forney's Weekly Press,* December 18, 1869.

13. Purvis, *The Purvis Family,* pp. 231, 335, 350.

14. Ibid., John Purvis to Mary Ryan Schubert, May 18, 1997, Library, Byberry Friends Meeting.

15. *The Purvis Family,* p. 216.

16. U.S. Bureau of Census, Charleston, 1810.

17. Jordan, *White Over Black,* pp. 144–145.

18. Bernard E. Powers Jr., *Black Charlestonians: A Social History 1822–1885* (Fayetteville: University of Arkansas Press, 1994), pp. 48–49; Ira Berlin, *Slaves Without Masters: The Free Negro in the Antebellum South* (New York: Pantheon Books, 1974), pp. 138, 215; see Larry Koger, *Black Slaveholders: Free Black Slave Masters in South Carolina, 1790–1860* (Jefferson, NC: McFarland and Company, 1985), pp. 74–75.

19. South Carolina Misc. Records, Secretary of State, Bills of Sale, Book 4F, pp. 105, 110. South Carolina Department of Archives and History, Columbia, SC.

20. South Carolina Misc. Records, Secretary of State, Bills of Sale, Book 4S. South Carolina Department of Archives and History, Columbia, SC. Purvis, *Purvis Family*, p. 336.

21. *Philadelphia Press*, August 3, 1890. Thomas Day, *The History of Sanford and Merton*. The book was a children's classic with a strong antislavery message.

22. South Carolina's Writers Project, *South Carolina: A Guide to the Palmetto State*, compiled by the WPA (New York: Oxford University Press, 1941), pp. 184–211.

23. Ibid.

24. Gerda Lerner, *The Grimké Sisters from South Carolina: Pioneers for Woman's Rights and Abolition* (New York: Shocken Books, 1971), pp. 13–17.

25. *South Carolina*, WPA Guide, pp. 192–195. Henry J. Cadbury, *Friendly Heritage: Letters from the Quaker Past* (Norwalk, CT: Silvermine Publishers, 1972) p. 328.

26. Powers, *Black Charlestonians*, pp. 52–53.

27. Berlin, Ira, *Generations of Captivity: A History of African-American Slaves* (Cambridge: The Belknap Press, 2003), p. 139.

28. Berlin, *Slaves Without Masters*, pp. 289–290; Berlin, *Generations of Captivity*, pp. 228–229.

29. Vincent Harding, *There is a River: The Black Struggle for Freedom in America* (New York: Harcourt Brace Jovanovich, 1981), pp. 65–72.

30. Gabriel Prosser led a slave revolt near Richmond, Virginia in 1800. Nat refers to Nat Turner, who led a slave uprising in Virginia in 1831.

31. *A Remonstrance Against the Proceedings of a Meeting held November 23, 1831, at Upton's in Dock Street* (Philadelphia: For Sale at No. 78, George Street, 1832). Probably written by Robert Purvis in conjunction with William Whipper and James Forten.

32. Purvis, *The Purvis Family*, p. 350.

Chapter 2. The City of Brotherly Love

1. U.S. Bureau of the Census for Philadelphia, 1810, 1820.

2. Gary B. Nash, "Slaves and Slaveholders in Colonial Philadelphia," in *Race, Class and Politics: Essays on American Colonial Revolutionary Society*, ed. Gary B. Nash (Urbana and Chicago: University of Illinois Press, 1986), pp. 91–118.

3. Julie Winch, ed., *The Elite of Our People: Joseph Willson's Sketches of Black Upper Class Life in Antebellum Philadelphia* (University Park, PA: Pennsylvania State University Press, 2000), pp. 23–24.

4. Julie Winch, "You Have Talents—Only Cultivate Them," in *The Abolitionist Sisterhood: Women's Political Culture in Antebellum America*, eds. Jean Fagan Yellin and John C. Van Horne (Ithaca, New York: Cornell University Press, 1994), pp. 105–106.

5. Henry J. Cadbury, "Negro Membership in the Society of Friends," *Journal of Negro History*, 21 (1936): 151–213.

6. Winch, *The Elite of Our People*, p. 122, n. 7.

7. Margaret H. Bacon, *History of the Pennsylvania Society for Promoting the Abolition of Slavery, The Relief of Negroes Unlawfully Held in Bondage; and for Improving the Condition of the African Race* (Philadelphia: Pennsylvania Abolition Society, 1959); also Jeffrey Nordlinger Bumbrey, ed., *A Guide to the Microfilm Publication of the Papers of the Pennsylvania Abolition Society at the Historical Society of Pennsylvania* (Philadelphia: The Historical Society of Pennsylvania, 1976).

8. Bacon, *Pennsylvania Abolition Society*, p. 111; Robert Purvis, *A Tribute to the Memory of Thomas Shipley, the Philanthropist, Delivered at St. Thomas Church, November 23, 1836* (Philadelphia: Merrihew and Gunn, Printers, 1836).

9. Anonymous, *A Brief Sketch of the Schools for Black People and their Descendants Established by the Religious Society of Friends in 1770* (Philadelphia: Friends Book Store, 1867).

10. See Maria J. Lindhorst, "Sarah Mapps Douglass: The Emergence of an African American Educator/Activist in Nineteenth Century Philadelphia" (PhD diss., Pennsylvania State University, 1995).

11. Smedley, *History of the Underground Railroad*, p. 354. William Pervis's [sic] account, Pennsylvania Abolition Society, Board of Education, Clarkson School, Tuition Account Book, 1820, Historical Society of Pennsylvania.

12. Edwin Wolf, 2nd, *Portrait of an American City* (Philadelphia: Stackpole Books, 1970), pp. 120–146.

13. Ibid.

14. Emma Lapsansky, "'Since They Got Those Separate Churches: Afro-Americans and Racism in Jacksonian Philadelphia, "*African Americans in Pennsylvania: Shifting Historical Perspectives*, eds., Joe William Trotter Jr. and Eric Ledell Smith, (University Park, PA: Pennsylvania State University Press, 1991), p. 97; John Runcie, "Hunting the Nigs," in *Pennsylvania History*, 39 (April 1972): 203, 215.

15. Julie Winch, *A Gentleman of Color: The Life of James Forten* (New York: Oxford University Press, 2002), pp. 112–113.

16. Margaret H. Bacon, *Sarah Mapps Douglass: Faithful Attender of Quaker Meeting: View from the Back Bench* (Philadelphia: Quaker Press, 2003), p. 3.

17. Philadelphia City Directory; John Purvis, *The Purvis Family*, p. 216.

18. William Purvis, Will dated August, 1824, proved October 18, 1826, box 9, page 5, Philadelphia County Wills, Philadelphia City Archives (Philadelphia, PA: City Hall).

19. Poulson, *American Daily Advertiser*, October 4, 1826; *Charleston City Gazette*, October 12, 1826; *Columbia S.C. Telescope*, October 17, 1826.

20. Purvis, *The Purvis Family*, p. 216.

21. Harriet Miller, Robert and Joseph Purvis *v.* John Purvis, Charleston County Court of Equity, Decree 1834, #36. South Carolina Department of History and Archives, Columbia, SC.

22. School Records, Amherst College and Amherst Academy, Amherst, MA. Letter from Daria D'Arienzo, Archivist of Amherst College, to Margaret Hope Bacon, December 21, 1994.

23. *Philadelphia Press*, August 3, 1890. Letters from Daniel Lombardo, the Jones Library, Amherst, MA, November 16, 1995, and Ruth T. Degenhardt, the Berkshire Athenaeum, Amherst, MA, October 31, 1995 to Margaret H. Bacon.

24. Poulson, *American Daily Advertiser*, April 7, 1828.

25. Ibid.

26. William Purvis Jr. will dated April, 1828, proved April 10, 1928, box 9, p. 189, Philadelphia County Wills. Philadelphia County Deeds, A. M. Book 29, p. 187.

27. William Jacob Walls, *The African Methodist Episcopal Zion Church: Reality of the Black Church* (Charlotte, NC: A. M. E. Zion Publishing House, 1885), pp. 47–48, 50, 52, 63, 68, 82, 89–90. 117, 121–122, 124, 127, 129, 133, 148, 172–173, 301, 483, 567, 572.

28. Ibid. *Lib*, February 14, 1835.

29. Ibid. In 1837, Robert Purvis took a fugitive slave to his mother's house on Seventh Street. Smedley, pp. 356–361. *History of the Underground Railroad*, Fran Wilcox, "Robert Purvis, Underground Railroader," *Bucks County Panorama* (March, 1978): 19–20, 51–54. *Friends Intelligencer*, 55, no. 11 (March 12, 1898): p. 181.

30. William Miller, Harriet Miller, Robert and Joseph Purvis *v.* John and Robert Purvis, Charleston County Court of Equity, Decree #74, 1836. South Carolina Department of History and Archives, Columbia, SC.

31. "Members of the Executive Committee of the Pennsylvania Anti-Slavery Society," Friends Historical Library, Swarthmore College. Photograph; "Robert Purvis," Sophia Smith Collection, Smith College: National Antislavery Standard, November 20, 1860; Elizabeth Cady Stanton, Susan B. Anthony, and Matilda Joslyn Gage, *History of Woman Suffrage* (New York: Fowler, 1881–1922), 2: 358.

32. St. Thomas Episcopal Church, Parish Registry, 1828.

33. See Merton L. Dillon, *Benjamin Lundy and the Struggle for Negro Freedom* (Urbana: University of Illinois Press, 1966).

34. Ibid., pp. 106, 143.

35. See P. J. Staudenraus, *The African Colonization Movement, 1816–1865* (New York: Columbia University Press, 1961).

36. Dillon, *Benjamin Lundy,* pp. 94, 169.

37. Ibid., p. 145. William Lloyd Garrison (1805–1879) was born in Newburyport, MA. See Wendell Phillip Garrison and F. J. Garrison, *William Lloyd Garrison, 1805–1879: The Story of His Life told by His Children* (New York: The Century Company, 1885–89). Also Henry Mayer, *All on Fire: William Garrison and the Abolition of Slavery* (New York: St. Martin's Press, 1998).

38. Letter from Lucretia Mott to James Miller McKim, May 8, 1834, Mott Papers, Friends Historical Library, Swarthmore College.

39. *Genius of Universal Emancipation,* June, 1823, p. 171.

40. Robert Purvis, *A Tribute to the Memory of Thomas Shipley* (Philadelphia: Merrihew and Gunn, 1836).

Chapter 3. Present at the Beginning

1. Robert Purvis, *Remarks on the Life and Character of James Forten, Delivered at Bethel Church, March 30, 1842* (Philadelphia: Merrihew and Thompson, 1842), pp. 5–6.

2. Purvis, *Remarks on the Life of James Forten,* pp. 7–9; Winch, *A Gentleman of Color,* pp. 50–76.

3. Winch, *Gentleman of Color,* pp. 50–76.

4. Winch, *Gentleman of Color,* pp. 121–122.

5. *Poulson, American Daily Advertiser*, September 12, 1831; Parish Registry, St. Thomas Episcopal Church, October 1824–July 1842.

6. Philadelphia County Deeds A M, Book 26, p. 469. Philadelphia County Archives. For this and other deeds executed by Robert Purvis, I am indebted to Julie Winch.

7. Sarah Forten to Elizabeth Whittier, 10 September 1836; Pickard Papers; Winch, *A Gentleman of Color*, p. 273. *Philadelphia Press*, August 3, 1890.

8. Lucretia Mott to James Miller McKim, 8 May 1834. Mott Manuscripts, Friends Historical Library, Swarthmore College. Hereafter, Mott Papers.

9. Rosalind Cobb Wiggins, *Captain Paul Cuffe's Logs and Letters, 1810–1817* (Washington, DC: Howard University, 1996), pp. 58–59.

10. Paul Cuffe to James Forten, 29 January 1815; James Forten to Paul Cuffe, 25 January 1817, in Wiggins, *Captain Paul Cuffe's Logs*, pp. 309, 502.

11. Purvis, *Remarks on the Life of James Forten*, pp. 14–15.

12. James Forten, Robert Purvis and William Whipper, *A Remonstrance Against the Proceedings of a Meeting held November 23, 1831, at Upton's Dock Street* (Philadelphia, Library Company of Philadelphia).

13. *Lib*, December 10, 1831. Forten, et al., *A Remonstrance*, pp. 6–7.

14. Forten, et al., *A Remonstrance*, p. 7.

15. Ibid.

16. Julie Winch, *The Elite of Our People*, p. 136.

17. Memorial by James Forten, Robert Purvis and William Whipper "to the Honorable Senate and House of Representatives of the Commonwealth of Pennsylvania." *Lib*, April 14, 1832.

18. Ibid.

19. Ibid.

20. Howard Bell, *A Survey of the Negro Convention Movement, 1830–1861* (New York: Arno Press, 1969), pp. i–12. Winch, *Elite*, pp. 91–92.

21. Bell, *Survey of Negro Conventions*, p. 7; Benjamin Quarles, *Black Abolitionists* (New York: Oxford University Press, 1969), pp. 107.

22. Ibid.

23. Bell, *1832 Minutes and Proceedings of Second Annual Convention*, pp. 15–20.

24. Bell, *1832 Minutes and Proceedings of Second Annual Convention*, pp. 9–11.

25. Julie Winch, *The Elite*, pp. 113, 150.

26. Bell, *1833 Minutes and Proceedings of the Third Annual Convention*, pp. 22, 29, 30.

27. Ibid., p. 22.

28. Ibid., p. 29.

29. Joseph Dailey to Robert Purvis: 12 April 1833, 21 May 1833, 15 August 1833, Anti-Slavery Papers, Boston Public Library.

30. Robert Purvis to R.R. Gurley, 2 December 1833. Library of Congress.

31. Robert Purvis to editor, *Pennsylvania Freeman*, 24 December 1840.

32. William Lloyd Garrison to Robert Purvis, 12 May; 30 May, 1832. Anti-Slavery Papers, Boston Public Library.

33. William Lloyd Garrison to "My dear Purvis," 22 June 1832. Anti-Slavery Papers, Boston Public Library.

34. Ibid.

35. William Lloyd Garrison to Robert Purvis 10 December 1832. Anti-Slavery Papers, Boston Public Library.

36. Henry Mayer, *All on Fire*, p. 149.

37. Robert Purvis to Rowland Johnson, 22 August 1879. Anti-Slavery Papers, Boston Public Library.

38. William Lloyd Garrison to Robert Purvis, 30 April 1833. Anti-Slavery Papers, Boston Public Library.

39. James McCrummill, a free black from Virginia, was a prosperous barber and dentist.

40. *The Abolitionist*, December, 1833. Declaration of Sentiments, American Anti-Slavery Society, Adelphi Hall, December 4, 1833.

41. *Friends Intelligencer*, April, 1898.

42. *Philadelphia Press*, August 3, 1890.

43. *The Abolitionist*, December, 1833.

44. Ibid.

45. Minutes, Philadelphia Female Anti-Slavery Society, December, 1833. Pennsylvania Abolition Society Papers (hereafter PAS), Historical Society of Pennsylvania, Microfilm Edition, Philadelphia, PA, 1976, reel 30.

46. Carolyn Williams, "The Female Anti-Slavery Movement" in *The Abolitionist Sisterhood*, eds. Jean Fagin Yellin and John C. Van Horne (Ithaca: Cornell University Press, 1994), p. 162.

47. *NASS*, April 16, 1870.

48. See Records of the Philadelphia Young Men's Anti-Slavery Society and the Philadelphia Anti-Slavery Society: Pennsylvania Abolition Society. Microfilm edition, 1975, reel 31.

49. Ibid., Microfilm, reel 31.

Chapter 4. World Traveler

1. William Lloyd Garrison to Robert Purvis, 20 May 1834, in *The Letters of William Lloyd Garrison*, eds. Walter Merrill and Louis Ruchames (Cambridge: The Belknap Press, 1971–1979), 1: 342–343.

2. Elliot Cresson (1796–1854), a Philadelphia merchant, served as secretary of the Pennsylvania Colonization Society in 1829; he developed the Young Men's Colonization Society in 1834. In 1837 he became vice president of the Pennsylvania Colonization Society. In 1834, he was in Great Britain for the colonization cause. C. Peter Ripley, ed., *Black Abolitionist Papers*, 5: I: 37 (Chapel Hill, NC: University of North Carolina Press, 1985–1991).

3. Report of the organizing meeting of the Pennsylvania Colonization Society, October 1829 (Philadelphia: Library Company of Philadelphia); Early Lee Fox, "The American Colonization Society 1817–1840." Baltimore: Johns Hopkins University Studies in Historical and Political Science, 1919, ser. 37, no. 13 (1919): 60-61, 99, 110-111.

4. *Philadelphia Press*, August 3, 1890.

5. Ibid. For Cope Line see Eliza Cope Harrison, ed., *Philadelphia Merchant: The Diary of Thomas P. Cope, 1800–1851* (South Bend IN: Gateway Editions, 1978).

6. *Lib*, August 23, 1834, p. 135.

7. Ibid.

8. William Wilberforce (1759–1833) was an English philanthropist and antislavery crusader.

9. Daniel O'Connell (1775–1847) was an Irish patriot and abolitionist.

10. The Rev. John Scoble, of Newark, England, was Secretary of the British and Foreign Antislavery Society.

11. *Lib*, August 23, 1834, p. 135.

12. George Thompson to Robert Purvis, 10 November 1834. Anti-Slavery Papers, Boston Public Library.

13. Philadelphia Female Anti-Slavery Society incoming correspondence, 1834–1837. Microfilm edition 1976, reel 31.

14. Harriet Miller, Robert and Joseph Purvis *v.* John Purvis, Charlestown County Court of Equity, Decree #36, 1834, South Carolina Department of History and Archives.

15. *Philadelphia Press*, August 3, 1890.

16. Ibid.

17. Ibid.

18. Abby Hopper to "My dear Brother," 28 November 1834. Gibbons Papers, Friends Historical Library, Swarthmore College.

19. John Runcie, "'Hunting the Nigs' in Philadelphia: The Race Riot of 1834," *Pennsylvania History*, 39 College Park, PA (April, 1972): 190–193.

20. Lucretia Mott to Phoebe Post Willis, 13 September, 1834, *Selected Letters of Lucretia Coffin Mott*, ed. Beverly Palmer, University of Illinois Press. 2002. Champaign, IL.

21. Bucks County Records, Deed Bk. 59, p. 510. Bucks County Courthouse, Doylestown, PA. For this and many following records of deeds I am grateful for the generosity of Julie Winch.

22. Bucks County Deed Bk. 59, p. 510; b. 61, p. 544; Bucks County Mortgage Bk. 17, p. 191; Bucks County Courthouse, Doylestown, PA; Burlington County Deed Bk. Y3, p. 546; B. A., p. 521: Burlington County Court House, Mt. Holly, NJ.

23. Winch, *Gentleman of Color*, p. 271; Bucks County Deed Bk. 63, p. 171. Bucks County Courthouse, Doylestown, PA.

24. Philadelphia County Deeds Bk. 28, p. 58; Bk. 26, p. 231; Bk. 4, p. 718. Philadelphia City Archives, Philadelphia, PA.

25. Ibid., Bk. 70, pp. 575–576.

26. Ibid., Bk. 26, p. 231; Bk. 10, p. 86; Bk. 36, p. 111.

27. Ibid., Bk. 6, pp. 721, 723, 725; Bk. 8, p. 724.

28. *Fifth Annual Convention for the Improvement of the Free People of Colour, Held in Wesley Church, Philadelphia, 1st to 5th of June 1835* (Philadelphia: William G. Gibbons, 1835), pp. 4, 6, 12, 15, 18, 19.

29. Ibid., p. 14.

30. *Minutes of the Fourth Annual Convention for the Improvement of the Free People of Colour in the United States, Held by Adjournment in the Asbury Church, New York from the 2nd to the 13th of June Inclusive* (New York: By Order of the Convention, 1834).

31. *National Enquirer and Constitutional Advocate of Liberty,* August 24, 1836.

32. Ibid.

33. See Julie Winch, *Philadelphia's Black Elite, Activism, Accommodation and the Struggle for Autonomy, 1787–1848* (Philadelphia: Temple University Press, 1988), Chap. 6, for more on this subject.

34. Letter to the Honorable S. C. Pomeroy, Government Colonization Agent; *Lib,* September 12, 1862.

35. Dorothy Porter, *Early Negro Writing, 1760–1837* (Boston: Beacon Press, 1971), pp. 200–248. *Constitutional Advocate of Universal Freedom,* September 14, 1837.

36. *Colored American,* March 15, 1838. Ripley, et al., eds. *Black Abolitionist Papers,* 3: 262–263.

37. *NASS,* September 10, 1840.

38. Ibid.

39. *NASS,* October 1, 1840.

40. *NASS,* October 1, 1840; May 6, 1841.

41. *National Reformer,* November, 1838–December, 1839.

42. *National Reformer,* January–February, 1839, p. 75.

43. *Pennsylvania Freeman,* September 8, 1841. Howard Bell, "The American Moral Reform Society, 1836–1841," in *The Journal of Negro Education,* 27 (Winter 1958): 34–40.

44. See Howard Bell, *Proceedings of the National Negro Conventions, 1830–1864* (New York: Arno Press, 1969).

45. *Lib,* September 24, 1836, p. 155.

46. *A Tribute to the Memory of Thomas Shipley the Philanthropist,* delivered at St. Thomas's Episcopal Church, November 23, 1836.

47. *Tribute,* p. 7.

48. Ibid., p. 9.

49. Ibid., pp. 10–11.

50. Ibid., p. 14.

51. Ibid. (Purvis lists names given to the various settlements sponsored in Africa by the American Colonization Society. Elliott Cresson, a Philadelphian active in the Colonization Society, insisted on naming a port after himself.)

52. *Tribute*, p. 15.

53. Ibid., p. 17.

Chapter 5. *"We are Not Intruders Here"*

1. *National Enquirer and Constitutional Advocate of Universal Liberty*, February 11, 1837.

2. See William Cohen, "The Pennsylvania Anti-Slavery Society" (master's thesis, Columbia University, 1960). Microfilm, reel 1.

3. See Julie Winch, *Philadelphia's Black Elite*, pp. 135–137.

4. Ibid., Robert Purvis, *Appeal of Forty Thousand Citizens Threatened with Disfranchisement, to the People of Pennsylvania* (Philadelphia: Merrihew and Gunn, Printers, 1838), p. 6.

5. *Proceedings and Debates of the Convention of the Commonwealth of Pennsylvania to Propose Amendments to the Constitution, Commenced at Harrisburg on the Second Day of May, 1837* (Harrisburg: Parker, Barrett and Parke, 1837–1839), 1: 35.

6. *Proceedings and Debates*, 1: 270.

7. *Proceedings and Debates*, 5: 414; Winch, *Black Elite*, p. 138.

8. *Proceedings*, 9: 259. Edwin Bronner, *Thomas Earle As a Reformer* (Philadelphia: International Printing Company, 1948), p. 78.

9. Census of the Condition of Colored People in Philadelphia in 1847, taken by N. Kite. PAS, Miscellaneous Papers, Microfilm Edition, reel 31.

10. In addition to Purvis, the committee consisted of James Cornish, J. C. Bowers, Robert B. Forten, J. G. Bias, James Needham, and John P. Burr; *Pennsylvania Freedman*, March 22, 1838.

11. Purvis, *Appeal of Forty Thousand Citizens*.

12. Ibid., p. 1.

13. Ibid., p. 1.

14. Purvis, *Appeal of Forty Thousand Citizens*, p. 4.

15. Purvis, *Appeal of Forty Thousand Citizens*, p. 10.

16. Ibid.

17. Ibid.

18. Ibid., p. 12.

19. Ibid., pp. 13–14.

20. Purvis, *Appeal of Forty Thousand Citizens*, p. 15.

21. Ibid., p. 17.

22. William Penn, founder of Pennsylvania; Benjamin Franklin, author, inventor, diplomat; Dr. Benjamin Rush, noted physician and humanitarian; William Rawle, humanitarian; Thomas Wistar, prison reformer; Roberts Vaux, businessman and humanitarian. All except Penn were members of the Pennsylvania Abolition Society.

23. Purvis, *Appeal of Forty Thousand Citizens*, p. 18.

24. *Pennsylvania Freeman*, August 29, 1839.

25. Ibid.

26. *Lib*, July 25, 1835.

27. Ibid.

28. *Lib*, August 1, 1835.

29. Minutes, 18 June 1847; 19 December 1864; Minute Book of the Board of Managers of Pennsylvania Hall, in "A Temple of Amalgamation: The Burning of Pennsylvania Hall," in *Proclaim Liberty! Anti-Slavery and Civil Rights in Pennsylvania, 1688–1887*, Ira Brown. (University Park, PA: 2000), p. 216.

30. Ibid., 206–208. Margaret H. Bacon, *Valiant Friend: The Life of Lucretia Mott* (New York: Walker and Company, 1980), p. 78.

31. Dorothy Sterling, ed., *Turning the World Upside Down: The Anti-Slavery Convention of American Women, Held in New York City May 9–12, 1837* (New York: Coalition of Publishers for Employment, 1987).

32. Gerda Lerner, *The Grimké Sisters from South Carolina: Pioneers of Woman's Rights and Abolition* (New York: Schocken Books, 1971), pp. 240–242.

33. See Samuel Webb, ed. *History of Pennsylvania Hall, which was Destroyed by a Mob, on the 17th of May, 1838* (Philadelphia: Merrihew and Gunn, Printers, 1838): Lerner, *Grimké Sisters*, pp. 240–242.

34. Webb, *History of Pennsylvania Hall*, p. 13.

35. *Proceedings of the Second Annual Anti-Slavery Convention of American Women, Held in Philadelphia, May 15, 6, 17 and 18, 1838* (Philadelphia: Merrihew and Gunn, Printers, 1838).

36. Webb, *History of Pennsylvania Hall*, p. 70.

37. Brown, "A Temple of Amalgamation," p. 211.

38. Ibid., p. 211.

39. Webb, *History of Pennsylvania Hall*, p. 117.

40. Lerner, *The Grimké Sisters*, p. 246.

41. Dorothy Sterling, *Ahead of Her Time: Abby Kelley and the Politics of Antislavery* (New York: W. W. Norton Co. Inc., 1991) p. 64.

42. Brown, "A *Temple of Amalgamation*," p. 212.

43. Bacon, *Valiant Friend*, p. 86.

44. Brown, "A *Temple of Amalgamation*," p. 214.

45. Robert Purvis to Rowland Johnson on 22 August 1879. Anti-Slavery Papers, Boston Public Library.

46. Robert Purvis to Joseph Sturge, *A Visit to the United States in 1841* (London: Hamilton, Adams, and Co., 1841), pp. 45–47.

47. Brown, "A Temple of Amalgamation," p. 216.

48. Lucretia Mott to Edward M. Davis, June 18, 1838; Palmer, *Selected Letters*, p. 43.

49. Lucretia Mott and Anna Coffin to David Wright, June 2, 1838 (Mott Papers).

50. *Proceedings of the Third Anti-Slavery Convention of American Women* (Philadelphia: Merrihew and Gunn, Printers, 1839), p. 6.

51. *Lib*, May 10, 1839.

Chapter 6. To Aid the Fleeing Slave

1. Ira Brown, *Proclaim Liberty!: Anti-Slavery and Civil Rights in Pennsylvania, 1688–1887* (University Park, PA, 2000), p. 53.

2. *Philadelphia Press*, August 3, 1890; Smedley, *History of the Underground Railroad*, p. 355.

3. Fran Wilcox, "Robert Purvis: Bucks County Underground Railroader," *Bucks County Panorama* (March 1978): pp. 19–20, 51–54.

4. Smedley, *History of the Underground Railroad,* p. 356.

5. Wilcox, "Purvis, Underground Railroader," p. 20.

6. Joseph Borome, "The Vigilant Committee of Philadelphia," *Pennsylvania Magazine of History and Biography* 92: (1968) 321. Smedley, p. 357.

7. Ibid.

8. *Constitutional Advocate of Universal Freedom,* August 3, 1837.

9. Smedley, *History of the Underground Railroad,* p. 359.

10. *Constitutional Advocate of Universal Freedom,* August 3, 1837; *Bucks County Intelligencer,* August 9, 1837.

11. Smedley, *History of the Underground Railroad,* p. 361.

12. Robert Purvis, *Testimonial of Gratitude to David Paul Brown, in Mother Bethel Church in 1841* (Pennsylvania: David Paul Brown Papers. Historical Society of Pennsylvania).

13. *National Enquirer,* August 10, 1837; Borome, "The Vigilant Committee," p. 323.

14. *National Enquirer,* September 19, 1837.

15. *Pennsylvania Freeman,* July 26 and Dec. 27, 1838.

16. Winch, *Black Elite,* p. 149.

17. Minutes of the Vigilant Committee of Philadelphia, 14 December 1840. (Pennsylvania: Leon Gardiner Collection File 8B. Historical Society of Pennsylvania).

18. Minutes of the Vigilant Committee 25 April 1841 (Pennsylvania: Leon Gardiner Collection, File 8B, Historical Society of Pennsylvania); Borome, "The Vigilant Committee" p. 324.

19. Borome, "The Vigilant Committee," pp. 331–332.

20. Ibid., p. 335.

21. Ibid., p. 341.

22. Ibid., p. 343.

23. Ibid.

24. *NASS,* May 13, 1841. Minutes of The Vigilant Committee, 12 June 1841; Borome, "The Vigilant Committee," p. 343.

25. Minutes, Philadelphia Female Anti-Slavery Society. June, 1839–February, 1843. PAS Misc. Papers, reel 31.

26. Ibid. Wilbur H. Siebert, *The Underground Railroad from Slavery to Freedom* (New York: Macmillan, 1899), p.10; "The Vigilant Committee," p. 346. *New York Times*, April 16, 1898.

27. William Still, *The Underground Railroad* (Philadelphia: Porter and Coates, 1872), p. 711.

28. Seibert, *Underground Railroad*, p. 153; Smedley, *History of the Underground Railroad*, p. 355.

29. Robert Purvis to Sydney Gay, 15 July 1858. Sydney Howard Gay Papers, Rare Books and Manuscripts, Columbia University.

30. *Pennsylvania Freeman*, October 31, 1838. See William Cohen, *The Pennsylvania Anti-Slavery Society* (master's thesis, Columbia University, 1960).

31. Sterling, *Ahead of Her Time*, p. 105; Keith Melder, *Beginnings of Sisterhood: The American Woman's Rights Movement 1800–1850* (New York: Shocken Books: 1977), pp. 108–112.

32. Frederick Douglass (1817–1895) was one of the signers of the original Declaration of Woman's Independence at the Seneca Falls Convention in 1848.

33. Antoinette Brown Blackwell (1825–1921), first woman to be ordained as a minister in the United States, was a supporter of equal rights.

34. Abby Kelley Foster (1810–1887) was an abolitionist lecturer. In 1840, her appointment to a committee of the American Anti-Slavery Society led to a schism in that organization and the withdrawal of the more conservative members into the American and Foreign Anti-Slavery Society. Robert Purvis supported her appointment.

35. *Report of the International Council of Women, 1888, Published by the National Woman's Suffrage Association* (Washington, DC: Rufus H. Darby, Printer, 1888).

36. Sterling, *Ahead of Her Time*, p. 105.

37. Elizabeth Cady Stanton, *Eighty Years & More* (New York: Schocken Books, 1971), p. 83.

38. Quarles, *Black Abolitionists*, pp. 76–77.

39. Ibid., p. 77.

40. Phillip Lapsansky, "Bias in Art has a Long Tradition," *Philadelphia Inquirer*, May 16, 1988.

41. Phillip Lapsansky, "Bias in Art," *Philadelphia Inquirer*.

42. Ibid., Quarles, *Black Abolitionists*, p. 77.

43. *Pennsylvania Freeman*, April 21, 1841.

44. Lapsansky, "Bias in Art."

45. Philadelphia County Deeds, bk. 23, p. 184; bk. 16, p. 265. Philadelphia City Archives. I am indebted to Julie Winch for all these citations.

46. Philadelphia County Deeds, bk. 18, p. 458. Philadelphia City Archives.

47. Philadelphia County Deeds, bk. 29, p. 482. Philadelphia City Archives.

48. Philadelphia County Deeds, bk. 18, p. 459. Philadelphia City Archives.

49. Philadelphia County Deeds, bk. 19, p. 114. Philadelphia City Archives.

50. Philadelphia County Deeds, bk. 23, p, 184. Philadelphia City Archives.

51. Philadelphia County Deeds, bk. 24, p. 275: bk. 23, p. 558. Philadelphia City Archives.

52. Philadelphia County Deeds, bk. 23, p. 558. Philadelphia City Archives.

53. Philadelphia County Deeds, bk. 24, p. 491. Philadelphia City Archives.

54. Philadelphia County Deeds, bk. 36, p. 111. Philadelphia City Archives.

55. Burlington County Book A, p. 521. Burlington County Courthouse, Mt. Holly, NJ.

56. Philadelphia County Deeds, bk. 42, p. 282. Philadelphia City Archives.

57. *Pennsylvania Freeman*, November 17, 1841.

58. Ibid.

59. Ibid.

60. *Philadelphia Press*, April 16, 1898.

Chapter 7. A Time of Loss

1. Winch, *Gentleman of Color*, p. 321.

2. *Colored American*, August 29, 1840.

3. *North Star*, October 6 and 13, 1848. Interview with Robert Purvis, conducted by Edward Magill, former president of Swarthmore College, *Friends Intelligencer*, 55 (March 12,1898): 181.

4. Winch, *Gentleman of Color*, pp. 336–337.

5. Ibid, pp. 326–327.

6. *Pennsylvania Freeman*, January 17, 1839; September 6, December 8, 1841. *Lib*, May 15, 1840.

7. *Lib*, March 18, 1842. Copied from the *Demosthenian Shield*.

8. Lucretia Mott to Richard D. and Hannah Webb, Philadelphia, February 25–March 12, 1842. Anti-Slavery Papers. BPL. Palmer, p. 115.

9. Ibid.

10. *NASS*, March 17, 1842.

11. *Lib*, March 11, 1842.

12. *NASS*, March 24, 1842; *PF*, April, 1842.

13. *Remarks on the Life and Character of James Forten, Delivered at Bethel Church, March 30, 1842* (Philadelphia: Merrihew and Thompson, 1842), p. 3.

14. *Remarks*, p. 8.

15. *Remarks*, pp. 8–9.

16. *Remarks*, p. 10.

17. *Remarks*, pp. 11–12.

18. *Remarks*, p. 12.

19. Ibid.

20. *Remarks*, p. 17.

21. *Remarks*, pp. 17–18.

22. *NASS*, July 21, 1842.

23. Winch, *Gentleman of Color*, pp. 333–338.

24. Winch, *Gentleman of Color*, pp. 338–344.

25. *Act of Incorporation and Constitution of the Pennsylvania Society for the Abolition of Slavery*. Membership (1775–1859), p. 35. (Philadelphia: Merrihew and Thompson, 1860).

26. Philadelphia Female Anti-Slavery Society Minutes, PAS Microfilm Edition, Philadelphia PA, 1976, reel 31.

27. Proceedings of the Anti-Slavery Convention of American Women: 1838; 1839 (Philadelphia, 1838, 1839).

28. Minutes Philadelphia Female Anti-Slavery Society, June 15, 1841; June 23, 1841. PAS. Microfilm Edition, Philadelphia, PA. 1976, reel 31.

29. The Colored Free Produce Society was organized in February, 1831, and the Colored Female Free Produce Society in May of that year. *Genius of Universal Emancipation* (February, May, August, 1831).

30. Janice Sumler-Lewis, "The Forten-Purvis Women of Philadelphia and the American Anti-Slavery Crusade," *Journal of Negro History*, 66 (1981–1982): 281.

31. Annual Meeting of the American Anti-Slavery Society, May, 1853. *NASS*, May 13, 1853.

32. Julie Winch, "You Have Talents—Only Cultivate Them: Philadelphia's Black Female Literary Societies and the Abolitionist Crusade," in *The Abolitionist Sisterhood*.

33. *NASS*, August 18, 1842.

34. Winch, *Black Elite*, p. 149.

35. Ibid.

36. Ibid., Joseph Borome, "The Vigilant Committee of Philadelphia," p. 326.

37. *Philadelphia Press*, August 3, 1890.

38. Borome, "Vigilant Committee." Robert Purvis to Henry Wright, 22 August 1842. Anti-Slavery Papers, Boston Public Library.

39. Robert Purvis to Henry Wright, 22 August 1842. Anti-Slavery Papers, Boston Public Library.

40. Ibid.

41. Ibid.

Chapter 8. Gentleman Farmer

1. Philadelphia County Deeds, bk. 8, p. 351; p. 353, bk. 10, p. 303; bk. 10, p. 91; Box 24, p. 202. Courtesy of Julie Winch.

2. Robert and Harriet Purvis to Lester Comly, Ezra Comly and Jesse James, Trustees of Byberry Transpontine Meeting of Friends, Philadelphia County Deed Book, RLL 8:351, January 7, 1873. Philadelphia County Archives, Philadelphia.

3. Letter to author from Beatrice J. Walton, Librarian of Byberry Monthly Meeting, 12–03–2002.

4. Notes by Myra Hall, a longtime member of Byberry Monthly Meeting. Information from Beatrice Walton, Librarian, Byberry Monthly Meeting Library.

5. Ibid.

6. Robert Purvis to Mrs. M. W. Chapman, 24 September 1845, Anti-Slavery Papers, Boston Public Library.

7. John White Chadwick, ed., *A Life For Liberty: Anti-Slavery and Other Letters of Sallie Holley* (New York: Putnam, 1899), p. 102.

8. William Lloyd Garrison to Helen Garrison 6-10-1862; Walter Merrill and Louis Ruchames, *The Letters of William Lloyd Garrison* (Cambridge: The Belknap Press, 1971-1981), 5: 95; Dorothy Sterling, *Ahead of Her Time*, p. 250; Aaron Powell, *Personal Reminiscences of the Anti-Slavery and Other Reforms and Reformers* (New York: Cauldron Press, 1899), p. 150.

9. Powell, *Personal Reminiscences*, p. 150.

10. Will of Robert Purvis, signed October 14, 1887, codicils October 27, 1887 and May 3, 1894. Probated April 30, 1898. Philadelphia County Wills, Will Book 200, p. 291, No. 661. Philadelphia County Archives.

11. *NASS*, January 1, 1859, To the editor of the *Germantown (Pa.) Telegram*.

12. Ibid.

13. Ibid.

14. Federal Agricultural Bureau of the Census, 1850 and 1860. Courtesy of Julie Winch.

15. *Maryland Colonization Journal*, October 1846; *Pennsylvania Freeman*, December 8, 1853; *Quarles, Black Abolitionists*, p. 134.

16. Chadwick, *A Life for Liberty*, p. 102.

17. Henry Cadbury, "Negro Membership in the Society of Friends," *Journal of Negro History*, 21 (1936): 151-213. The author indicated that Robert Purvis might have joined Byberry Meeting. An extensive search of the records, however, reveals that he did not. See also the Burial Records for Fair Hill Burial Ground, and Minutes of Bristol Monthly Meeting, which lists him as a non-Quaker. Meeting Records, Friends Historical Library, Swarthmore College.

18. Ibid. See Margaret Hope Bacon, "New Light on Sarah Mapps Douglass and Her Reconciliation with the Society of Friends" *Quaker History* (Spring, 2001).

19. Margaret H. Bacon, *Abby Hopper Gibbons: Prison Reformer and Social Activist* (Albany: State University of New York Press, 2000), pp. 39-42.

20. *Pennsylvania Yearly Meeting of Progressive Friends, Proceedings*, 1853-1868. Friends Historical Library, Swarthmore College: Progressive Friends of Longwood Burial Records, Chester County Visitors Bureau, Kennett Square, PA.

21. Philadelphia County Deeds, R. L. L. Box 39, p. 283; Deeds, AWM Book 51, p. 549. Information from Beatrice Walton, Librarian, Byberry Monthly Meeting. William Wells Brown, *The Black Man: His Antecedents, His Genius and His Achievements* (New York: Thomas Hamilton 1863), p. 256.

22. *Pennsylvania Freeman,* November 25, 1847.

23. *Maryland Colonization Journal,* October, 1846, p. 211.

24. *North Star,* October 6 and 13, 1848. See Chapter 4, footnote 41.

25. *North Star,* December 10, 1848.

26. Philadelphia Female Anti-Slavery Society minutes, March 14, 1844; December 12, 1844; February 13, 1848. PAS, Microfilm Edition, reel 30.

27. Georgiana Bruce attended several meetings of the Pennsylvania Anti-Slavery Society with Harriet. She may have been the wife of William Bruce, listed in the U.S. Census of 1850 for Philadelphia as a waiter, living at South Street above Eighth Street. Records of the Byberry Friends School. Information from Beatrice Walton, Librarian, Byberry Monthly Meeting.

28. "Byberry School," unpublished paper from the Byberry Meeting Library. Information from Beatrice Walton, Librarian, Byberry Monthly Meeting.

29. Ibid.

30. Byberry School Reunion, 1906–1907. Item by Charles Purvis, information from Beatrice Walton, Librarian, Byberry Monthly Meeting.

31. Ibid.

32. *Pennsylvania Freeman,* February 10, 1848. Purvis claimed that his sons had been abused by a teacher, with the support of the school principal, on the basis of their color.

33. Ibid.

34. *Lib,* September 16, 1853.

35. Ibid.

36. Information from Beatrice Walton, Librarian, Byberry Monthly Meeting.

37. Benjamin Quarles, *Black Abolitionists,* p. 114.

38. Lucretia Mott to Joseph and Ruth Dugdale, 12 July 1850. Palmer, *Selected Letters,* pp. 204–206.

39. Hattie Purvis to Ellen Wright, 16 January 1856. Garrison Papers, Smith College.

40. Joseph C. Martindale, *Byberry and Moreland History* (Philadelphia: George W. Jacobs, & Co., 1901), p. 182.

41. *Pennsylvania Freeman*, December 8, 1853.

42. Martha Coffin Wright to David Wright, 4 December 1853. Garrison Papers, Smith College.

43. Winch, *Gentleman of Color*, p. 372.

44. *Public Ledger*, December 17, 1845; Philadelphia County Wills, Will Book 18, p. 170, no. 264. Education and Employment Statistics of the Colored People of Philadelphia 1856, PAS; Microfilm Edition, Philadelphia, 1976; reel 26; Pinckney, ed., Register of St. Phillips Church 1810–1822, p. 53; U.S. Census, 1870 Charleston, p. 381.

45. Minutes, Philadelphia Female Anti-Slavery Society, January 17, 1841; September 19, 1842; March 9, 1843. PAS Microfilm, reel 30; Lucretia Mott to Martha Coffin Wright, 21 January 1868. Mott Papers. FHL. From *Selected Letters*, Palmer.

46. Minutes Philadelphia Female Anti-Slavery Society, 12 January, 1854. PAS. Microfilm, reel 30.

47. Minutes, Philadelphia Female Anti-Slavery Society, 9 January 1851. PAS, Microfilm Edition, reel 30.

48. *Public Ledger*, July 4, 1843.

49. *Public Ledger*, July 4, 1843.

50. See William Cohen, "The Pennsylvania Anti-Slavery Society," 1960.

51. Robert Purvis to Miller McKim, 21 October 1844. Peter Ripley and George Carters, eds, *Black Abolitionist Papers*, Microfilm Edition, New York, 1981. Vol. 44, frame 0944.

52. Cohen, "The Pennsylvania Abolition Society."

53. Minutes, Pennsylvania Anti-Slavery Society, 1845, 1847. PAS, Microfilm Edition, reel 30.

54. Philip S. Foner and George F. Walker, Pennsylvania Convention of 1848, in Foner, Philip S. and Walker, George F., *Proceedings of the Black State Conventions 1840–1865* (Philadelphia: Temple University Press, 1979). Pennsylvania Convention of 1848.

55. Ibid., pp. 123–125.

56. "Appeal to the Colored Citizens of Pennsylvania," Philip S. Foner and George F. Walker, p. 128.

57. Ibid., p. 127.

58. Memorial to Robert Purvis, April 18, 1898. Gardiner Collection, 8B, Historical Society of Pennsylvania.

59. William Still, *The Underground Railroad*, p. 20; Lucretia Mott to Joseph and Ruth Dugdale, 28 March 1849. Mott Papers, Friends Historical Library, Swarthmore College, as in Palmer, *Selected Letters*, pp. 178–182.

Chapter 9. *"This Wicked Law"*

1. *Pennsylvania Freeman*, October 31, 1850.

2. Ibid.

3. Jerome A. Borome, "The Vigilant Committee of Philadelphia," 321–337.

4. Quarles, *Black Abolitionists*, p. 201. *Pennsylvania Freeman*, October 24, 1850.

5. *NASS*, October 31, 1850.

6. *NASS*, May 29, 1851. *Public Ledger*, May 15, 1851.

7. *Frederick Douglass' Paper*, June 16, 1851.

8. *Frederick Douglass' Paper*, June 26, 1851; T. T. Purvis, *Hagar: The Singing Maiden and Other Stories* (Philadelphia: Walton, 1881), pp. 111–115.

9. Still, *Underground Railroad*, p. 349. See Jonathon Katz, *Resistance at Christiana* (New York: Thomas Y Crowell, 1974). Also Thomas Slaughter, *Bloody Dawn: The Christiana Riot and Racial Violence in the Antebellum North* (New York: Oxford University Press, 1991).

10. Ibid.

11. *Pennsylvania Freeman*, October 16, 1851. Margaret H. Bacon, *Valiant Friend*, p. 172.

12. Borome, "The Vigilant Committee," p. 326.

13. *Pennsylvania Freeman*, January 16, 1851. The case of the Crafts, a very light-skinned woman and her darker husband, who had escaped as master and servant, had recently attracted national attention.

14. Ibid.

15. Gerrit Smith (1797–1874) was a wealthy manufacturer and philanthropist who worked with William Lloyd Garrison but later championed advancing antislavery in the political arena, serving one term in Congress. *Pennsylvania Freeman*, January 16, 1851; April 29, 1852; May 13, 1852.

16. *Frederick Douglass' Paper*, April 29, 1852.

17. Sarah Pugh to Mary Estlin, November 29, 1853, in Quarles, *Black Abolitionists*, p. 134, footnote 39.

18. *Pennsylvania Freeman*, December 8, 1853.

19. Still, *Underground Railroad*, pp. 73–84.

20. Ibid.

21. Ibid.

22. Ibid.

23. Bell, *Colored Conventions*, 1853, 1855.

24. Ibid, 1855, p. 20.

25. Ibid., p. 10.

26. Garrison to Purvis, April 9, 1854 and April 21, 1854; Merrill and Ruchames, *The Letters of William Lloyd Garrison*, 4: 296, 299.

27. *Lib*, May 19, 1854.

28. Ibid.

29. *NASS*, April 16, 1870.

30. *The North Star* was combined with the *Liberty Line Paper* and became *Frederick Douglass' Paper* in June of 1851.

31. *Frederick Douglass' Paper*, May 20, 1852.

32. *Lib*, September 16, 1853.

33. Ripley, *Black Abolitionist Papers*, 1: 419; *NASS* January 13, 1855.

34. *NASS*, January 13, 1855.

35. *Lib*, December 29, 1854.

36. *Lib*, June 13, 1856.

37. Ibid.

38. *NASS*, February 14, 1857.

39. Ibid.

40. *Anti-Slavery Bugle*, April 11, 1857.

41. Ibid.

42. *NASS*, May 23, 1857.

43. Ibid.

44. American Antiquarian Society, Worcester, MA, Miscellaneous Anti-Slavery Collection. "Call for a National Convention."

45. *NASS*, January 31, 1857; *Bucks County Intelligencer*, January 17, 1857; *Doylestown Democrat*, January 27, 1857.

46. Winch, *Gentleman of Color*, p. 363. Information on Joseph from genealogical records in possession of John Purvis of Fife.

47. Winch, *Gentleman of Color*, p. 364.

48. Brenda Stevenson, ed., *Journals of Charlotte Forten Grimké* (New York: Oxford University Press, 1987), July 6, 1858, p. 322.

49. Raymond W. Logan and Michael R. Winston, *Dictionary of American Negro Biography*, New York: W. W. Norton Co. Inc. 1982, p. 529; *Bucks County Intelligencer*, August 28, 1857; *Doylestown Democrat*, September 15, 1857.

50. Information from Beatrice Walton, Librarian, Byberry Monthly Meeting. Lucretia Mott to Martha Coffin Wright, 9th mo. [September] 7th, 1857. Palmer, 262–263.

51. Ibid.

Chapter 10. *"Are We Not Men?"*

1. See Brenda Stevenson, ed. *The Journals of Charlotte Grimké*.

2. Ibid., p. 345.

3. Ibid., September 18, 1858, p. 339.

4. Ibid., August 25, 1858, p. 333; September 19, p. 339.

5. Ibid., December 11, 1858, January 30, 1859, p. 352.

6. Ellen Wright to Martha Coffin Wright, December 13, 1858. In Harriet Alonso, *Growing Up Abolitionist: The Story of the Garrison Children* (Amherst: University of Massachusetts Press, 2002), p. 188.

7. Ellen Wright's diary, entry for January 12, 1859; Winch, *A Gentleman of Color*, p. 359.

8. Ellen Wright to Anna Davis, December 29, 1859; Alonso, *Growing Up Abolitionist*, p. 188.

9. Ellen Wright to Anna Davis, January 6, 1860; Alonso, *Growing Up Abolitionist*, p. 188.

10. Brenda Stevenson, ed., *The Journals of Charlotte Grimké*, p. 356. See Stanley W. Campbell, *The Slave Catchers: Enforcement of the Fugitive Slave Law, 1850–1860* (Chapel Hill, NC: University of North Carolina Press, 1968).

11. Ibid.

12. *NASS*, April 16, 1859.

13. Ibid.

14. Brenda Stevenson, ed., *Journals of Charlotte Forten Grimké*, p. 357.

15. Stevenson, *Journals of Charlotte Forten Grimké*, p. 358. Daniel Webster to William Still, Ripley et al, *Black Abolitionist Papers*, 2: 409.

16. Robert Purvis Jr. to C. A. Walbern, February 22, 1859, Jenks Papers, Friends Historical Library, Swarthmore College.

17. *NASS*, December 10, 1859; Quarles, *Black Abolitionists*, p. 243.

18. Alexander Crummell (1819–1898), black clergyman, scholar and activist, became interested in the development of Liberia and spent two decades there.

19. *Weekly Anglo-African*, April 21, 1860.

20. *NASS*, May 12, 1860.

21. Ibid., Robert Purvis, *Speeches and Letters Published by the Request of the Afro-American League* (n.d.:, n.p. Rare Books, University of Pennsylvania).

22. Ibid., *The Merchant of Venice*, 3.1. in *Shakespeare, The Complete Works*, ed. George Bagehawe Harrison (New York: Harcourt, Brace and Company, 1948) p. 597.

23. Ibid.

24. *Philadelphia Press*, October 27, 1860.

25. Ibid.

26. Ibid.

27. *Philadelphia Bulletin*, October 27, 1860.

28. *Philadelphia Press*, October 27, 1860.

29. Purvis to Miller McKim, October 28, 1860. Miller McKim Letters, Cornell University, Ithaca, New York; *Philadelphia Dispatch*, October 28, 1860; *NASS*, October 30, 1860.

30. Miller McKim to the *Philadelphia Press* in *NASS*, November 10, 1860.

31. See Bayard Taylor, *A Journey to Central Africa: or, Life and Landscapes from Egypt to the Negro Kingdoms of the White Nile* (New York: Putnam, 1852).

32. *NASS*, November 17, 1860.

33. *NASS*, November 24, 1860.

34. *NASS*, December 4, 1860.

35. *Philadelphia Freeman*, February 16, 1854.

36. Jenkins papers, Friends Historical Library, Swarthmore College, *Friends Intelligencer*, 76 (1918): 238. U.S. Bureau of Census for Philadelphia, 1860, ward 23, p. 973.

37. *NASS*, May 25, 1861.

38. *NASS*, November 2, 1861.

39. Ibid.

40. Benjamin Quarles, *The Negro in the Civil War* (Boston: Little Brown, 1953), pp. 32–35; 71–74.

41. See Willie Lee Rose, *Rehearsal for Reconstruction: The Port Royal Experiment* (Indianapolis: The Bobbs-Merrill Company, Inc. 1964); Stevenson, *Journals of Charlotte Forten Grimké*, October 27, 1862, p. 382–392.

42. *Lib*, April 4, 1862.

43. William Lloyd Garrison to Helen, June 10, 1862; Merrill and Ruchames, *The Letters of William Lloyd Garrison*, 5: 95.

44. Stevenson, *Journals of Charlotte Forten Grimké*, p. 364.

45. Samuel Clarke Pomeroy (1816–1891) served under President Lincoln in charge of emigration.

46. *Lib*, September 12, 1862.

47. Ibid.

48. Ibid.

49. Ibid.

Chapter 11. *"A Proud Day for the Colored Man"*

1. *NASS*, January 24, 1863.

2. *NASS*, May 16, 1863.

3. Edward Bates (1793–1869) was attorney general under President Abraham Lincoln.

4. William Henry Seward (1801–1872) was U.S. Secretary of State (1861–1869).

5. Edwin Stanton (1814–1869), U.S. Secretary of War under Abraham Lincoln, and later Andrew Johnson.

6. *NASS*, May 16, 1863.

7. Ibid.

8. Following the liberation of the offshore islands of South Carolina by Union troops, a black regiment was raised. The First South Carolina Volunteers, under Thomas Wentworth Higginson, were the first black troops to serve in the Civil War.

9. The Massachusetts 54th Regiment was the first black regiment mustered into U.S. service. Under Colonel Robert G. Shaw. It went into action at Fort Wagner, South Carolina in 1863, sustaining heavy losses. Shaw himself died in the attack.

10. George Henry Thomas was a Major General in the Civil War. He fought in Tennessee.

11. *NASS*, May 16, 1863.

12. *NASS*, February 14, 1873. Sarah Lester to William Still, April 21, 1863, in Ripley, *Black Abolitionist Papers*, 2: 515, n. 519; George Luther Stearns (1809–1867) was a Boston businessman and abolitionist who backed John Brown in his attempt to raise a slave insurrection at Harper's Ferry.

13. Richard P. Hallowell (1835–1904) recruited troops for the Massachusetts 54th and 55th, but was too ill to serve. Three of his brothers fought in the Civil War.

14. The army insisted that all black troops be under the command of white officers.

15. Robert Purvis to unknown, February 18, 1863. Peter Ripley and George Carter, eds., *Black Abolitionists Papers*, 1830–1865, Microfilm Edition, New York, reel 14, frame 0744.

16. Robert Purvis to Elizabeth Gay, June 7, 1863. Sydney Howard Gay Papers, Rare Books and Manuscripts, Columbia University.

17. Stevenson, *Journals of Charlotte Forten Grimké*, p. 494.

18. Quarles, *The Negro in the Civil War*, pp. 223–224.

19. David Jenks Morrison, *A Guidebook to Historic LaMott* (Cheltenham, PA: Cheltenham Township Historical Commission. 1974).

20. Ibid.

21. Milliken's Bend was a Civil War battle fought in Louisiana under General George H. Thomas, in which African-American troops participated.

22. A decisive Civil War battle was fought at Port Hudson, Louisiana in 1863 under General Nathaniel P. Banks, in which African-American troops played a major role.

23. *Lib*, September 11, 1863.

24. *Lib*, May 13, 1864.

25. Ibid.

26. Winch, *Gentleman of Color*, p. 366.

27. Philip S. Foner, "The Battle to End Discrimination Against Negroes on Philadelphia Streetcars," *Pennsylvania History*, 40, 41 (July and October, 1973); Margaret Hope Bacon, *Valiant Friend: The Life of Lucretia Mott*, 3rd ed. (Philadelphia: Friends General Conference, 1999), p. 210.

28. Minutes, Philadelphia Female Anti-Slavery Society, 1862–1867, PAS Microfilm Edition, reel 30.

29. *Philadelphia Press*, April 1, 1865; William Still, "A Brief Narrative of the Struggle for the Rights of the Colored People of Philadelphia in the City Railway Cars, and a Defense of William Still" (Philadelphia: n.p., 1867).

30. Hugh Davis, "Pennsylvania State Equal Rights League and the Northern Black Struggle for Equality, 1864–1877," in *The Pennsylvania Magazine of History and Biography*, 126, no. 4 (2002): 611–634.

31. Harry C. Silcox, "Nineteenth Century Philadelphia Black Militant Octavius Catto, (1839–1871), *Pennsylvania History*, 44 (January 1977): 53–76.

32. Davis, "Pennsylvania State Equal Rights League," pp. 611–634.

33. Roger Lane, *William Dorsey's Philadelphia and Ours: On the Past and Future of the Black City in America* (New York: Oxford University Press, 1993), p. 111.

34. Ibid.

35. Robert Purvis to Parker Smith, Esq., Feb 22, 1867. Copy of letter, Leon Gardiner Collection, 8B, Historical Society of Pennsylvania.

36. See Iver Bernstein, *The New York Draft Riots: Their Significance in American Society and Politics in the Age of the Civil War* (New York: Oxford University Press 1990).

37. Henry Mayer, *All on Fire: William Garrison and the Abolition of Slavery* (New York: St. Martin's Press, 1998), p. 529.

38. Ibid, p. 557.

39. *Proceedings of the American Anti-Slavery Society at its Third Decade, held in the City of Philadelphia Dec. 3rd and 4th, 1863* (Phonographic report by Henry M. Parkhurst). Friends Historical Library, Swarthmore College.

40. *NASS*, December 12, 1863, p. 2.

41. *Proceedings*, p. 112.

42. *Proceedings*, p. 77.

43. The Board of Education and the Committee of Employment, PAS, Microfilm, reel 27.

44. Lucretia Mott to Martha Coffin Wright, April 19,1864. Mott Papers, Friends Historical Library, Swarthmore College.

45. *Lib*, May 26, 1865.

46. Ibid.

47. William Lloyd Garrison to Helen Garrison, February 16, 1866; *Garrison Letters*, 5: 390.

48. Francis Jackson (1789–1861) was a Boston merchant, and president of the Massachusetts Anti-Slavery Society. *NASS*, August 10, 1867.

49. *NASS*, August 10, 1867.

50. Ibid.

51. *NASS*, March 16, 1867.

52. Garrison to Helen, June 8, 1868, *Garrison Letters*, 6: 62–63.

53. Ibid.

54. Robert Purvis to Wendell Phillips, November 8, 1864. Papers of Wendell Phillips, Harvard University Library. bMS AM 1953 (1014), Cambridge, MA.

55. *NASS*, February 15, 1868.

56. *NASS*, June 6, 1868.

Chapter 12. *"Equality of Rights for All"*

1. *Oberlin College Catalogue of Students, 1833–1908*, p. 377; William Simmons, *Men of Mark: Eminent, Progressive and Rising* (New York: Arno Press, 1968), pp. 690–693; *NASS*, April 17, 1869, April 16, 1870.

2. *Oberlin College Catalogue of Students, 1833–1908*; p. 377; Graduates of Howard University, p. 301. Willard B. Gatewood, *Aristocrats of Color* (Fayetteville, AR: University of Arkansas Press, 2000), p. 127.

3. Dorothy Porter, *Early Negro Writing 1760–1837* (Boston: Beacon Press, 1971), pp. 200–248. *Report of the International Council of Women, 1888, published by the National Woman Suffrage Association, Washington, DC* (Washington, DC: Rufus H. Darby, printer, 1888), pp. 342–344.

4. Elizabeth Cady Stanton, Susan B. Anthony, Matilda Joslyn Gage, *History of Woman Suffrage*, 6 vols. (New York: Fowler, 1881–1922), 2: 182.

5. Stanton, Anthony, Gage, *History of Woman Suffrage*, 2: 183.

6. Ibid., 2: 382.

7. Ibid., 2: 383.

8. *Report of the International Council of Women*, assembled by the National Woman Suffrage Association, Washington, DC (Washington, DC: National Woman Suffrage Association, 1888).

9. Stanton, Anthony, Gage, *History of Woman Suffrage*, 4: 136.

10. Mary Grew, *James Mott, A Biographical Sketch* (New York: William P. Tomlinson, Publishers, 39 Nassau Street, 1868), p. 19.

11. *Report of the International Council of Women*, assembled by the National Woman Suffrage Association, Washington, DC (Washington, DC: National Woman Suffrage Association, 1888).

12. Martha Coffin Wright to David Wright, January 27, 1869, Garrison Papers, Smith College.

13. Ibid.

14. Stanton, Anthony, Gage, *History of Woman Suffrage*, 2: 358.

15. Ibid.

16. Ibid., 2: 418–419.

17. Ibid., 4: 163.

18. *Forney's Weekly Press*, December 18, 1869.

19. *Sunday Dispatch*, December 19, 1869.

20. Will of Harriet Miller, First will Jan. 16, 1846, codicil May 11, 1868. Probated December 17, 1868. Philadelphia County Archives.

21. St. Thomas Church Parish Register, 1853–1893; Records, Parrish House, St. Thomas Church, Philadelphia; Fair Hill Burial Ground, Friends Historical Society, Swarthmore College.

22. Francis Butler Simkins and Robert Hilliard Woody, *South Carolina During Reconstruction* (Chapel Hill, NC: The University of North Carolina Press, 1932), p. 46.

23. *NASS*, August 29, 1868.

24. Ibid.

25. Logan and Winston, *Dictionary of American Negro Biography*, p. 107.

26. *NASS*, July 3, 1869.

27. John Mercer Langston (1829–1897) was a lawyer and educator, who later taught at Howard University and served as ambassador to Haiti.

28. Robert Purvis to Wendell Phillips, September 9, 1867. Wendell Phillips Papers, Harvard University Library. bMS AM 1953 (1014), Cambridge, MA.

29. Ibid., September 18th, 1867, Wendell Phillips Papers, Harvard University Library. bMS AM 1953 (1014), Cambridge, MA.

30. *NASS*, October 23, 1869.

31. Letter to Fellow Abolitionists signed by Robert Purvis, Lucretia Mott, William Still, and Benjamin Bacon. Mott Papers, Friends Historical Library, Swarthmore College.

32. *NASS*, April 3, 1869.

33. *NASS*, April 16, 1870.

34. Ibid.

35. Ibid.

36. Ibid.

37. Ibid.

38. *Philadelphia Press*, April 27, 1870.

39. Roger Lane, *Roots of Violence in Black Philadelphia, 1860–1900* (Cambridge: Harvard University Press, 1986), p. 53; *Philadelphia Press*, April 26, 1870.

40. *Philadelphia Press*, April 26, 1870.

Chapter 13. The Freedmen's Savings Bank

1. Roger Lane, *Roots of Violence in Black Philadelphia, 1860–1890*, pp. 45–46; Harry C. Silcox, "Nineteenth Century Philadelphia Black Militant: Octavius Catto, (1839–1871) *Pennsylvania History*, 44 (January, 1977): 53–76.

2. Ibid., pp. 212, 214.

3. *Public Ledger*, October 14, 1871.

4. Harry Silcox, "The Black 'Better Class' Political Dilemma: Prototype Isaiah C. Wears," in *Pennsylvania Magazine of History and Biography*, 113 (January 1989): 62–64.

5. Lane, *Roots of Violence*, p. 46.

6. *Philadelphia Press*, October 9, 1871.

7. Ibid.

8. Ibid.

9. John W. Forney, *Anecdotes of Public Men* (New York: Harper Brothers, 1873), pp. 336–339.

10. *Philadelphia Press*, March 11, 1874; March 18, 1874.

11. S. A. Newby to William Still, March 18, 1874. Leon Gardiner Papers, Historical Society of Pennsylvania.

12. M. A. S. Carr to William Still, May 11, 1874 in Alberta Norwood, "Negro Welfare in Philadelphia, Especially as Illustrated by the Career of William Still," (master's thesis, University of Pennsylvania, 1931), p. 172; Roger Lane, *William Dorsey's Philadelphia and Ours*, p. 106.

13. Purvis to Gerrit Smith, February 1,1871. Gerrit Smith Papers, Special Collections, Research Center, Syracuse University Library, Syracuse, New York.

14. *Philadelphia Press*, May 14, 1873.

15. *Voice of Peace*, July 1873, p. 14.

16. U.S. Bureau of Census, Washington, DC 1870; Willard B. Gatewood, *Aristocrats of Color: The Black Elite, 1880–1890* (Fayetteville: University of Arkansas Press, 2000), p. 168.

17. U.S. Bureau of Census for Washington County, Maine, 1840, 1850. Memorial Services Colored Orphans Home, Washington, DC, 1899. I am indebted to Dr. Marie Agnew-Marcelli for this information. U.S. Bureau of Census, Washington, DC, 1870, 1880; Edward James, Janet James and Paul Rover, eds., *Notable American Women, 1607–1950* (Cambridge, MA: The Belknap Press, 1971), p. 96.

18. Memorial Services for Anne M. Purvis, at Colored Orphans Home, Tuesday, May 9, 1899. African-American Perspectives: Pamphlets from the Daniel A. P. Murray Collection, 1818–1997. Library of Congress, Washington, DC.

19. Gatewood, *Aristocrats of Color*, p.168.

20. Michael B. Winston, "Charles Purvis" in *Dictionary of American Negro Biography*, Rayford W. Logan and Michael R. Winston, eds. (New York: W. W. Norton Co. Inc., 1982), pp. 507–508.

21. William S. McFeeley, *Frederick Douglass* (New York: W. W. Norton Co. Inc., 1991), p. 296.

22. Gatewood, *Aristocrats of Color*, p. 127; Winch, *Gentleman of Color*, p. 362; NASS, March 4, 1871.

23. Holt, *Black Over White*, pp. 150, 162.

24. Forney, *Anecdotes*, pp. 338–339.

25. Genealogical information supplied by John Purvis of Fife, Scotland, and Reginald Pitts.

26. Simkins and Woody, *South Carolina Reconstruction*, pp. 516–523.

27. Thomas Holt, *Black Over White*, p. 203.

28. Ibid.

29. *Philadelphia Times*, December 14, 1880.

30. *See* George R. Bentley, *A History of the Freedmen's Bureau* (New York: Farrar, Strauss and Giroux: New York, 1974); Walter Fleming, *The Freedmen's Saving Bank: A Chapter in the Economic History of the Race* (Chapel Hill, NC: University of North Carolina, 1927) pp. 101–102.

31. William McFeeley, *Frederick Douglass*, pp. 282–284.

32. Fleming, *The Freedmen's Saving Bank*, pp. 102–103.

33. McFeeley, *Douglass*, p. 280.

34. Fleming, *The Freedmen's Saving Bank*, p. 115.

35. Ibid., pp. 118, 119.

36. Records, Depositors of Freedmen's Bank, United States Archives, Microfilm. Charleston Free Negro Capitation tax books, 1860–1870, South Carolina Department of Archives and History, Columbia, SC.

37. Fleming, *The Freedmen's Saving Bank*, p. 104.

38. Ibid.

39. Ibid.

40. Ibid., p. 105.

41. Fleming, *The Freedmen's Saving Bank*, pp. 108–112.

42. Fleming, *The Freedmen's Saving Bank*, p. 121.

43. Robert Purvis to Frederick Douglass, Manuscript Division, Library of Congress, August 29, 1878.

44. Fleming, *The Freedmen's Saving Bank*, p. 112.

45. Frederick Douglass, *Life and Times of Frederick Douglass* (New York: n.p., 1892), p. 418. Charles B. Purvis to Frederick Douglass, July 1, 1886, Douglass Papers, Library of Congress.

46. Deed SN-21-2, Robert Purvis, grantee, to John A. McDowell, grantor, June 24, 1873. Recorder of Deeds, Philadelphia County Deed Book, LW 143–509. April 1, 1881. Philadelphia County Archives.

47. Winch, *Gentleman of Color*, p. 365.

48. *Public Ledger*, June 12, 1875; Records of the Fair Hill Burial Ground, p. 222. Friends Historical Library, Swarthmore College.

49. Charles B. Purvis to Francis Grimké, August 27, 1922. Francis Grimké Papers, Moorland-Springarn Research Center, Howard University.

50. Records of Fair Hill Burial Ground, p. 238. Friends Historical Library, Swarthmore College.

51. *Bucks County Intelligencer*, March 20, 1878; Byberry Friends Meeting Library; *Friends Intelligencer*, 1898, 1900; *Christian Recorder*, February 7, 1884.

52. T. T. Purvis, *Abi Meredith* (Philadelphia: Friends Book Association, 1878); *Hagar: The Singing Maiden.*

53. Bristol Preparative Meeting of Men and Women Friends, October 23,1878; Bristol Monthly Meeting of Women Friends, November 1, 1878: November 29, 1878 Monthly Meeting Records, Friends Historical Library, Swarthmore College.

54. Ray Allen Billington, "Charlotte Forten Grimké," *Notable American Women*, 2: 97.

55. Anonymous, *Centennial Anniversary of the Pennsylvania Society for Promoting the Abolition of Slavery, the Relief of Free Negroes Unlawfully Held in Bondage; and for Improving the Condition of the African Race* (Philadelphia: Grant, Faires, & Rogers, printers, 1875), p. 33.

56. See Philip S. Foner, "Black Participation in the Centennial of 1876," *Negro History Bulletin*, 39, no. 2. February, 1976, pp. 533–538.

57. Stanton, Anthony and Gage, *History of Woman Suffrage*, 3: 93.

58. Ibid., p. 493.

Chapter 14. *"We are To the Manner Born"*

1. Logan and Winston, *Dictionary of American Negro Biography*, p. 508.

2. Wolf, *Philadelphia, Portrait of an American City* (Philadelphia: Stackpole Books, 1970), pp. 236–238.

3. Ibid., pp. 245–246.

4. Ibid., p. 236.

5. Lane, *Dorsey*, p. 203.

6. Lane, *Roots*, p. 64: *Philadelphia Press*, August 23, 1881.

7. Ibid.

8. Ibid.

9. Lane, *Dorsey*, p. 217.

10. Lane, *Roots*, p. 67.

11. *Philadelphia Press*, January 3, 1889.

12. Ibid.

13. Ibid.

14. *Philadelphia Times*, May 18, 1886.

15. Ibid.

16. Ibid.

17. Ibid.

18. Ibid.

19. *Philadelphia Times*, August 19, 1890; August 26, 1890.

20. Ibid.

21. *Philadelphia Press*, November 29, 1890.

22. *Philadelphia Press*, April 21, 1891.

23. Ibid.

24. Lane, *Roots*, p. 82.

25. Robert Purvis to William Lloyd Garrison. November 18, 1878. "Our friend Davis" refers to Edward M. Davis. Anti-Slavery Papers, Boston Public Library.

26. Robert Purvis to William Lloyd Garrison December 2, 1878, Anti-Slavery Papers, Boston Public Library.

27. Robert Purvis to William Lloyd Garrison, March 4, 1879. Anti-Slavery Papers, Boston Public Library.

28. *Philadelphia Ledger*, November 26, 1880.

29. Anonymous, *Report on the Semi-Centennial of the Founding of the American Anti-Slavery Society*, Friends Historical Library, Swarthmore College. Also, Daniel Neall Papers, Friends Historical Library, Swarthmore College.

30. Ibid.

31. Edward M. Davis to Dear Friends, December 5, 1883. Daniel Neall Papers, Friends Historical Library, Swarthmore College.

32. Daniel Neall to Edward M. Davis, n.d. Neall Papers. Friends Historical Library, Swarthmore College.

33. Ira Brown, *Mary Grew: Abolitionist and Feminist* (Selingrove: Susquehanna University Press, 1984), p. 159.

34. Brown, *Grew*, p. 161.

35. T. T. Purvis, *Hagar: The Singing Maiden*, p. 256; Stanton, Anthony, Gage. *History of Woman Suffrage*, 4: 898. Friends Historical Library, Swarthmore College. *Report of the International Council of Women, 1888*, pp. 342–344.

36. *International Council of Women Report*, p. 342.

37. Ibid.

38. Ibid.

39. Ibid.

40. *The Voice of Peace*, issue of July, 1873, p. 14.

41. William Still, *The Underground Railroad*, p. 737; Robert Purvis to William Still, January 30, 1866. Leon Gardiner Collection, 9G, Folder 17, Historical Society of Pennsylvania.

42. Smedley, *History of the Underground Railroad*, editors' preface.

43. Siebert, *The Underground Railroad*, pp. 10, 346.

44. John Greenleaf Whittier to Robert Purvis, August 2, 1890. Whittier Papers, Friends Historical Library, Swarthmore College.

45. *Philadelphia Press*, August 3, 1890.

46. Will of Robert Purvis, signed October 14, 1887, two codicils, dates October 27, 1887 and May 3, 1894, probated April 30, 1898. Philadelphia County Wills, Will Book 200, p. 291, will 661 (1898) Philadelphia City Archives.

47. Robert Purvis to Mrs. Elizabeth Gay, Philadelphia, September 7, 1896. Sydney Howard Gay Papers, Rare Books and Manuscripts, Columbia University.

48. Ibid.

49. Winch, *Gentleman of Color,* p. 365; Information on Sterling Paper Company courtesy of Reginald Pitts.

50. Charles B. Purvis to Francis Grimké, February 20, 1910, Purvis-Grimké Letters, Morland-Springarn Research Center, Howard University, Washington, DC.

51. *The Unitarian Year Book, 1917* (Boston: American Unitarian Association, 1918), pp. 127–128.

52. Edward H. Magill, "The Underground Railroad," *Friends Intelligencer,* 55: n. 11 (March 12, 1898).

53. Ibid.

54. Ibid.

55. Ibid.

Chapter 15. *"His Magnificent Record"*

1. *Philadelphia Press,* April 16, 1898.

2. *Philadelphia Bulletin,* April 16, 1898.

3. *New York Times,* April 16, 1898.

4. *The Woman's Journal,* April 23, p. 132.

5. Ibid.

6. Frederick A. Hinckley, *Sermon preached at the Funeral of Robert Purvis by Rev. Frederick A. Hinckley of Philadelphia, Pennsylvania on Friday, April 15, 1898 at Spring Garden Unitarian Church* (Washington, DC: Judd and Detweiler, printers, 1898), p. 4.

7. Ibid., p. 7.

8. Ibid., p. 8.

9. Ibid., p. 9.

10. Ibid., p. 9, "Truth for authority" was the motto of Robert Purvis's mentor, Lucretia Mott.

11. Robert Purvis, Fair Hill Burial Ground records, p. 390, April 18, 1898. Friends Historical Library, Swarthmore College.

12. Hattie Purvis to Samuel May, Jr. May 28, 1898. This letter is pasted inside a copy of the Hinckley Funeral Sermon, at the American Antiquarian Society in Worcester, Massachusetts. I am indebted to Julie Winch for a copy.

13. *Friends Intelligencer,* 55 (1898): 299, 336.

14. Leon Gardiner Collection, American Negro Historical Association, 10G. Historical Society of Pennsylvania, Philadelphia.

15. Isaiah Wears to American Negro Historical Association, Leon Gardiner Collection, 8B, Historical Society of Pennsylvania, Philadelphia.

16. Ibid.

17. Ibid.

18. Ibid.

19. Stanton, Anthony and Gage, *History of Woman Suffrage,* 4: 345.

Bibliography

Alonso, Harriet. *Growing Up Abolitionist: The Story of the Garrison Children.* Amherst: University of Massachusetts Press, 2002.

Bacon, Jacqueline. "Rhetoric and Identity in Absalom Jones and Richard Allen's Narrative of the Proceedings of the Black People During the Late Awful Calamity in Philadelphia." *The Pennsylvania Magazine of History and Biography* 125, (Spring 2001).

Bacon, Margaret Hope. *History of the Pennsylvania Society for Promoting the Abolition of Slavery: The Relief of Negroes Unlawfully Held in Bondage: and for Improving the Condition of the African Race.* Philadelphia: Pennsylvania Abolition Society, 1959.

——. *Rebellion at Christiana.* New York: Crown, 1975.

——. *Valiant Friend: The Life of Lucretia Mott.* New York: Walker & Company, 1980.

——. "One Great Bundle of Humanity: Frances Ellen Watkins Harper 1825–1911." *Pennsylvania Magazine of History and Biography* 113, No. 1. (January 1989).

——. "The Double Curse of Sex and Color: Robert Purvis and Human Rights." *Pennsylvania Magazine of History and Biography.* No. 1–2 (January, April, 1997).

——. *Abby Hopper Gibbons: Prison Reformer and Social Activist.* Albany: State University of New York Press, 2000.

——. "New Light on Sarah Mapps Douglass and Her Reconciliation with the Society of Friends." *Quaker History* (Spring 2001).

——. *Sarah Mapps Douglass: Faithful Attender of Quaker Meeting: View from the Back Bench*. (Philadelphia: Quaker Press, 2003.

Baron, Salo W., and Joseph L. Blau, eds. *The Jews of the United States, 1790–1840: A Documentary History*. New York: Columbia University Press, 1963.

Bell, Howard. *Proceedings of the National Negro Conventions, 1830–1864*. New York: Arno Press, 1969.

——. *A Survey of the Negro Convention Movement 1830–1861*. New York: Arno Press, 1969.

——. "The American Moral Reform Society, 1836–1841." *The Journal of Negro Education* 27 (1958).

Bentley, George R. *A History of the Freedmen's Bureau*. New York: Octagon Books, 1974.

Berlin, Ira. *Slaves Without Masters: The Free Negro in the Antebellum South*. New York: Pantheon Books, 1974.

——. *Many Thousands Gone: The First Two Centuries of Slavery in North America*. Cambridge, MA: The Belknap Press, 1998.

——. *Generations of Captivity: A History of African-American Slaves*. Cambridge, MA: The Belknap Press, 2003.

Berman, Myron. *Richmond Jewry, 1769–1976*. Charlottesville, VA: University of Virginia, 1979.

Bernstein, Ira. *The New York Draft Riots: Their Significance in American Society and Politics in the Age of the Civil War*. New York: Oxford University Press, 1990.

Biographical Directory of the United States Congress, 1774–1989. Washington, DC: U.S. Government Printing Office.

Biographical Encyclopedia of Pennsylvania in the Nineteenth Century. Philadelphia: Galaxy Publishing, 1874.

Blassingame, John W., and Mae G. Henderson, eds. *Antislavery Newspapers and Periodicals*. Boston: G.K. Hall, 1970.

Bordewich, Fergus M. *Bound for Canaan: The Underground Railroad and the War for the Soul of America*. New York: HarperCollins, 2005.

Borome, Joseph. "Robert Purvis and His Early Challenge to American Racism." *Negro History Bulletin* 30 (1967): 8–10.

——. "The Vigilant Committee of Philadelphia." *Pennsylvania Magazine of History and Biography* 92 (July 1968: 320–351).

Bronner, Edwin. *Thomas Earle as a Reformer*. Philadelphia: International Printing Company, 1948.

Brown, Ira. *The Negro in Pennsylvania History*. University Park, PA: Pennsylvania Historical Association, 1970.

———. *Mary Grew, Abolitionist and Feminist*. Selingrove: Susquehanna University Press, 1984.

———. *Proclaim Liberty! Anti Slavery and Civil Rights in Pennsylvania 1688–1887*. University Park, PA: 2000.

Brown, William Wells. *The Black Man, His Antecedents, His Genius and His Achievements*. New York: Thomas Hamilton, 1863.

Bumbrey, Jeffrey Nordlinger, ed. *A Guide to the Microfilm Publication of the Papers of the Pennsylvania Abolition Society at the Historical Society of Pennsylvania*. Philadelphia: The Historical Society of Pennsylvania, 1976.

Cadbury, Henry J. "Negro Membership in the Society of Friends." *Journal of Negro History* 21 (1936):151–213.

———. *Friendly Heritage: Letters from the Quaker Past*. Norwall, CT: Silvermine Publishers, 1972.

Campbell, John. *Negro-Mania, Being an Examination of the Falsely Assumed Equality of the Races of Man*. Philadelphia: Campbell and Power, 1851.

Campbell, Stanley W. *The Slave Catchers: Enforcement of the Fugitive Slave Law, 1850–1860*. Chapel Hill, NC: University of North Carolina Press, 1968.

Centennial Anniversary of the Pennsylvania Society for Promoting the Abolition of Slavery, the Relief of Negroes Unlawfully Held in Bondage; and for Improving the Condition of the African Race. Philadelphia: Grant, Faires & Rogers, Printers, 1875.

Chadwick, John White, ed. *A Life For Liberty: Anti-Slavery and Other Letters of Sallie Holley*. New York: Putnam, 1899.

Child, Maria L. *Isaac Hopper: A True Life*. Boston: John P. Jewett, 1859.

Cohen, William. "The Pennsylvania Anti-Slavery Society." Master's thesis, Columbia University, 1960.

Davis, Hugh. "Pennsylvania State Equal Rights League and the Northern Black Struggle for Equality, 1864–1877." *The Pennsylvania Magazine of History and Biography* 126, No. 4 (2002), 611–634.

Dillon, Merton Lynn. *Benjamin Lundy and the Struggle for Negro Freedom*. Urbana, IL: University of Illinois Press, 1966.

Douglass, Frederick. *Life and Times of Frederick Douglass.* New York: n.p., 1892.

Du Bois, W. E. B. *The Souls of Black Folk.* New York: Blue Heron Press, 1953.

"Earliest Extant Minute Book of the Spanish and Portuguese Congregation Shearith Israel in New York 1728-1760." *Publications of the American Jewish Historical Society* 21, No.5 (1913).

Ezekiel, Herbert T., and Gaston Lichenstein. *The History of the Jews of Richmond from 1769 to 1917.* Richmond, VA: H.T. Ezekiel, 1917.

Fifth Annual Convention for the Improvement of the Free People of Colour, Held in Wesley Church, Philadelphia, 1st to 5th of June, 1835. Philadelphia: William G. Gibbons, 1835.

Finley, Robert. *Thoughts on the Colonization of Free Blacks.* Washington, DC: The American Colonization Society, 1816.

Fleming, Walter. *The Freedman's Savings Bank: A Chapter in the Economic History of Race.* Chapel Hill, NC: University of North Carolina, 1927.

Foner, Philip. "The Battle to End Discrimination Against Negroes on Philadelphia Streetcars:" *Pennsylvania History* 40, 41 (July and October 1973).

——. "Black Participation in the Centennial of 1876." *Negro History Bulletin* (1976).

Foner, Philip S., and George F. Walker. *Proceedings of the Black State Conventions 1840–1865.* Philadelphia: Temple University Press, 1979.

Forney, John W. *Anecdotes of Public Men.* New York: Harper Brothers, 1873.

Forten, James, Robert Purvis, and William Whipper. *To the Honorable Senate and House of Representatives of the Commonwealth of Pennsylvania.* Philadelphia: n.p., 1832.

——. *A Remonstrance Against the Proceedings of a Meeting held November 23, 1831 at Upton's Dock Street.* Philadelphia: Library Company of Philadelphia, 1832.

——. *Fourth Annual Convention for the Improvement of the Free People of Colour in the United States, Held by Adjournment in the Asbury Church, New York from the 2nd to the 13th of June, 1834, inclusive.* New York, by order of the Convention, 1834.

Fox, Early Lee. "The American Colonization Society, 1817–1840." *Studies in Historical and Political Science* 37, No. 13 (1919: 60–62, 99, 110–111).

Garrison, Wendell Phillip and F. J. Garrison. *William Lloyd Garrison, 1805–1879: The Story of His Life Told by His Children.* New York: The Century Company, 1885–1889.

Gatewood, Willard B. *Aristocrats of Color*. Fayetteville, AR: University of Arkansas Press, 2000.

Goodman, Paul. *Of One Blood: Abolitionism and the Origins of Racial Equality*. Berkeley, CA: University of California Press, 1998.

Grew, Mary. *James Mott, A Biographical Sketch, by Mary Grew*. New York: William P. Tomlinson, 1868.

Hagy, James William. *This Happy Land: The Jews of Colonial and Antebellum Charleston*. Tuscaloosa, AL: The University of Alabama Press, 1993.

Harding, Vincent: *There is a River: The Black Struggle for Freedom in America*. New York: Harcourt Brace Jovanovich, 1981.

Harper, Ida Husted. *Life and Work of Susan B. Anthony*. Salem, NH: Ayer Co., 1983.

Harrison, Eliza Cope, ed. *Philadelphia Merchant: The Diary of Thomas P. Cope, 1800–1851*. South Bend, IN: Gateway Editions, 1978.

Hinckley, Frederick Allen. *Sermon Preached at the Funeral of Robert Purvis by the Rev. Frederic A. Hinckley on Friday, April 15, 1898, at Spring Garden Unitarian Church*. Washington, DC: Judd and Detweiler, 1898.

Holt, Thomas. *Black Over White: Negro Political Leadership in South Carolina During Reconstruction*. Urbana, IL: University of Illinois Press, 1977.

International Council of Women. *Report of the International Council of Women: Assembled by the National Woman Suffrage Association*. Washington, DC: n.p., 1888.

Jacobs, Harriet. *Incidents in the Life of a Slave Girl, Written by Herself*. Edited by L. Maria Child. Introduction by Jean Fagan Yellin. Cambridge: Harvard University Press, 2000.

James, Edward, Janet James, Paul Rover, eds. *Notable American Women, 1607–1950*. Cambridge, MA: The Belknap Press, 1971.

Jordan, Winthrop. *White Over Black: American Attitudes Toward the Negro, 1550–1812*. Chapel Hill, NC: The University of North Carolina Press, 1968.

Katz, Jonathon. *Resistance at Christiana*. New York: Thomas Y Crowell, 1974.

Koger, Larry. *Black Slaveholders: Free Black Slave Masters in South Carolina, 1790–1860*. Jefferson, NC: McFarland and Company, 1985.

Kohut, George A. "Oldest Tombstone Inscriptions of Philadelphia and Richmond." *Proceedings of the American Jewish Historical Society* 6 (1898): 111.

Lane, Roger. *Roots of Violence in Black Philadelphia, 1860–1900.* Cambridge, MA: Harvard University Press, 1986.

———. *William Dorsey's Philadelphia and Ours: On the Past and Future of the Black City in America.* New York: Oxford University Press, 1993.

Lapsansky, Emma. *Neighborhoods in Transition: William Penn's and Urban Reality.* New York: Garland Publishers, 1994.

———. *"Since They Got Those Separate Churches." African Americans in Pennsylvania: Shifting Historical Perspectives.* Editors Joe William Trotter, Jr., and Eric Ledell Smith. University Park, PA: Pennsylvania State University Press, 1997.

Lapsansky, Philip. "Bias in Art Has a Long Tradition." *Philadelphia Inquirer* (May 16, 1988).

Lapsansky, Philip, Richard Newman, Patrick Rael, eds. *Pamphlets of Protest: An Anthology of Early African Americans Protest Literature, 1790–1869.* New York: Routledge and Kegan Paul, 2001.

Lerner, Gerda. *The Grimké Sisters from South Carolina: Pioneers of Woman's Rights and Abolition.* New York: Charleston Shocken Books, 1971.

Lindhorst, Maria J. "Sarah Mapps Douglass: The Emergence of an African American Educator/Activist in Nineteenth Century Philadelphia." PhD diss., Pennsylvania State University, 1995.

Logan, Rayford W. and Michael R. Winston. *Dictionary of American Negro Biography.* New York: W.W. Norton & Co., 1982.

[Laura M. Lovell] *Report of a Delegate to the Anti-Slavery Convention of American Women.* Boston, MA: n.p., 1838.

McFeeley, William S. *Frederick Douglass.* New York: W.W. Norton & Co., 1991.

McPherson, James M. *The Struggle for Equality.* Princeton, NJ: Princeton University Press, 1964.

———. *Battle Cry of Freedom: The Civil War Era.* New York: Oxford University Press, 1991.

Martindale, Joseph C. *Byberry and Moreland History.* Philadelphia: n.p., 1867.

Mayer, Henry. *All on Fire: William Garrison and the Abolition of Slavery.* New York: St. Martin's Press, 1998.

Melder, Keith. *Beginnings of Sisterhood: The American Woman's Rights Movement 1800–1850.* New York: Shocken Books, 1977.

Merrill, Walter, and Louis Ruchames, eds. *The Letters of William Lloyd Garrison.* Cambridge, MA: The Belknap Press, 1971–1981.

Minutes and Proceedings of the First Annual Convention of the People of Colour In These United States, Held by Adjournment in the City of Philadelphia, from the Sixth to the Eleventh of June, Inclusive, 1831. Philadelphia: by Order of the Committee of Arrangements, 1831.

Minutes and Proceedings of the Second Annual Convention of the Free People of Colour in These United States, Held by Adjournment in the City of Philadelphia, from the 4th to the 13th of June, Inclusive, 1832. Philadelphia: by Order of the Convention, 1832.

Minutes and Proceedings of the Third Annual Convention of the Free People of Colour in these United States, Held by Adjournment in the City of Philadelphia, from the 3rd to the 13th of June, Inclusive, 1833. Philadelphia: by Order of the Convention, 1833.

Minutes of the Fifth Annual Convention for the Improvement of the Free People of Colour, in the United States, Held by Adjournment in the Wesley Church, Philadelphia, from the First to the Fifth of June, Inclusive, 1835. Philadelphia: William P. Gibbons, 1835.

Minutes of the State Convention of Colored Citizens of Pennsylvania, Convened at Harrisburg, December 13th, 1848. In Philip S. Foner and George. E. Walker, eds. *Proceedings of the Black State Conventions, 1840–1865,* 2 Vols. Philadelphia: Temple University Press, 1979–81.

Morrison, David Jenks. *A Guidebook to Historic LaMott.* Cheltenham [Pa.] Township Historical Commission, 1974.

Nash, Gary B. *Forging Freedom: The Formation of Philadelphia's Black Community, 1720–1840.* Cambridge, MA: Harvard University Press, 1988.

———, ed. *Race, Class and Politics: Essays on American Colonial Revolutionary Society.* Urbana and Chicago, IL: University of Illinois Press, 1986.

———. "Slaves and Slaveholders in Colonial Philadelphia." In *Race, Class and Politics: Essays on American Colonial Revolutionary Society.* Urbana and Chicago, IL: University of Illinois Press, 1986.

Norwood, Alberta. "Negro Welfare in Philadelphia, Especially as Illustrated in the Life of William Still." Master's thesis, University of Pennsylvania, 1931.

Palmer, Beverly, ed. *Selected Letters of Lucretia Coffin Mott.* Urbana: University of Illinois Press, 2002.

Penny, Sherry H., and James D. Livingston. *A Very Dangerous Woman: Martha Wright and Women's Rights.* Boston: University of Massachusetts Press, 2004.

Pinckney, Elise, ed. *Register of St. Philip's Church, Charlestown, South Carolina 1810–1822*. South Carolina: National Society of Colonial Dames of America in the State of South Carolina, 1973.

Porter, Dorothy, ed. *Early Negro Writing, 1760–1837*. Boston: Beacon Press, 1971.

Powell, Aaron. *Personal Reminiscences of the Anti-Slavery and Other Reforms and Reformers*. New York: Cauldron Press, 1899.

Powers, Bernard E. Jr. *Black Charlestonians: A Social History 1822–1885*. Fayetteville, AR: University of Arkansas Press, 1994.

Proceedings of the American Anti-Slavery Convention, Assembled at Philadelphia, December 4, 5, and 6, 1833. Philadelphia: n.p., 1833.

Proceedings of the American Anti-Slavery Society at its Third Decade, Held in the City of Philadelphia, Dec. 3rd and 4th, 1863. (Phonographic report by Henry M. Parkhurst). Swarthmore, PA: Friends Historical Library, Swarthmore College.

Proceedings of the Board of the Progressive Friends at Longwood, 1853–1868. Swarthmore, PA: Friends Historical Library, Swarthmore College.

Proceedings of the Colored National Convention, Held in Franklin Hall, Sixth Street Below Arch, Philadelphia, October 16th, 17th, and 18th, 1855. Salem, NJ: By Order of the Convention, 1856.

Proceedings and Debates of the Convention of the Commonwealth of Pennsylvania to Propose Amendments to the Constitution, Commenced at Harrisburg, on the Second Day of May, 1837. 13 Vols. Harrisburg, PA: Parker, Barrett and Parke, 1837–1839.

Proceedings of the First Anti-Slavery Convention of American Women, Held by Adjournment in the City of New York from the 9th to the 12th of May, 1837. New York: William S. Dorr, 1837.

Proceedings of the Second Anti-Slavery Convention of American Women, Held in Philadelphia, May 15th, 16th, 17th and 18th, 1838. Philadelphia: Merrihew and Gunn, 1838.

Proceedings of the Third Anti-Slavery Convention of American Women, Held in Philadelphia, May 1st, 2d, and 3d, 1839. Philadelphia: Merrihew and Gunn, 1839.

Purvis, John, ed. *The Purvis Family 1694–1988*. Tillicoultry, Scotland: n.p., 1988.

Purvis, Robert. *A Tribute to the Memory of Thomas Shipley, the Philanthropist, Delivered at St. Thomas Church, November 23rd, 1836*. Philadelphia: Merrihew and Gunn, Printers: 1836.

———. *Appeal of Forty Thousand Citizens, Threatened with Disfranchisement, to the People of Pennsylvania*. Philadelphia: Merrihew and Gunn, Printers, 1838.

——. "Appeal to the Voters of the Commonwealth of Pennsylvania (1848)." In Philip S. Foner and George F. Walker, *Proceedings of the Black State Conventions 1840–1865*. Philadelphia: Temple University Press, 1979.

——. *Remarks on the Life and Character of James Forten, Delivered at Bethel Church, March 30, 1842*. Philadelphia: Merrihew and Thompson, 1842.

——. *Testimonial of Gratitude to David Paul Brown, in Mother Bethel Church in 1841*. University Park, PA: Historical Society of Pennsylvania (1841).

——. *Speeches and Letters of Robert Purvis, Published by the Request of the Afro-American League*. Philadelphia: University of Pennsylvania, Rare Books, n.d. and n. p.

——, with James Forten, William Whipper. *Memorial to the Honorable Senate and House of Representatives of the Commonwealth of Pennsylvania, in General Assembly Met, the Memorial of the Subscribers, Free People of Colour, Residing in the City of Philadelphia*. Philadelphia: n.p., 1833.

Purvis, T. T. *Abi Meredith*. Philadelphia: Friends Book Association, 1878.

——. *Hagar, The Singing Maiden, and Other Stories and Rhymes*. Philadelphia: Walton, 1881.

Quarles, Benjamin. *Black Abolitionists*. New York: Oxford University Press, 1975.

——. *The Negro in the Civil War*. Boston: Little Brown, 1956.

Ripley, C. Peter et al., eds. *Black Abolitionist Papers*. 5 Vols. Chapel Hill, NC: University of North Carolina, 1985-92.

Rose, Willie Lee. *Rehearsal for Reconstruction: The Port Royal Experiment*. Indianapolis, IN: The Bobbs-Merrill Company, Inc., 1964.

Runcie, John. "Hunting the Nigs in Philadelphia: The Race Riot of 1834." In *Pennsylvania History* 39 (April, 1972) 203, 215; University Park, PA: Pennsylvania State University.

Siebert, Wilbur H. *The Underground Railroad from Slavery to Freedom*. New York: n.p., 1899.

Silcox, Harry C. "The Black 'Better Class' Political Dilemma: Prototype Isaiah C. Wears." In *Pennsylvania Magazine and History and Biography* 113 (January 1989).

——. "Nineteenth Century Philadelphia Black Militant: Octavius Catto (1839-1871)." *Pennsylvania History* 44, no. 1 (January 1977).

Simkins, Francis Butler and Robert Hilliard Woody. *South Carolina During Reconstruction*. Chapel Hill: The University of North Carolina Press, 1932.

Simmons, William. *Men of Mark: Eminent, Progressive and Rising*. New York: Arno Press, 1968.

Slaughter, Thomas. *Bloody Dawn: The Christiana Riot and Racial Violence in the Antebellum North*. New York: Oxford University Press, 1991.

Smedley, Robert C. *History of the Underground Railroad in Chester and Neighboring Counties of Pennsylvania*. Lancaster, PA, 1883.

Smith, Eric Ledell, and Joe William Trotter, Jr., eds,. *African Americans in Pennsylvania: Shifting Historical Perspectives*. Harrisburg, PA. Pennsylvania Historical and Museum Commission: Penn State University Press, 1997.

South Carolina's Writers Project. *South Carolina: A Guide to the Palmetto State*. New York, Oxford University Press, 1941.

Stanton, Elizabeth Cady. *Eighty Years and More*. New York: Shocken Books, 1971.

Stanton, Elizabeth Cady, Susan B. Anthony, and Matilda Joslyn Gage. *History of Woman Suffrage*. 6 Vols. New York: Fowler, 1881–1922.

Staudenraus, P. J. *The African Colonization Movement,1816–1865*. New York: Columbia University Press, 1961.

Stauffer, John. *The Black Hearts of Men: Radical Abolitionists and the Transformation of Race*. Cambridge MA: Harvard University Press, 2002.

Stearns, Frank Preston. *The Life and Public Service of George Luther Stearns*. Philadelphia: Lippincott and Co., 1907.

Sterling, Dorothy. *Ahead of Her Time: Abby Kelley and the Politics of Antislavery*. New York: W. W. Norton Co., Inc., 1991.

——. *The Making of an Afro-American: Martin Robinson Delany, 1812–1885*. New York: De Capo Press, 1996.

——, ed. *We Are Your Sisters: Black Women in the Nineteenth Century*. New York: W. W. Norton Co., Inc., 1984.

——, ed. *Turning the World Upside Down: The Anti-Slavery Convention of American Women, Held in New York City, May 9–12, 1837*. New York: Coalition of Publishers for Employment, 1987.

Stevenson, Brenda, ed. *Journals of Charlotte Forten Grimké*. New York: Oxford University Press, 1987.

Stewart, James Brewer. *Wendell Phillips: Liberty's Hero*. Baton Rouge, LA: Louisiana University Press, 1986.

Still, William. *The Underground Railroad*. Philadelphia: Porter and Coates, 1872.

———. "A Brief Narrative of the Struggle for the Rights of the Colored People of Philadelphia in the City Railway Cars, and a Defense of William Still." Philadelphia: n.p., 1867.

Sturge, Joseph. *A Visit to the United States in 1841.* London: Hamilton, Adams & Co., 1842.

Sumler-Lewis, Janice. "The Forten-Purvis Women of Philadelphia and the American Anti-Slavery Crusade." *Journal of Negro History* 66 (1981–1982).

Taylor, Bayard. *A Journey to Central Africa: Or, Life and Landscapes from Egypt to the Negro Kingdoms of the White Nile.* New York: Putnam, 1852.

Walls, William Jacob. *The African Methodist Episcopal Church: Reality of the Black Church.* Charlotte, NC: A. M. E. Zion Publishing, 1885.

Webb, Samuel, ed. *History of Pennsylvania Hall, Which was Destroyed by a Mob on the 17th of May, 1838.* Philadelphia: 1838.

Wiggins, Rosalind Cobb. *Captain Paul Cuffe's Logs and Letters, 1808–1817: A Black Quaker's "Voice from within the Veil."* Washington, DC: Howard University Press, 1996.

Wilcox, Fran. "Robert Purvis, Bucks County Underground Railroader." *Bucks County Panorama* (March 1978).

Wilkinson, Frederick D. *Directory of the Graduates of Howard University 1870–1963.* Washington DC: Howard University Press, 1965.

Wilknamanayake, Marina. *A World in Shadow: The Free Black in Antebellum South Carolina.* Columbia, SC: University of South Carolina Press, 1973.

Williams, Carolyn. "The Female Anti-Slavery Movement." In *The Abolitionist Sisterhood: Women's Political Culture in Antebellum America.* Edited by Jean Fagin Yellin and John C. Van Horne. Ithaca, NY: Cornell University Press, 1944.

Winch, Julie. *A Gentleman of Color: The Life of James Forten.* New York: Oxford University Press, 2002.

———. *The Elite of Our People, Joseph Willson's Sketches of Black Upper Class Life in Antebellum Philadelphia.* State Park, PA: Pennsylvania State University Press, 2000.

———. "You Have Talents—Only Cultivate Them." In *The Abolitionist Sisterhood: Women's Political Culture in Antebellum America.* Edited by Jean Fagin Yellin and John C. Van Horne. Ithaca: Cornell University Press, 1994.

———. *Philadelphia's Black Elite: Activism, Accommodation and the Struggle for Autonomy, 1787–1848.* Philadelphia: Temple University Press, 1988.

Wolf, Edwin. *Philadelphia: Portrait of an American City*. Philadelphia: Stackpole Books, 1970.

Yellin, Jean, ed. *Incidents in the Life of a Slave Girl, Written by Herself, by Harriet A. Jacobs: Edited by L. Maria Child, Now with "A true tale of slavery" by John S. Jacobs*. Cambridge, MA: Harvard University Press, 2000.

———. *Harriet Jacobs: A Life*. New York: Basic Civitas Books, 2004.

Yellin, Jean Fagan, and John C. Van Horne, eds. *The Abolitionist Sisterhood: Women's Political Culture in Antebellum America*. Ithaca: Cornell University Press, 1994.

Index